Off with Her Head!

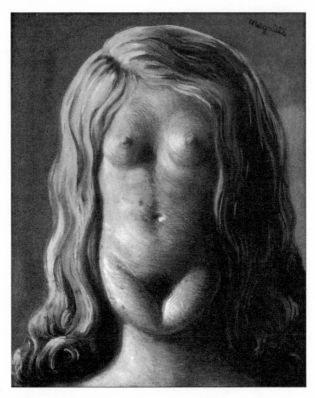

René Magritte, *Le Viol* (The Rape), c. 1945.
(© 1994 C. Herscovici/ARS, New York; Giraudon/Art
Resource, New York)

Off with Her Head!

*The Denial of Women's Identity in Myth,
Religion, and Culture*

EDITED BY

Howard Eilberg-Schwartz
and Wendy Doniger

UNIVERSITY OF CALIFORNIA PRESS
Berkeley   Los Angeles   London

University of California Press
Berkeley and Los Angeles, California

University of California Press, Ltd.
London, England

© 1995 by
The Regents of the University of California

Library of Congress Cataloging-in-Publication Data

Off with her head! : the denial of women's identity in myth, religion, and culture / edited
by Howard Eilberg-Schwartz and Wendy Doniger.
   p.   cm.
   Includes bibliographical references and index.
   ISBN 0-520-08839-5 (alk. paper). — ISBN 0-520-08840-9 (pbk. : alk. paper)
   1. Head—Social aspects.   2. Women—Identity.   3. Hair—Social aspects.
   4. Psychoanalysis.   I. Eilberg-Schwartz, Howard, 1956–   II. Doniger, Wendy.
   GT498.H43034   1995
   305.42—dc20   95-13310
                                                                                                  CIP

Printed in the United States of America
9 8 7 6 5 4 3 2 1

To our mothers, with love,
Joan Schwartz
and
Rita Roth, 1909–1991

CONTENTS

ACKNOWLEDGMENTS

These essays were first presented at a panel at the American Academy of Religion. Jo Glorie believed they should be published as a book and she became our editor at Paragon Press. She offered numerous important critical comments on an early draft of the manuscript and many of the papers take account of her queries and concerns. When Paragon was sold, we lost Jo as our editor. Without her early support and commitment, this book would never have seen the light of day. Fortunately, Doug Abrams Arava at the University of California Press got behind the project and helped see it through to the end. We are grateful to both Jo and Doug for the support.

Introduction

The Spectacle of the Female Head

Howard Eilberg-Schwartz

In the quest to understand femininity—what it is and how it is made—much scholarly attention has been devoted to the representation of women's bodies, especially to their reproductive and sexualized bodies, to wombs, vaginas, and breasts.[1] But it would be a mistake to think that it is simply the reproductive or erotic parts of the female body which are at issue in the representation of femininity. The female head is a particularly rich and important site in the symbolization of gender and in the linking of gender to the transcendent values of specific cultural or religious systems. For the head, which is potentially separable from the body, poses special dilemmas when it belongs to a woman. This book is about those dilemmas. It explores the role of the female head as a cultural and religious symbol, the kinds of significance it carries, and the diverse ways in which it is integrated into cultural and religious meanings. This volume thus looks at the other half of woman: the anatomical part of the female body that gives women a voice and an identity and that thereby threatens to unmake and disrupt the classic gender distinctions that have linked men to speech, power, identity, and the mind. If the head is typically thought of as masculine, then what is to be made of the female head? Our contention is that the objectification of woman as a sexual body necessarily requires coming to terms with the presence of her head.

Decapitation is one way of solving the dilemma. Removing the female head relieves woman of both identity and voice and reduces her to a mere sexual and reproductive body. But there are other, less obvious, forms of beheading. The eroticization of the female head extends the body, turning the head into an alluring and sexually provocative organ. In this way, the female head becomes part of a woman's genitalia. To see a woman's face, to look at her hair, to hear her voice, is imagined as an erotic experience.

1

Eroticization of the head is thus a form of beheading, since it depicts women as nothing more than a sexual and erotic body. Magritte's painting *The Rape* (see frontispiece) illustrates just how the eroticization of the female head can lead to its submersion and disappearance into the body. The eyes become breasts, the nose a navel, the mouth a vagina. What women speak, eat, and see is nothing but desire. Speaking to a woman is a form of sex, seeing her hair a violation of modesty. This sort of erotic symbolism is one of the motivations behind the practices of veiling a woman's face and/or hair and avoiding the sound of her voice. Ironically, of course, the eroticism of the female hair or face is intensified and partially created by the very acts of veiling that are intended to keep female sexuality under wraps. What is forbidden to the gaze is that much more tantalizing to the imagination.[2]

Covering the female head is not the only practice which simultaneously presupposes and creates its eroticism. Cosmetics and hairstyling, instead of hiding the female head, draw the gaze to it and highlight its features. These practices are enmeshed in the same eroticism as is the practice of veiling. But instead of resisting desire, they play on and provoke it. To be made up is to invite looking, to draw attention to the face and head, to signify the desire to be seen and admired. And it is precisely the desire to be looked at rather than the desire to look which is signaled by cosmetics. It is no accident that movies sometimes depict women as more erotic when they remove their glasses. To wear glasses is to be a viewer, to remove them is to become the object of the gaze.[3] A woman becomes a "looker" when she draws the attention of the desiring male gaze. Ironically, then, the display of the female face can be another form of decapitation, turning the female head into a symbol of desire, rather than a symbol of identity and of the capacity for speech and language. The techniques that draw attention to women's heads may be precisely the mechanisms by which women lose their heads, and the techniques for hiding the female head can help turn it into a symbol of desire.

It is the treatment of the female head, its decapitation, covering, highlighting, and eroticization, that is the subject of this book. In the process of exploring these themes, the focus will be turned to different parts of the female head: the hair, the face, the mouth, and the voice. What each of these essays shows is how the representation of the female head is critical to the depiction of femininity and how gender in turn is the ground for and the symbol of much wider religious and cultural significances.

DESIRE, DISPLACEMENT, AND GENERATIVITY

In understanding the meanings of the female head in the context of gender and religious symbolism, this book returns to, is partly inspired by, and fundamentally criticizes the psychoanalytic theory of upper and lower body displacement. According to Freud's episodic reflections on the subject, the head is one of the symbols to which the repressed desires of the lower body are transferred and expressed in disguised form.

Freud's speculations about the erotic symbolism of the head and hair spawned an interesting debate between psychoanalysts and anthropologists over both the extent of and the reasons for the sexual meaning of hair. These essays pose a critique of that debate and should be read as a commentary upon it. While this book confirms the frequent association of the female head and the vagina, it fundamentally reinterprets the meaning of that association, by making gender the operative category for thinking about its significance.

As is well known, Freud saw the upper body, particularly the head, as a symbol for the lower body and its desires. He worked this association out in different ways. In his *Three Essays on the Theory of Sexuality* (1905) he explored the process by which the mouth, which serves as an erogenous zone in early childhood, is repudiated on the way to maturity when the libido is concentrated in genital sexuality. The association of genital symbolism with the mouth can thus be interpreted as a symbolic return to the site of an original eroticism. Freud's views on the connection of the lower and upper body were also grounded in his understanding of evolutionary theory and embryology and were influenced by the writings of Wilhelm Fliess.[4] Later Freud came to believe that the symbolic displacement from the lower to the upper body was the result of repression. When the desires of the lower body could not be admitted into consciousness, they found indirect expression and relief through other symbols, including, among other things, the head. In his case study of Dora (1909), for example, Freud assumed that the symptoms affecting her mouth were symbols of erotic desires which she could not consciously acknowledge. Subsequently, Freud was to formulate his understanding of the Oedipus complex and to seek evidence for it in Greek myth—which, like dreams, he believed had escaped the monitoring of the conscious.

The convergence of all of these assumptions led Freud to see Medusa's head as a symbol of castration. Medusa was one of the Gorgons of Greek mythology, monsters that were portrayed in Greek art as winged female creatures with snakes for hair and with large sinister teeth and a protruding tongue. Medusa was the only Gorgon to be mortal. When Perseus cut off her head, two sons sprang from her blood. And her decapitated head had the power to turn to stone anyone who gazed on it. Freud's terse reflections on Medusa's head were published posthumously and may have been notes for a longer and more extensive treatment.[5] Not surprisingly, Freud interpreted Medusa's head as evoking castration anxiety:

> To decapitate = to castrate. The terror of Medusa is thus a terror of castration that is linked to the sight of something. Numerous analyses have made us

familiar with the occasion for this: it occurs when a boy, who has hitherto been unwilling to believe the threat of castration, catches sight of the female genitalia, probably those of an adult, surrounded by hair, and essentially those of his mother.

It is important to note that it was the decapitated *female* head that Freud believed provoked castration anxiety in males. Medusa's gaping mouth and her long curly hair symbolized the female genitals, the sight of which Freud believed generated male castration anxiety. In *The Unconscious Significance of Hair,* Charles Berg, a psychoanalyst, developed Freud's insights into a cross-cultural theory of hair practices. Drawing on ethnographic evidence, Berg argued that castration anxiety was behind various hair practices the world over, irrespective of a person's gender.

The psychoanalytic tradition thus posed a variety of important questions: Is there a recurring symbolic displacement between the upper and lower body? If such a recurring symbolism exists, is there an alternative to the psychoanalytic explanation? To what extent is such erotic symbolism confined to the female head? And what are the implications if the male head is entangled in a similar symbolism?

ANTHROPOLOGICAL REFLECTIONS ON HAIR SYMBOLISM

As the discussion moved beyond the confines of psychoanalytic discourse and into the discipline of anthropology, other scholars found confirmation for certain aspects of the psychoanalytic interpretation. In his essay "Magical Hair," the British social anthropologist Edmund Leach argues that while Berg drew on outdated ethnographic sources, more reliable ethnographies frequently confirm the erotic symbolism of hair. Leach notes that in many different contexts cutting the hair is associated with asceticism. Shaved heads frequently signify that the person is expected to have no sexual relations, while long, unkempt hair signifies unrestrained sexuality. Leach concludes that the anthropologist has to agree that hair is indeed a symbol of desire. But symbolic meanings, Leach argues, have public rather than private and personal significance and are thus accessible to the consciousness of agents.[6] The cutting of the hair is therefore a public statement with public meanings, and does not necessarily say anything about the unconscious.

Leach overstates his case by seeming to deny that public meanings can also have private or personal significance, and by assuming that the connection between hair cutting and asceticism is always something of which actors are consciously aware.[7] Still, he provides an impressive array of examples that seem to bear out the connection of the head and the genitals. While Leach sometimes follows Berg's emphasis on the phallic significance of the head and hair, he also imperceptibly shifts the discussion (at least at times) by talking about the ways in which hair signifies desire generally and not the penis specifically. In sometimes freeing hair of its specifically phallic associations, Leach is able to see that the cutting of female hair has female desire, and not male desire, as its referent.[8] A woman's shorn hair has to do with her own asceticism and not male castration anxiety. Ironically, then, while Leach understands himself to be confirming the symbolism that psychoanalysis had revealed, he actually reinterprets it in important ways. To say that the hair is symbolic of desire generally is fundamentally different from seeing it as a symbol of castration anxiety.

Leach's argument has evoked responses of two kinds. In *Medusa's Hair*, Gananath Obeyesekere, a psychoanalytically oriented anthropologist, argues that Leach went too far in his rejection of the psychoanalytic paradigm. Studying female Hindu ascetics who had grown long matted locks and thus resembled "Medusa," Obeyesekere argues that these matted locks are "phallic" symbols and indicate the marriage of these women to a male God. The life histories of these women and personal interviews with them reveal that each had suffered severe personal trauma related to marriage and sexuality, traumas which led to the women's asceticism and symbolic marriage to a god. These "psychological" symbols, as Obeyesekere calls them, are phallic symbols which spring spontaneously from the personal unconscious of these women, though they may take on public meanings subsequently. Leach was therefore mistaken in assuming that all symbols are public and conscious.

By contrast, two other social anthropologists, C. R. Hallpike and Mary Douglas, argue that Leach did not go far enough in breaking with the psychoanalytic paradigm.[9] Hair does not so much represent desire as symbolize social control and deviance. Shorn hair signifies a person who is constrained by social rules (a monk, a soldier, a prisoner in jail). Long hair signifies a person who stands outside the rules (certain kinds of ascetics, hippies, women). Wearing long hair also symbolizes being more like animals and hence closer to nature. In general, this understanding of hair symbolism flows from the presuppositions of British social anthropology, which sees religious and cultural symbolism as reflecting the tensions and powers inherent in the social structure. Douglas understands the connection between hair and control as part of a larger symbolic process in which the human body often symbolizes society in general, particularly the boundaries of the social body.[10]

There are exceptions which disprove the universality of either Douglas's or Hallpike's theory. But the question is whether there are enough positive examples to make the transcultural nature of the phenomenon significant. Both theories are supported by an impressive array of examples. An exception proves only that a symbolism is not universal; it does not prove that the association is unreal.[11] Although Hallpike and Douglas offer their interpretations as an alternative to a sexual understanding, the two views are in fact compatible. Sexual asceticism is obviously one extreme form of social control. When symbolizing desire, therefore, hair may simultaneously signify a relationship to social control. The long hair of hippies signified both the breaking of norms generally and "free love" specifically. But these two symbolisms may vary independently. Jewish law, for example, forbids men from cutting their hair or shaving during the period of mourning, a period in which they must also forgo sexual relations. In this case, the growing of the hair occurs while the Jew is outside his normal status and exempt from religious duties (such as saying certain prayers) which are otherwise obligatory. Here, however, the growing of the hair does not signal unrestrained sexuality but the reverse: the restraint of desire. Thus the erotic and the socially deviant meanings of hair are potentially but not necessarily convergent.

GENDERED MEANINGS OF THE FEMALE HEAD

In this debate about the significance of hair, gender has unfortunately remained of secondary concern. Consequently, the discussion has missed the ways in which the head and hair symbolize different things for men and for women. And in missing this asymmetrical treatment of men and women's heads, the theoretical discussion has been misleading.

In her important essay "Castration or Decapitation?" Hélène Cixous responds to this imbalance from within psychoanalytic theory. She suggests that the fear of decapitation could be regarded as the female equivalent of castration anxiety. "If man operates under the threat of castration, if masculinity is culturally ordered by the castration complex, it might be said that the backlash, the return, on women of this castration anxiety is its displacement as decapitation, execution, of woman, as loss of her head."[12] Women can only keep their heads "on the condition that they lose them, lose them, that is, to complete silence, turned into automatons." Women are denied the privilege of speech, and when they do speak what they say is regarded as simply idle chatter.

Cixous's description of "decapitation anxiety" as a female equivalent to male fears of castration is intended as a blow at psychoanalytic theory with its near-exclusive focus on male gender development.[13] Castration anxiety, of course, was the foundational concept in Freud's understanding of a boy's psychic development. It was the fear of losing the penis, Freud believed, that made the boy renounce his incestuous wishes for his mother, a founding act of culture, and come to identify with his father. Psychoanalysis never generated an equivalent concept for female development. Indeed, Freud suggested that because women did not fear losing an organ, their superego did not develop to the same degree. Because they had nothing to lose, they did not gain as much. By suggesting that there is a corresponding female fear of loss, Cixous subverts the understanding of gender construction that informs psychoanalytic theory. If women fear losing an organ, then their fears and the psychic consequences of those fears can become the object of analysis and attention. Women can no longer be viewed as passively acquiescing to their gender identities (as in the Freudian model) but as actively responding to the threat of losing their heads. Cixous thus denies the lack which psychoanalytic theory ascribes to women: lacking a penis does not mean that women "lack a lack," as she puts it; the task of becoming a woman is in fact fraught with a greater potential loss than the task of becoming a man.

Cixous thus employs the concept of beheading as a way of redressing the imbalance of psychoanalytic theory and exposing it as an example of a tradition that itself decapitates women by silencing female experience.[14] To be silent, to have no subjectivity, is to be decapitated. More specifically, Cixous's essay can be read as a reinterpretation and critique of Freud's reflections on Medusa's head. She follows Freud in seeing a connection between castration anxiety and female decapitation. But rather than viewing female decapitation as a symbol of castration anxiety, Cixous treats it as an effect: the beheading of women is the result of male fears about castration. Cixous thus rejects Freud's conclusion that Medusa's decapitation is simply a story about male fears. Instead, it is a symptom of the real dangers that women face in a culture that is anxious about the powers of masculinity. From Cixous's perspective, Freud's misreading of Medusa is illustrative of this very problem, for he erases the meaning of Medusa's head for female experience.

In this understanding of Cixous's essay, the concept of decapitation would appear to depend logically on the concept of castration anxiety and thus be problematic for those who find the psychoanalytic perspective unconvincing. "*If* man operates under the threat of castration . . . it *might* be said that the backlash . . . is its displacement as decapitation" (emphasis supplied).[15] But what if man does not operate under the threat of castration anxiety? What if psychoanalytic theory is a fiction, a modern myth, as many interpreters of culture reasonably assume? Should the concept of decapitation still play a central role in feminist analysis? Cixous does not answer this question directly. But the truth or nontruth of psychoanalytic theory may be beside the point. The power and continuing influence of psychoanalytic discourse and the psychoanalytic institution is itself sufficient reason to contest psychoanalytic theory.[16] Like other post-Lacanian feminist theorists in France, Cixous engages psychoanalytic theory not because of its truth but because of its power. And one of the most powerful ways of destabilizing a practice is by undermining it from within, on its own terms.

Whatever Cixous's intentions, we believe it would be a mistake to treat the concept of "decapitation" simply as a successful stratagem for subverting male privilege in psychoanalytic theory. The concept of female decapitation is a much more powerful analytic tool and points to a phenomenon which, though not universal, does have cross-cultural significance. This becomes evident as we translate from the overly anatomical language of castration anxiety into symbolic language about the prowess of masculinity. Restated, Cixous can be interpreted as saying that male fears about losing their manhood (and their power, which is much the same thing)[17] are frequently dealt with by removing or covering the female head, that is, by denying women the power of identity, language, thought, and selfhood. We are not talking here about a threat of actual decapitation, although in certain contexts that threat is real. Rather, we are dealing with symbolic processes, how women's heads are imagined, in myth, stories, plays, religious texts, and medical manuals, and how these symbolic processes are enacted in practices that affect women's power, subjectivity, and identity.

Reformulated, then, the debate regarding the sexual meaning of hair has failed to take seriously the way in which sexuality is itself a public symbol. Sexuality is shot through with conceptions of power, vitality, divinity, language, and so forth. As Leach insightfully observes,

> For society, sexuality itself is a 'symbol' rather than a first cause; it 'stands for' the creative reproductive element in the world at large. For the psycho-analyst sex comes first. Therefore in the Hindu context, the head represents the phallus and the *linga* represents itself. The anthropologist repudiates this cause-and-effect interpretation. God (i.e. Society) comes first and *linga* and the head alike both represent the power of God.[18]

Obeyesekere seems to miss this point when he argues that some symbols, such as the matted locks of female Hindu ascetics, are continually born anew from the personal unconscious. For the gods, too, are imagined in some cases to have matted locks. The women who sprout matted locks are thus *appropriating* a characteristic of the gods themselves. While the appropriation of such symbols may be motivated by deep personal and even inner psychic struggles, the symbols do not spring spontaneously from the unconscious; they already are pre-endowed with cultural meanings, which may or may not be consciously articulated. Hair is associated with sexuality because both are associated with ideas about generativity, life, and vitality. And it is precisely here that the question of gender reasserts itself, for notions of generativity, divinity, power, and life are thoroughly gendered. We are then in a circle from which there is no hope of escape. To privilege any one of these—whether desire, gender, generativity, or divinity—is arbitrarily to break out of an interlocking and circulating set of symbols. The repression and displacement theory breaks the circle and grounds the symbolism in blocked desire. But if desire itself is developed within and is mediated by cultural symbols, such as images of divinities, notions of gender, and ideas about power, then any entrance into this circulation of signs is an arbitrary one. To pull on any symbol is to pull on all of them.

In seeing the symbolism of the head as entangled in gendered meanings, we thus return to where we began: to the difference between the female and the male head. The theory of displacement does not explain why there should be a differential treatment of men's and women's heads. It is only through attention to gender, and the realization of how symbols of desire, power, and generativity enter into the construction of men and women, that such differences in erotic symbolism can be explained. Eroticizing the female head is one way in which the power of speech and thought can be denied to women. And this is one reason why the female head is in fact more of a pub(l)ic spectacle than the male head.

The chapters which follow explore these themes in several different religious, mythological, and cultural contexts. The first two essays, by Doniger and Lang, focus on the symbolism of the female head in Hindu, Buddhist, and Tantric mythology and practice. The other chapters probe one or more of the religious or cultural traditions that originated in the Mediterranean: the mythology and practices of the Greeks and Romans (Levine and Richlin), the religious symbolisms of Judaism (Eilberg-Schwartz), Christianity (D'Angelo), and Islam (Delaney). In this way, these essays widen the scope of and thus correct what has been a feminist stereotyping of Islam.[19] They show that the eroticization of the hair, which is presupposed by veiling practices, also lies at the heart of various Western traditions including early Christianity, Judaism, and Greek and Roman society.

While most of these chapters focus on ancient traditions, Delaney explores the above meanings in the ethnographic context of a Turkish village, thus providing a window into how these symbols work in the practical flow of everyday life. The meaning of the female head is examined in different cultural domains: in religious mythology (Doniger, Levine, Richlin, Lang), religious practice (Delaney, D'Angelo, Eilberg-Schwartz), religious poetry (Lang), and medical and cosmetic manuals (Richlin).

All of these chapters reveal ways in which the symbolization of the female head is connected to women's loss of subjectivity and identity. In "Put a Bag over Her Head," Doniger explores how Hindu myths of decapitation dehumanize women. She follows the fate of these severed heads, how they get recombined with the bodies of women of different castes and what effects such recombinations have on the status of the newly formed woman.

Doniger's reflections on the severed female head provide the point of departure for the subsequent chapters, which take up the meanings of the female head when it is still attached to the body. Four of the chapters (Lang, Delaney, Levine, and D'Angelo) discuss the polyvalent meanings of female hair, and in particular how the erotic associations of hair are intertwined in larger religious, cultural, and political meanings. At one level all of these essays confirm that hair has erotic and sexual significance. More importantly, however, they show how this generalization simply misses what is most interesting, namely, the way in which sexual desires are themselves part and parcel of wider layers of symbolism. But it is not just the hair that has sexual significance. The female head itself is also in some sense viewed as a genital organ whose exposure is considered shameful (Delaney, D'Angelo, Eilberg-Schwartz, Richlin). And it is not just the hair that is eroticized but also the female voice and mouth (Eilberg-Schwartz and Richlin).

Generally speaking, these essays reflect how men make sense of the female head. In explicating this symbolism, there is therefore a danger of assuming the position of the desiring (presumably male) subject and thereby becoming complicitous in the very phenomenon being described.[20] To see female practices of making up and covering over as simply expressions of male control or phallocentrism is to participate in the process of decapitation, of denying women agency in these practices. Because these practices are multivalent and carry many meanings for both agents and observers, they are continually under renegotiation and reappropriation. They have no meaning that is fixed once and for all. Like all practices, their meanings emerge through their strategic employment.[21] A practice can simultaneously be a sign of women's debasement and decapitation even as it is a source of their resistance to control and objectification. The female head, precisely because of its importance, can become a site of contestatory practices that undo and threaten the ruling symbolic system, a point made by D'Angelo in her essay on the Christian women who prophesied bareheaded at Corinth.

In exploring how the female head is symbolized, these chapters keep in view both the larger transcultural processes by which the symbolisms of the female head tend to converge and also the local and culturally specific meanings that operate in different cultural and religious contexts. These essays demonstrate how the symbolization of the female head is overdetermined: entangled in much wider cultural meanings, in ideas about generativity, procreation, animality, divinity, power, nationality, and religion. What is intriguing is both the cross-cultural convergence of these symbolisms and their unique modes of expression in each local context. This volume, then, poses a fundamental critique of the psychoanalytic theory of displacement, by making gender the operative category through which the entanglement of upper and lower body symbolisms is conceptualized and understood. The essays give substantial support to Cixous's claim that "decapitation" should be a central concept in the understanding of how femininity is made and unmade. But they also show how the full meaning of decapitation cannot be understood outside of much wider frames of cultural reference.

NOTES

1. See, for example, Millet 1970, O'Brien 1981, Spellman 1982, Laqueur 1990.
2. See, for example, Steele 1985 on the issue of eroticism and clothing.
3. Doane 1982.
4. See Geller 1992.
5. Freud 1922.
6. Geertz 1973 makes a similar kind of argument about the public nature of symbols and their accessibility to understanding by an interpreter.
7. See Obeyesekere 1981, whose views I return to below.
8. Hallpike 1972 and Delaney (this volume) criticize Leach for treating the cutting of female hair as linked to castration anxiety. A more sympathetic reading of Leach, I suggest, reveals that he was already moving well beyond the psychoanalytic model, though at times his language had not yet caught up with his insight.
9. Hallpike 1972 and Douglas 1966, 1970:65–82.
10. Douglas 1966:115.
11. Eilberg-Schwartz 1990:87–114.
12. Cixous 1981:43.
13. See Kuhn 1981.
14. The equation of male castration anxiety with female fear of decapitation also has the consequence of equating the female head with the phallus.
15. Cixous 1981:43.
16. See Grosz 1990:1–19.
17. MacKinnon 1987:4, for example, argues that gender difference is simply a reflection of power relations. Without differential power relations there cannot be two genders.
18. Leach 1958:159.
19. See Lazreg 1990.
20. On this danger, see Butler 1990 and Wittig 1980, 1981, 1982.
21. See Bourdieu 1977.

REFERENCES

Berg, Charles
    1951   *The Unconscious Significance of Hair.* London: Allen and Unwin.
Bourdieu, Pierre
    1977   *Outline of a Theory of Practice.* New York: Cambridge University Press.
Butler, Judith
    1990   *Gender Trouble.* New York: Routledge.
Cixous, Hélène
    1981   "Castration or Decapitation?" Trans. Annette Kuhn. *Signs* 7(1):41–55.

Doane, Mary Ann
1982   "Film and the Masquerade: Theorising the Female Spectator." *Screen* 23:3–4, 74–88.
Douglas, Mary
1966   *Purity and Danger.* London: Routledge and Kegan Paul.
1970   *Natural Symbols.* New York: Pantheon.
Eilberg-Schwartz, Howard
1990   *The Savage in Judaism: An Anthropology of Israelite Religion and Ancient Judaism.* Bloomington: Indiana University Press.
Freud, Sigmund
1950 [1922] "Medusa's Head." In *Collected Papers,* ed. by James Strachey, 5:105–6. London: Hogarth Press.
1905   "Three Essays on the Theory of Sexuality." *Standard Edition,* ed. by James Strachey, 7:123–243. London: Hogarth Press.
1909   "Notes upon a Case of Obsessional Neurosis." *Standard Edition,* ed. by James Strachey, 10:151–318. London: Hogarth Press.
Geertz, Clifford
1973   "Religion as a Cultural System." In *The Interpretation of Cultures,* 87–125. New York: Basic Books.
Geller, Jay
1992   "(G)nos(e)ology: The Cultural Construction of the Other." In *People of the Body: Jews and Judaism from an Embodied Perspective,* ed. by Howard Eilberg-Schwartz, 243–82. Albany: State University of New York Press.
Grosz, Elizabeth
1990   *Jacques Lacan: A Feminist Introduction.* London and New York: Routledge.
Hallpike, C. R.
1972   "Social Hair." In *Reader in Comparative Religion,* ed. by William A. Lessa and Evon Z. Vogt, 99–104. New York: Harper and Row.
Kuhn, Annette
1981   "Introduction to Hélène Cixous's 'Castration or Decapitation?' " *Signs* 7(1):36–40.
Laqueur, Thomas
1990   *Making Sex.* Cambridge: Harvard University Press.
Lazreg, Marnia
1990   "Feminism and Difference: The Perils of Writing as a Woman on Women in Algeria." In *Conflicts in Feminism,* ed. by Marianne Hirsch and Evelyn Fox Keller, 326–48. New York: Routledge.
Leach, Edmund
1958   "Magical Hair." *Man: Journal of the Royal Anthropological Institute* 88:147–68.
MacKinnon, C. A.
1987   *Feminism Unmodified.* Cambridge: Harvard University Press.
Millet, Kate
1970   *Sexual Politics.* Garden City, N.Y.: Doubleday.
Obeyesekere, Gananath
1981   *Medusa's Hair: An Essay on Personal Symbols and Religious Experience.* Chicago: University of Chicago Press.

O'Brien, Mary
   1981   *The Politics of Reproduction.* Boston: Routledge and Kegan Paul.
Spellman, Elizabeth
   1982   "Woman as Body: Ancient and Contemporary Views." *Feminist Studies*
             8(1):109–32.
Steele, Valerie
   1985   *Fashion and Eroticism.* New York: Oxford University Press.
Wittig, Monique
   1980   "The Straight Mind." *Feminist Issues* 1(1):103–11.
   1981   "One Is Not Born a Woman." *Feminist Issues* 1(2):47–54.
   1982   "The Category of Sex." *Feminist Issues* 2(2):63–68.

ONE

❦

"Put a Bag over Her Head"
Beheading Mythological Women

Wendy Doniger

INTRODUCTION

From ancient myth to contemporary culture, the metaphor of beheading has been used to express the dehumanizing of women. Beheading involves a double darkness: it ensures not merely the blindness of the beheaded person (deprived of the power of vision) but the invisibility of that person (deprived of the face which reveals his or her identity to the other), which amounts to the blindness of the other person, the one who views the beheaded person. The mythologically beheaded woman is seen (or at least partially seen) but does not see; she is blinded and those who have beheaded her are blinded to her real nature. She is transformed from a seeing subject to a merely seen object, a demeaned and faceless body. The blindness is inflicted on the beheaded person, the victim (the object), by someone else; but the blindness of the victimizer (the subject) is self-inflicted. Both the perpetrator and the victim are degraded, through the loss of their individuality and identity and through the incompleteness that the blindness of each inflicts upon the other.

This essay will explore the implications of the beheading and blinding of women in myths from ancient India and in early and contemporary America. In juxtaposing these materials I wish to argue that the two cultures, despite their distance in time and space, share certain underlying attitudes to women's heads, attitudes which should therefore be regarded as cross-cultural, though not necessarily universal. But at the same time I wish to demonstrate the ways in which the two different cultures—and, indeed, the various different subcultures within them—modify those attitudes in highly significant ways.

THE MYTH OF THE TRANSPOSED HEADS IN INDIA

There is a corpus of Hindu myths in which a man splits a high-caste woman against her will, dividing her into a head and a body, each endowed with life, which may then join with the supplementary parts of her shadow "double" to form two other women (or goddesses), each consisting of two vividly contrasting halves. This story, retold in many versions in India, has a great deal to teach us about the dichotomizing of women and of goddesses. It juggles the different aspects of a human woman, on two levels: on the literal level, there is an interaction between a goddess and a woman; on the symbolic level, an implicit parallelism and contrast between the structure of a goddess and the structure of a woman. Let us therefore ask what the story tells us, first about the split between aspects of a goddess, then about the correlated split between classes of human society, and finally about the split between aspects of a human woman.

The great Sanskrit epic, the *Mahābhārata,* tells the story of a human princess:

> Renuka, the daughter of a king, was the wife of the paradigmatic chaste (and notoriously irascible) sage Jamadagni, and she was renowned for her chastity. One day as she bathed in the river she caught sight of a king playing in the water with his queen, and Renuka desired him. As a result of this unchaste thought, she lost her senses and became wet in the water. When she returned home, her husband immediately noticed her excitement, became enraged, and commanded his five sons to kill their mother.
>
> The first four refused, and he cursed them to lose their senses and to become like birds and animals, like numb, inanimate creatures. Then the fifth son, Parasurama ["Rama with the Axe"], obediently cut off his mother's head. When Jamadagni offered Parasurama a reward for this obedience, Parasurama chose that his mother would rise up alive, that no one would remember her murder, that no one would be touched by the evil, and that his brothers would return to their normal state. All this was granted.[1]

Renuka's sons are indirectly injured by her fall and by the subsequent anger of her husband; they are said to lose their senses (the very same word used to describe what happened to Renuka in the water—or, as we might say, to lose their heads, as she is soon to do literally) and to become like animals. One might think that this implies a state of natural sexuality, such as Renuka was denied, but the text also says that the sons are made numb, inanimate, impotent (*jada*); they are condemned to a bestial, mindless asexuality. Magic intervenes, however, and Renuka and her four sons are restored to wholeness by the fifth son, Parasurama. But Parasurama, Rama with the axe (the Lizzie Borden of Hindu mythology), is still torn between obedience to his two warring parents. The father uses the son to hurt the unchaste mother, and although the son specifically begs that there be no memory of the murder nor any effect of the evil, it is not entirely clear

whether the evil consists in the murder or in the original lapse of chastity—
or, therefore, whether Parasurama is asking that Renuka, or he himself, or
everyone else, should never again experience lust.

Beheading is seldom fatal in a Hindu myth. In the *Mahābhārata* story,
nothing really happens; at the end, all wrongs are righted. All that is lost
when the head has been restored is memory—perhaps not merely the
memory of the murder, but also the memory of the sexual *vision* that threatened Renuka's integrity as a chaste wife, by threatening to unveil in her
the conflicting image of the erotic woman. For in India, where seeing (*dar-
shan*) is inextricably connected with touching, Renuka's troubles begin
when she merely *sees* the handsome king.

The opposition between the chaste and the erotic woman is further
expressed through a series of oppositions between the head and the body
in the myth, but it is not clear what is symbolized by this opposition. The
structure of this theme seems to remain constant throughout a large corpus
of myths about beheadings: the head is severed from the body; *something* is
cut away from something else. But what is that something? Unlike the widespread pattern of myths in which a human head is removed and replaced
with the head of an animal, here the exchange is more subtle, a woman's
head for a woman's head: Renuka simply gets back her own head again.
Woody Allen, as always, nicely expresses this quandary in his description of
the mythical beast called the Great Roe, which has the body of a lion and
the head of a lion, but not the same lion.[2]

When the story of Renuka is told and retold in South India, it becomes
an important origin myth about the transformation of a human woman
into the Kannada or Telugu goddess variously known as Ellamma, Allamma,
or Mariamma:

> A sage's wife, Mariamma, was sentenced by her husband to death. At the
> moment of execution she embraced an outcaste woman, Ellamma, for her
> sympathy. In the fray both the outcaste woman and the Brahmin lost their
> heads. Later, the husband relented, granted them pardon, and restored their
> heads by his spiritual powers. But the heads were transposed by mistake. To
> Mariamma (with a Brahmin head and outcaste body) goats and cocks but not
> buffaloes were sacrificed; to Ellamma (outcaste head and Brahmin body) buf-
> faloes instead of goats and cocks.[3]

This story ends up with two sets of mixed women and makes use of both
sets of heads and torsos, thus further splitting the goddess into two contrasting goddesses. The goddesses are, as usual, named after their heads,
not their bodies, a pattern to which we will return. From the Hindu standpoint, the purpose of this myth is to explain the relationship between certain high-caste and low-caste goddesses. European scholars have seen it as
a metaphor for the fusion of Aryan (northern and Indo-European) and

Dravidian (southern and non-Indo-European) cults and/or for "transpositions in the 'great' and 'little' traditions."[4] But that is not all that the myth is about.

For these expanded meanings, let us turn to a vivid version of the story that was retold by Pierre Sonnerat in the eighteenth century, recorded from an oral Tamil tale, in which the goddess is named not Mariamma but Mariatale. The following text is several times removed from the original telling: it is my translation of the eighteenth-century Frenchman's translation from the oral Tamil. But despite its mixed provenance as a kind of multicultural document in itself, the text is valuable because of the ingenuity with which it presents an image that is meaningful to all three cultures, the image of the women with transposed heads. And since this central image is, as we have seen, attested in other texts whose provenance is not sullied by the French connection, I think we may take the central points, at least, as evidence of Hindu thinking:

> Mariatale was the wife of the ascetic Jamadagni and mother of Parasurama. This goddess ruled over the elements, but she could only keep this empire as long as her heart remained pure. One day she was fetching water from a pool, and, following her usual custom, was rolling it up in a ball to carry it home. She happened to see on the surface of the water several male demigods [Gandharvas], who were sporting gymnastically [here one suspects a French euphemism] right under her head. She was taken by their charms, and desire entered her heart. The water that she had already collected immediately turned to liquid and mingled back with the water of the pool. She could no longer carry it home without the help of a bowl. This impotence revealed to Jamadagni that his wife had ceased to be pure, and in the excess of his anger, he commanded his son to drag her off to the place set aside for executions, and to cut off her head.
>
> This order was executed; but Parasurama was so afflicted by the loss of his mother that Jamadagni told him to go and get her body, to join to it the head that he had cut off, and to whisper in its ear a prayer that he taught him, which would immediately revive her. The son ran in haste, but by a singular oversight, he joined the head of his mother to the body of an outcaste woman who had been executed for her crimes—a monstrous assemblage, which gave to this woman the virtues of a goddess and the vices of an unfortunate wretch. The goddess, having become impure through this mix, was chased out of her house and committed all sorts of cruelties; the gods, seeing the ravages that she was causing, appeased her, by giving her the power to cure smallpox and promising her that she would be supplicated for this disease. . . . Only her head was placed in the inner sanctuary of the temple, to be worshipped by Indians of good caste; while her [outcaste] body was placed at the door of the temple, to be worshipped by outcastes. . . . Mariatale, having become impure through the mixing of her head with the body of an outcaste, and fearing that she would no longer be adored by her son Parasurama, begged the gods to grant her another child. They gave her Kartavirya; the outcastes divide

their worship between his mother and him. This is the only one of all the gods to whom are offered cooked meats, salted fish, tobacco, and so forth, because he came from the body of an outcaste.[5]

Mariatale's divine half reflects the unreasonable image of the entirely pure wife, symbolized by the impossible ability to roll water up, solid and dry, with nothing to sustain it. This is itself an image that cannot be sustained; the woman's natural emotion is expressed in the vision of the water that melts back into its natural liquidity and mingles again with the waters of the pool from which it was unnaturally frozen. This image may be an expansion of the simpler one that occurs in the *Mahābhārata,* in which Renuka "lost her senses and became wet in the water."

In Sonnerat's version of the myth, unlike the Telugu/Kannada telling, there is only one mixed woman, created by the fusion of Mariatale's head and the body of the outcaste woman, although a more complex interaction between the high-born goddess, the criminal outcaste woman, and their two sons is involved. The fused woman is a monster, impure and destructive, disease incarnate—ambivalent disease, whose outcaste, human body brings the fever that is cooled by the grace of the divine head. This is the most basic of all theological doubles: she is the goddess who both brings disease and removes disease, the lord who giveth and taketh away, the *mysterium fascinans et tremendum* that Rudolf Otto (in *Das Heilige*) describes as the essence of the sacred—in this case, a creature with a head that is *fascinans* and a body that is *tremendum.* (A variant of this coincidence of opposite supernatural powers may be seen in the ability of Jamadagni, the husband of Mariatale, both to remove heads and to restore them to life.) So great is the tension within her that she does not remain integrated in ritual; she is split up once again, the divine head at last purified by being divorced from its polluting body, and the outcaste body made literally liminal, placed on the doorstep, forever marking the pale of the Hindu society that sees woman as a divine-headed and outcaste-bodied monster.

Mariatale's class is not specified, but is merely said to be pure in contrast with the outcaste; Mariatale begins as a goddess in contrast with a mortal, but she becomes mixed, half goddess and half outcaste. The outcastes further split their worship between the impure body of the goddess and the son born of that *body*—that is, not born of the divine part of her at all. For the son of the divine head and body is pure, while the son of the divine head and the outcaste body is impure; the son's quality is determined not by his mother's head but by her body (though it is the father's head that gives the son his social status). Mariatale's head remains divine (and hence relatively pure) while her body becomes lower-caste (and hence relatively impure).

How is Mariatale's sexual ambivalence related to the mixture of castes in her head and body? Lower-caste women here, as often, represent the more erotic side of a woman. And since the body is lower-caste, we might assume that it is therefore the site of her eroticism, that the head is rational and chaste, the body emotional and lustful. The Tamil text seems to be saying that the head is pure, the body polluted. On this model, beheading might mean that the woman *can't think* (straight) any more, that her sexuality has destroyed her rationality. But, on the other hand, in India, particularly but not only Tantric India, the head is where semen is stored—and women, as well as men, have sexual seed that is stored in the head.[6] It may well be, therefore, that by removing Mariatale's (sexual) head, the *body* becomes purified. On this model, beheading might make it possible for the woman to *think* (straight) again, freeing her rationality from her sexuality. There is, therefore, an ambivalence of caste parallel to the ambivalence of sexuality. But, in either case, the head is the source of Mariatale's identity and her legal status: if she has a divine head, she is a pure goddess. And her impure bottom half, the half that lusts for the demigod, is the human woman, the denied woman, the passionate woman, as polluting and despised as the outcaste. This half becomes the body of the finally integrated Mariatale, who is identified with the divine head but functions with an outcaste body.

THE MYTH OF THE BLINDFOLDED GODDESS

In a common variant of one thread of this myth, in which a high-caste woman is mistreated and as a result becomes transformed into an outcaste goddess, the theme of beheading is replaced by a series of different sorts of blindings. A. K. Ramanujan retells a story in this corpus, which I herewith summarize:

> A Brahmin girl began to menstruate before she was married; in keeping with the custom, her father blindfolded her eyes and left her in the jungle. A man who pitied the girl took her home and raised her as his own daughter. An outcaste fell in love with her, "dressed himself in Brahmin-style clothes," and married her. She bore him two sons. One day they spied on their father at work and saw him measuring peoples' feet and sewing sandals for them. Then they went home, gathered big leaves, and cut out the outlines of their feet, telling their mother, when she questioned them, "We are doing exactly what Daddy does." When she realized what caste of man she had married, her anger rose, and she grew bigger and bigger and became a terrifying goddess [a Mari, as in Mariamma]. She put out her tongue and went in search of her husband. Her children, terrified, hid themselves inside two goats, but she broke off the goats' heads and drank her children's blood. The outcaste man entered a he-buffalo, but she slit him open and drank his blood. She met a religious mendicant and told him to walk in front of her, not looking back; but he looked back, and she lashed out with her tongue at him, killed him, and drank his blood. She went on killing people, drinking their blood, until she came to rest.[7]

The Brahmin girl is blindfolded ostensibly so that she will not find her way home from the jungle, but really in order to blind her to what is being done to her, even as she will be "blinded" by the outcaste's change of clothing. The prohibition "Do not turn around and look at me" is a motif that we know not only from Lot's wife but also from Mélusine, Lohengrin, and Beauty and the Beast: "Do not ask to know who I am, do not look at me naked, do not shine a light at me, do not, in short, discover that I am supernatural." The violation of this prohibition is the mythological form of a violation that contemporary feminist thought has taught us to recognize as the male gaze. Thus the Mari is visually betrayed by three different men: her father, who blindfolds her; her husband, who masquerades for her; and the luckless mendicant, who looks at her when she tells him not to. Yet we would do well here to recall that there is also a powerful *female* gaze in these myths; it is by gazing, not by being gazed upon, that Renuka discovers and reveals her eroticism. Indeed, it is precisely because this female gaze is deemed unacceptable (by the male author of the text) that Renuka must be beheaded, her gaze "silenced," as it were. The principle is clear to see: women should be more gazed upon than gazing. In this particular myth of the Brahmin girl and the shoemaker, she responds to the limitation of her powers of sight by letting loose the powers of her destructive tongue.

The theological level of the myth of Mariatale or the myth of the blindfolded Brahmin woman is thus inextricably intertwined with the question of class. Indeed, this theodicy can be read from several points of view. From the woman's point of view, she is unjustly treated by various men, and driven to become a fierce goddess. But from the standpoint of Hindu society, the outcaste woman pollutes the goddess. These points of view merge in those myths that regard the outcaste man as the primary enemy of the Brahmin woman. In the tale of Mariatale, the woman has two enemies, who perform separately the two functions of the outcaste man in the myths of rape: the unfair Brahmin husband (the enemy in the woman's eyes) and the outcaste woman (the enemy in the eyes of Hindu caste law).

A strange inversion of the myth of the rape of a Brahmin woman by an outcaste man occurs in a contemporary story told by the hijras, bands of men whose sexuality is liminal in any of several different ways: they may be transvestites, male homosexual prostitutes, or eunuchs (or, indeed, more than one of these at once):

> Once there was a prince whose parents wanted to get him married. The boy did not want to get married, but his parents insisted. They selected this goddess as his wife, and the marriage took place. He was a very handsome boy, but the Mata was also a very beautiful lady. But after the marriage the husband and wife never joined together. On the first night, leaving the goddess alone in the nuptial room, the prince rode away into the forest. The goddess waited

till dawn and felt very angry that her husband had left her. This went on for some months.

The goddess felt very hurt and decided to investigate. So one night she followed him on a path to the forest clearing where the prince had been acting like the hijras. She was puzzled by what she had seen and returned home. When her husband returned, she said to him, "I want to ask you something, do not get angry at me. Don't you feel that you must have your wife by you?" Then the prince fell at her feet and told her, "Mother, if I had the urge for a wife and children, I wouldn't have left you and gone away. I am neither a man nor a woman, and that is the truth."

The goddess got very angry and said, "They have spoiled my life by hiding the facts, and therefore your life will also be spoiled. Hereafter, people like you should be *nirvan* [undergo emasculation in order to be reborn]." So saying, she cut off his genitals. After cutting off his genitals she said, "People like you, who are going to have this *nirvan,* should call me at that time." After this the prince took on the form of a woman.[8]

Here the goddess is infuriated not by a sexual attack but by the lack of it; the husband is not an outcaste masquerading as a Brahmin but simply a non-husband masquerading as a husband. And if we accept the Freudian concept of upward displacement, whereby blinding or beheading would stand for castration, the punishment in this case is a downward displacement of the beheading found in the South Indian stories: the masquerader is actually castrated. Here, as in many Hindu myths, "unsymbols" (or uncensored events) express on the manifest level what Freud expected to find only on the latent level. Sometimes a *linga* is just a good cigar.[9] Or, as Edmund Leach (cited by Eilberg-Schwartz in the Introduction) puts it, "The *linga* represents itself." We will return to the problem of upward/downward displacement and "unsymbols" in Conclusion B below.

BAGGING WOMEN IN SHAKESPEARE AND IN EARLY AND CONTEMPORARY AMERICA

Though, as we have seen, beheading is seldom fatal in myths, in more realistic versions of the theme beheading may be explicitly transformed into something less lethal—blindfolding the victim, or putting a bag over the victim's head. The latter is also a macho male fantasy, an antiromantic locker-room fantasy: "Put a bag over her head."

The phrase "put a bag over her head" is often attributed to Benjamin Franklin, who actually referred not to a bag but to a basket. He made this suggestion in the course of a letter, written on June 25, 1745, in which he advises a young friend to marry ("A single Man . . . resembles the odd Half of a Pair of Scissors") but, failing that, to "prefer old Women to young ones." Franklin gives seven reasons for this preference (the most notorious being that older women "are so grateful"), but the fifth is the one that concerns us in the context of beheading:

> In every Animal that walks upright, the Deficiency of the Fluids that fill the Muscles appears first in the highest Part. The Face first grows lank and wrinkled; then the Neck; then the Breast and Arms; the lower parts continuing to the last as plump as ever; so that covering all above with a Basket, and regarding only what is below the Girdle, it is impossible of two Women to know an old from a young one. And as in the Dark all Cats are grey, the Pleasure of Corporal Enjoyment with an old Woman is at least equal and frequently superior; every Knack being by Practice capable of improvement.[10]

The implication is that as the face dries up, the lower mouth gets wetter.

Putting a bag over her head is a way of gaining power over a woman by implying that no one particular woman has power over a man. But the "bag over her head" mentality can be used against men as well as women. (In a study of turtle-husbands, Stuart Blackburn refers, tongue in cheek, to "appendage-challenged heroes, such as our turtles and crabs and bodiless heads.")[11] Bagging the head mimics what is done to captives in war to make them helpless: unlike a blindfold, a bag over the head simultaneously blinds them, constrains their arms, and silences their mouths. Executioners traditionally wear bags over their heads, presumably to absolve them of any personal involvement in the act of killing.

A bag is quite literally placed over the head of the protagonist's alter ego in Shakespeare's *All's Well That Ends Well*. This protagonist, Bertram, is a great hypocrite, though not an obvious one; his foil, indeed his double, is provided by his sidekick Parolles, who is a blatant hypocrite. Bertram, married to Helena, refuses to sleep with her but makes an assignation with a young girl named Diana in Florence, a foreign city. Helena goes there and persuades Diana to allow her, Helena, to get into bed with Bertram in the dark, in Diana's place, and Bertram does not know the difference. Thus Bertram, thinking himself captured by a foreign woman in Florence, betrays his own wife, who is, unknown to him, present, masquerading in the dark as the woman with whom Bertram thinks he is deceiving her. Similarly, Parolles, blindfolded and thinking himself captured by the enemy, betrays his own friends, who are, unknown to him, present (who are, in fact, his captors). As the French lord says of Parolles, "A' will betray us all unto ourselves."[12] Parolles, with a blindfold (or, in most stage productions, literally a bag over his head), is a grotesque metaphor for blind lust: he does not know whom he is with. He believes that his captors are speaking a language he does not know. In the same way, Diana makes Bertram promise not to talk to her in bed ("Remain there but an hour, nor speak to me"),[13] eliminating any sensual contact at all but the sexual (since darkness stymies vision, and silence stymies hearing), and more specifically eliminating the voice that would identify her as an individual even when the male gaze has been silenced. Bertram falsely believes that he cannot speak to his "foreign" mistress, who is in fact his own wife, Helena, and does indeed speak his language. ("My wife does not understand me" is the modern version of this trope, traditionally repeated to a secretary.) The speech act and the sexual act are conflated, and a political betrayal is assimilated to a sexual betrayal. In Shakespeare's *Measure for Measure,* too, Isabella must find a substitute for her own maidenhead in order to keep Angelo from beheading her brother Claudio, and Claudio must find a substitute for his own head; and, like Parolles, the rake Lucio (another sort of double of Claudio, who eventually receives Claudio's punishment) slanders the Duke to the Duke himself when he (the Duke) has what amounts to a bag over his head: he is wearing the hood of a monk.

This same conflation of sexual and political dehumanization in the metaphor of bagging the head occurs in the contemporary film *The Crying Game.* In the opening part of this film, the prisoner, Jody, has a bag over his head, ostensibly so that he will not be able to recognize the people around him and identify them later if they should decide to set him free. But the bag serves another, more important, though less obvious, function: it prevents his captors from seeing him as an individual human being, a sight that might make it more difficult for them to murder him. Later, this mutual blindness is reflected, as in *All's Well,* in a sexual masquerade: Jody's captor eventually discovers that Jody's girl is, in fact, a boy. Thus the bag over Jody's head serves both the same manifest reason as the bag on Parolles (to blind a political prisoner) and the same latent reason (to hide a sexual masquerader).

The woman with a bag over her head gives a new meaning to the "bag lady," who is depersonalized not by her sexuality but by her poverty; here again, we see the conflation of sexual and political-economic forms of oppression. And the dishonoring of old women implicit in Franklin's satire lingers in our pejorative synecdoche "old bag," as in the gigolo's song in Cole Porter's *Kiss Me Kate:* "If my wife has a bag of gold, do I care if the bag be old?" The woman with the bag over her head is a pornographic image: she has no personality, no individualism. The fantasy of removing or bagging the head of a man or a woman is a fantasy that denies the power of the individual, reducing sexuality to pure animality. It is enshrined in a contemporary American culture that identifies the body with the person, a culture that also hides its public figures, male and female, behind sunglasses, which become symbolic of political power, criminal evil, and impersonal sexuality. As Eilberg-Schwartz remarks in the Introduction, "It is no accident that . . . women [are portrayed as] more erotic when they remove their glasses."

A contemporary sexist work, Bret Easton Ellis's *American Psycho,* uses images of blinding and beheading in the service of pornographic violence. At the height of his derangement, the protagonist parades naked around his apartment sexually attached to a severed head with both eyes scooped out and a pair of designer sunglasses over the holes. The physical form of sunglasses is relatively new and pleasantly utilitarian, but the symbolic echoes are very old indeed, and very violent.

CONCLUSION A: THE EYE AND THE TONGUE

Throughout these myths, there is a clear opposition between the female gaze and the female tongue. When the Brahmin woman's anger transforms her into the goddess Mari, she sticks out her tongue. When she finds a victim, it is said that "she lashed out with her tongue at him, killed him, and drank his blood." This is an ancient Hindu icon, which can be traced back to the ancient demoness named Long-tongue.[14] Long-tongue is a "male" woman, a woman with a phallus,[15] who also has multiple vaginas; she thus provides a precedent not only for the (female) *vagina dentata* of several demonic figures in Hindu mythology[16] but also for the (male) long tongue of Kali (who is thus depicted on many icons). The goddess (Devi) also disposes of the demon Raktabija ("Blood-semen"), from every drop of whose blood a new demon appears; to conquer him, the goddess emits multiforms of herself who extend their tongues to lick up each drop of his blood before it can fall to the ground.[17] The long tongue of Long-tongue, Kali, and Blood-semen's nemesis is in a certain sense a phallus, but it is also an antiphallic vagina. It is, moreover, the organ of language ("*langue,*" in both senses, in French). So, too, the phallus itself, as Lacan tells us, is a word, a "tongue" in the other sense of the word. The usual Sanskrit word for penis, *lingam,* primarily means "sign" or "characteristic" or, finally, "the image of a god or idol." That is, it is both a part of the body and a part of speech.

The god Indra subdues Long-tongue by creating for her a lover who has as many penises as she has vaginas. In another variant of this myth, Indra himself is said to have penises on every limb.[18] But in later mythology, Indra has not multiple penises but multiple vaginas, which he gets when a sage catches him in bed with his wife and curses him to have a thousand vaginas on his body (thus literally emasculating him, or at least effeminizing him; the curse may therefore be roughly equivalent to a castration). Later, this curse is modified and reduced to merely having a thousand eyes on his body, a stunning example of upward displacement.[19] But in other variants of the myth, Indra is actually castrated (and later restored with the testicles of a ram).[20] Indeed, in one variant Indra gets the vaginas *and* the eyes *and* the castration:

> Gautama cursed Indra, saying, "Since you have acted in this way for the sake of the female sexual organ, let there be a thousand of them on your body, and let your penis [*lingam*] fall." Then Indra praised the goddess in her aspect of Indraksi ["Eyes of Indra"], and she said, "I cannot destroy the evil created by a sage's curse, but I can do something so that people will not notice it: you will have a thousand eyes in the middle of the female organ, and you will have the testicles of a ram."[21]

These Indian texts validate Freud's concept of upward displacement, but they also suggest that it can, and must, be extended from its original androcentric formulation (beheading = castration, eyes = penis) to include the rest of the human race as well as a more ambivalent attitude to sexuality in general: beheading = the release or termination of sexuality, male or female; eyes = penis or vagina.

The old dichotomy between goddesses of the breast and goddesses of the tooth[22] might also here be supplemented, or even supplanted, by a distinction between the eye and the tongue. The Silent Woman, depicted headless on the sign of a New England restaurant of that name, is the beheaded woman. But she is also the raped woman who is silenced (as in the myth in which Tereus rapes Philomela and cuts out her tongue, and in Shakespeare's reworking of the myth in *Titus Andronicus*). The female impersonator in David Henry Hwang's *M. Butterfly* speaks eloquently of the rape mentality, the macho argument that "her eyes say yes when her tongue says no."[23] Vision is what the rapist trusts, the message of the eyes, communication on the animal level. Speech is what the rapist denies, the message of the tongue, the message on the cultural level of the individual. All cats are indeed gray in the night, but cats can't speak; women can, and hence are not alike.

CONCLUSION B: THE EYE AND THE GENITALS

The basic principle of upward displacement seems to apply cross-culturally, but the actual combinations vary in different cultures. Thus the genitals, male or female, or the sperm or the blood, may be associated with the head as a whole, with the eyes, with the nose (the protruding phallus), or with the mouth (particularly the tongue). The Greeks, for instance, tend to associate eyes with the phallus, the Hindus with the vagina (as well as the phallus). The Greeks blind the male child in punishment for the sexual sins of the father (Oedipus), while the Hindus blind the male child in situations where the mother has sinned (as in the stories of Pandu and Dirghatamas).[24] Whereas, in Greece, blinding occurs as punishment for a sexual sin, in India the sexual sin of a man may result in giving him *more* eyes (as in the story of the castration of Indra).[25]

The myths argue that blindness is both a cause of sexual sin and a result of sexual sin (the punishment for excessive sexual voyeurism, or incorrect visual sexual discrimination, judging by appearances or being taken in by a visual trick); the punishment fits the crime. Sexual mistakes may be the result of metaphorical blindness and may result in physical blindness. The female gaze is a double danger: the danger of looking at Medusa's head, and the danger of having her look at *you;* the dangerous woman with her dangerous eyes. Jean Delumeau tells how San Bernardo, who had a "horror of nudity," also "scolds anyone who too freely uses 'the eye' during conjugal relations. His words are startling: 'Look at me, do you see this eye? It was not made for marriage. What has the eye to do with marriage? Every time it desires to see obscene deeds, it is a deadly sin. For what is permissible to touch is not permissible to look at.' "[26]

These displacements can be mutual, even in simplistic physical terms, when, for instance, the cloth that usually covers the genitals is literally displaced to the head. A striking example of this displacement may be taken from the life and works of the surrealist painter René Magritte. In his painting *The Rape,* which Howard Eilberg-Schwartz glosses in the Introduction, a woman's facial features are replaced by breasts, a navel, and a triangle of pubic hair. Magritte said that in creating this image he had solved "the problem of woman." But events in Magritte's life give further meaning to the image. In 1912, when Magritte was only thirteen years old, his mother committed suicide by jumping off a bridge in Châtelet into a dreary stretch of the river Sambre. When her body was pulled from the water a couple of weeks later, Madame Magritte was nude because the currents had pulled up her nightdress and knotted it around her face. David Sylvester has argued that that memory was almost certainly a fantasy originating with the artist's governess, but it has often been cited as a source for Magritte's recurrent paintings of bare-chested women and hooded figures.[27]

CONCLUSION C: THE NECK AND THE WAIST

The myth of cutting a woman in half at the neck is often varied by cutting a woman in half at the waist. We have seen some of the meanings of the head severed from the body, and most of these will still apply when the top half also includes the breasts. But with the division at the waist another level of symbolism comes into play: the breast (mother) versus the genitals (whore). The division at the waist is common in mythology all over the world: mermaids, Naginis (Indian figures, cobras from the waist down, goddesses from the waist up), and centaurs. The sexual symbolism of the centaur persists in Shakespeare:

Down from the waist they are Centaurs,
Though women all above:
But to the girdle do the Gods inherit,
Beneath is all the fiend's: there's hell, there's darkness,
There is the sulphurous pit—burning scalding,
Stench, consumption: fie, fie, fie! pah! pah![28]

The centaur, which is divided at the waist in Greece and in Shakespeare, is often inverted and divided at the neck in India, where Buddhist sailors are plagued by women with the heads of horses and the bodies of women from the neck down.[29] There are significant differences between a horse-headed person and a person-torsoed horse. First of all, they are split in a different place: the Greek centaur is disproportionately horsey, for even though there is a whole human torso, and not just the head, there is an equine torso, too; there is everything of the horse up to the neck, four legs to the human's two arms. But more important, there is a different meaning to a human head and an animal head. When the head is that of a beast, it means that the mind is bestial. When the body is that of a beast, it means that the sexuality is that of the beast; for the animal body typically begins from the groin, so that the beast is an extension of the genitals.

In ancient Greece, however, sailors were plagued by another set of women divided at the waist, Scylla and Charybdis. Charybdis sucks men down into the dark water; Scylla has six heads, each with three rows of deadly teeth, with which she devours dolphins and dogs and people, and she is hidden up to the waist "in a hollow cave."[30] When Scylla fishes for Odysseus's men, she devours them as they scream and stretch out their hands "at her doors." Together, Scylla and Charybdis are a woman split in half: Scylla is the devouring upper mouth, the woman from the waist up, and Charybdis is the devouring lower mouth, the woman from the waist down. This double woman is further mirrored by the Symplagades or Plank-tae, rocks that crash together and smash ships between them,[31] a gross metaphor for the woman crushing the man with the walls of her womb as she contracts when he is inside her. This is misogyny squared: Scylla and Charybdis are a pair of nightmare women, each split in half, and Odysseus has to try to get between each of them and also between the pair of them, just as he has to get through the Planktae. Greek mythology teems with other groups of dangerous women who are part horse, part bird, and part snake, and the worst part of each (Harpies, Gorgons, Erinyes). The Sphinx is another deadly Greek split woman, part woman, part snake, part lion, and the worst part of each. Why is it that the male composite figures, like the centaurs, are all great heroes, while the female composite figures are man-eating monsters? The answer is embedded in these myths, an answer clear enough to those who have eyes to see and hear what the texts are saying to us.

NOTES

1. *Mahabharata* 3.116.
2. Allen 1976.
3. Ramanujan 1973:24–25.
4. Ibid., 24–25.
5. Sonnerat 1782:245–47.
6. O'Flaherty 1980:18, 21, 45–46, 87, 255–56.
7. Ramanujan 1986:58–61.
8. Nanda 1990:25–26.
9. Doniger 1993a.
10. Schuster 1940:159–62.
11. Blackburn 1993:30.
12. Shakespeare, *All's Well That Ends Well,* 4.1.92.
13. Ibid., 4.2.58.
14. *Jaiminiya Brahmana* 1.161–63; O'Flaherty 1985:101–3.
15. Roheim 1945:100–125.
16. *Skanda Purana* 1.2.27–29; O'Flaherty 1985:252–61.
17. O'Flaherty 1980:215; *Vamana Purana* 30.
18. *Kausitaki Brahmana,* 23.7.5–12.
19. *Kathasaritsagara* 17.137–48.
20. *Ramayana* 1.47.15–31.
21. *Padma Purana* 1.56.15–53.
22. O'Flaherty 1980:80–129.
23. Hwang 1988, Act 3.
24. Doniger 1993b.
25. Doniger 1992.
26. Delumeau 1990:436.
27. Sylvester 1992:60–61.
28. Shakespeare, *King Lear,* 4.6.123–29.
29. O'Flaherty 1980:216–18.
30. Homer, *Odyssey,* 12.101–10.
31. Homer, *Odyssey,* 12.60–72.

REFERENCES

Sanskrit Texts

Jaiminiya Brahmana
    1954   Edited by Raghu Vira and Lokesh Chandra. Nagpur: Sarasvati-vihara Series 31.
Kathasaritsagara
    1930   Bombay: Nirnara Sagara Press.
Kausitaki Brahmana
    1968   Wiesbaden: Harrassowitz.
Mahabharata, attributed to Vyasa
    1933–1969   Critical edition. Poona: Bhandarkar Oriental Research Institute.

Padma Purana
1893   Poona: Anandasrama Sanskrit Series 131.
Ramayana
1960–1975   Baroda: Oriental Institute.
Skanda Purana
1867   Bombay: Shree Venkatesvara Steam Press.
Vamana Purana
1968   Varanasi: All-India Kashiraj.

Texts in European Languages

Allen, Woody
1976   "Fabulous Tales and Mythical Beasts." In *Without Feathers*. New York: Random House.
Blackburn, Stuart
1995   "Coming Out of His Shell: Animal-husband Tales from India." Ms. Forthcoming in *Animal-Husband Tales: A Casebook*, ed. by Alan Dundes. New York: Wildman Press.
Delumeau, Jean
1990   *Sin and Fear: The Emergence of a Western Guilt Culture, 13th–18th Centuries*. New York: St. Martin's Press.
Doniger, Wendy
1992   "When God Has Lipstick on His Collar." Mackay Lecture, St. Lawrence University, 1991.
1993a   "When a Lingam Is Just a Good Cigar: Psychoanalysis and Hindu Sexual Fantasies." In *The Psychoanalytic Study of Society: Essays in Honor of Alan Dundes,* ed. by L. Bryce Boyer et al., 81–104. Hillside, N.J.: The Analytic Press.
1993b   "Begetting on Margin: The Paradox of the Levirate in Hinduism." Ms. Forthcoming in *Hindu Marriage*, ed. by Paul Courtright and Lindsey Harlan.
Ellis, Bret Easton
1991   *American Psycho*. New York: Vintage Books.
Hwang, David Henry
1988   *M. Butterfly*. New York: Dramatists Play Service, Inc.
Nanda, Serena
1990   *Neither Man Nor Woman: The Hijras of India*. Belmont, Calif.: Wadsworth.
O'Flaherty, Wendy Doniger
1980   *Women, Androgynes, and Other Mythical Beasts*. Chicago: University of Chicago Press.
1985   *Tales of Sex and Violence: Folklore, Sacrifice, and Danger in the Jaiminiya Brahmana*. Chicago: University of Chicago Press.
Ramanujan, A. K.
1973   *Speaking of Siva*. Harmondsworth: Penguin.
1986   "Two Realms of Kannada Folklore." In *Another Harmony: New Essays on the Folklore of India*, ed. by Stuart H. Blackburn and A. K. Ramanujan, 41–75. Berkeley and Los Angeles: University of California Press.

Roheim, Geza
    1945   *Eternal Ones of the Dream: A Psychoanalytic Interpretation of Australian Myth and Ritual.* New York: International Universities Press.
Schuster, M. Lincoln
    1940   *A Treasury of the World's Great Letters.* New York: Simon and Schuster.
Sonnerat, Pierre
    1782   *Voyages aux Indes Orientales.* Paris: L'auteur.
Sylvester, David
    1992   *Magritte: The Silence of the World.* New York: The Menil Foundation/ Harry N. Abrams.

TWO

Shaven Heads and Loose Hair

Buddhist Attitudes toward Hair and Sexuality

Karen Lang

The shaven heads of Buddhist monks and the long matted hair of female Hindu ascetics carry sexual meanings. But psychologists and anthropologists debate the nature of those meanings. As discussed in the Introduction, the debate concerns whether such practices have phallic meaning and, if so, whether actors are conscious of those meanings. Psychoanalytic theory explains both points in terms of castration anxiety: a shaven head is a symbolic castration and for this reason is adopted by ascetics who renounce their sexuality. By contrast, the growing and matting of hair is the denial of castration. Leach accepted this phallic interpretation, but insisted that the meanings were public and not related to the unconscious conflicts of the actors.[1]

But divergent ideas of chastity may lie behind these two symbolisms, as Gananath Obeyesekere argues in *Medusa's Hair*. Although the shaven head and matted hair both symbolize chastity, they are not interchangeable, for Hindu and Buddhist ideas of chastity are different. Hindu conceptions of chastity involve withholding sex to conserve semen; its conservation and the subsequent increase of power (*śakti*) is one of the major goals of Hindu ascetics. The Buddhist monk's notion of chastity is radically different: the total renunciation of sexuality; the Buddhist monk is sexless, a neuter.[2]

Obeyesekere develops this argument from his own ethnographic data on six female ascetics with matted hair. These six ascetic women describe their unkempt, lice-ridden locks of matted hair as a gift of the gods. For these women the locks of matted hair represent a visible manifestation of a bond of love between themselves and the gods who possess them. Writing within a psychoanalytic perspective, Obeyesekere interprets these matted locks as symbolic "penes stuck on the head." The matted hair is the god's *lingam,* the idealized penis, but this is not consciously recognized. Since none of the women he interviewed could even remotely associate their matted hair with male or female genitals, the correspondence, he concludes, must be unconscious. "If the head hair is the sublated penis emerging from the head," he asks, "what kind of penis is it? Gods, those idealized beings, cannot have penes like yours or mine," he tells us, revealing a distinct male bias in his orientation.[3] Obeyesekere has taken these matted locks, which he and others (including the ascetics themselves) regard as symbols of chastity, and from his own subjective gaze inferred a sexualized meaning.

In this paper I will argue that the psychoanalytic model of phallocentrism and castration does not explain adequately the complex secular and religious meanings of women's shaven heads and loose hair as found in Buddhist texts.

The frame of reference for those who study ancient texts also differs from that of both psychoanalysts and anthropologists. I am primarily concerned here with the experiences of people long dead, people whose lives and words have been edited and revised by others. It is difficult enough working with these centuries-old texts to try to recover what might have been the conscious motivation behind these religious figures' reported thoughts and actions. Far more difficult is any attempt to deal with their possible unconscious motivation. For these reasons, the major focus of my study involves conscious and explicit associations between hair and sexual behavior which these texts record.

The manner in which religious persons treat their hair can reveal something about their attitudes toward sexuality and about the means they choose for controlling the potent force of sexual desire. I will explore two alternative ways of treating the hair among female practitioners in the Buddhist tradition: the shaven head of the Buddhist nun and the loose hair of the Tantric adept (*siddha*).[4] Both shaven heads and loose hair can signify a celibate state; but they are not interchangeable symbols and the dichotomy they represent is not a mutually exclusive one. And both symbols are, of course, part of a larger network of related concepts. For the nun, shaving the head signifies a rite of separation, a turning away from the heat of sensual desire toward the coolness of nirvana. For the Tantric adept, loose hair signifies a different orientation, one that channels the heated power of sexuality and uses this force as a means of making spiritual progress toward enlightenment.

HEAD SHAVING AS A RITE OF SEPARATION

Leach classifies the removal of head hair as a rite of separation in which an individual separates himself from the world of his family and reorients himself toward another world.[5] This correlation between the severing of hair and the severing of family ties occurs also in the traditional biographies of the Buddha's life, which report that Prince Siddhārtha left his wife and young son behind, went out the palace gates, and cut off his long hair with his sword. This willful act of cutting the hair marked his transition from householder to ascetic. Men and women who follow his example similarly separate themselves from the world of their family and reorient themselves toward another world, that of the religious community. Cutting their hair signifies this renunciation of family life and willingness to assume a new orientation: the fulfillment of a chaste religious existence. In the collections of verses attributed to enlightened followers of the Buddha, the *Theragāthā* and the *Therīgāthā*, monks and nuns speak in similar ways about their renunciation of lay life. The monk Mahāpanthaka says: "I abandoned my children and my wife, my money and grain, I cut off my hair and beard, and went forth into the homeless state" (Thag. 512). Using the same formulaic pattern for speaking about renunciation, the nun Sakulā says: "I abandoned my son and daughter, my money and grain, I cut off my hair, and I went forth into the homeless state" (Thig. 98).[6] In these two statements and in many others that could be quoted from the Pāli canon, the cutting off of one's hair is a physical action that, in an unmistakable manner, marks the culmination of an individual's intention to leave home: like progeny, money, and material possessions, hair is something that belongs to householders. In several cases which serve as precedents for the disciplinary regulations codified in the *Vinaya*, when laymen complain angrily to the Buddha about the behavior of some of his female followers they refer to these nuns as "shaven-headed whores."[7] A shaven head thus becomes an external identifying mark that sets Buddhist monks and nuns apart from lay society.

Going forth from home to homelessness, the standard expression in Buddhist texts to describe an individual's choice of the religious life, indicates also a separation from a sexually active life and the resultant commitment to chastity. Hair that is long, and well-tended, signals a woman's sexual attractiveness. The authors of secular love poems often speak of their lovers' long, braided black hair, fragrant with the scent of white jasmine. In a reversal of the usual conventions of secular love poetry, in which the male poet describes the beauty of his young lover, the ex-courtesan Ambapālī describes how her own beauty has disappeared with age: "My hair adorned with flowers was fragrant like a scented box. Now because of old age it has the stench of dog's fur" (Thig. 253). In the past her hair was braided and decorated with gold pins; but now, she says, "my head is bald" (Thig. 255).[8] Hair was once part of this ex-courtesan's physical attractiveness; her bald head now signifies that she is no longer sexually attractive or available. Sumedhā, another of the enlightened nuns whose experiences the *Therīgāthā* records, chooses the chaste life of a nun over the sensual pleasures promised to her as the bride of a king: "Sumedhā cut her thick, soft, black hair with a knife, closed the palace door, and entered into her first meditation" (Thig. 480). She then develops an understanding of the concept of impermanence. The commentary to the verses of Sumedhā indicates that this meditation on her severed hair enables her to understand the impermanence of physical attraction.[9] This tradition of using a severed lock of hair as an object of meditation continues to the present day. In the ordination ceremony of a lay nun (dasa sil mata) in Sri Lanka, after a young woman's head is shaved, her preceptors ask her to look at a severed lock of her hair and meditate on impermanence.[10] The nun's continuing commitment to shaving her head indicates her control over her sexuality and her potential fertility. By altering her attractive appearance with the shaving off of her hair, a nun removes herself as a potential sexual threat to the monastic community.

Head shaving also marks the beginning of a monk's ordination ritual; it signals his readiness to take his place in a community (sangha) whose members shave their heads at least once a month. The act of shaving the head once a month, Charles Keyes says, symbolizes a renewed commitment to the monastic discipline; just as hair can grow again, sexual desire can re-emerge.[11] The rules laid down in the Vinaya for regulating the religious community forbid monks and nuns from growing their hair longer than two inches and from using combs or cosmetic applications to make it attractive.[12] Both the members of the religious community and the lay community which supports them associate a closely shaven head with a chaste life.[13]

HEAD SHAVING, CHASTITY, AND SYMBOLIC CASTRATION

Keyes considers the interpretation of head shaving as symbolic castration to be at odds with the regulations in the Vinaya regarding the sexual potency of the monastic community's members. There are explicit prohibitions against eunuchs entering the sangha; monks must be capable of performing sexually, while controlling completely the desire to do so. The ordination process, he argues, transforms those who undergo it into a new gender identity that is neither male nor female. The gender of the renunciant does not result from a biological sexual attribute, nor is it, he adds, "a consequence of physical mutilation."[14] It may seem that Keyes misses the point when he speaks as if what is at issue here is a physical castration and not a symbolic one, but his criticism is directed primarily against those who would read into a practice interpretations that the tradition itself does not support.

Similar concerns and prohibitions occur in the section of the Vinaya dealing with the ordination of women. The nuns who help the woman about to be ordained put on her new robes must examine her to see that she has the requisite female genitals. *Vinaya* regulations further prescribe that she not currently be menstruating, nor should she be "non-menstruous."[15] These regulations suggest that she, like the monk, should be capable of performing sexually while keeping sexual desire in check; they further suggest that she should be fertile, although her fertility must be controlled. At issue here is not castration—even symbolic—of genital organs but rather continued control over the mental organ which controls sexual responsiveness.

Buddhists believe that the mind wields power over all physical actions. For Buddhists the intention behind an action is the decisive factor which determines whether that action is moral or immoral. The initial prohibition in the *Vinaya* against sexual intercourse occurs after the Buddha is confronted with the case of a young monk, Sudinna. He is an only child whose parents very reluctantly give their consent to his ordination after he prepares to make good on his threat to starve himself to death if he does not receive their permission. His parents successfully persuade him to engage in sexual intercourse (three times) with his willing ex-wife in the hope of providing themselves with an heir. The Buddha severely criticizes Sudinna and tells him that it would have been better for him to have thrust his penis into the mouth of a poisonous snake or into a pit of blazing charcoal than into his ex-wife, for by breaking his commitment to chastity he will die and be reborn in hell.[16] After this initial case, the Buddha's judgment is sought on a wide assortment of sexual offenses that a monk might commit with women, with men, with animals, with demons, even with himself should he have a penis long enough to sodomize himself or a body supple enough to perform oral sex on himself.[17]

Similar regulations against sexual intercourse govern the sexual behavior of nuns. Any nun who receives sexual pleasure from any male, "asleep, awake, or dead," must be expelled from the religious community. The crucial factors in considering an act an offense that requires expulsion are that penetration, a breach of the body's integrity, occur, and that the act be consensual and voluntarily engaged in with the intention of fulfilling one's sensual desires. If the nun is unwilling or asleep when a man forces himself on her or if her mental faculties are impaired, no offense occurs.[18] Not only sexual intercourse but even touching any part of a man's body between the collarbone and the knees (including holding his hands) is an offense that results in expulsion, if the nun acts under the influence of passion. As Mohan Wijayaratna points out, sexual offenses involve "defeat" in the battle against the enemy of sensual desire; those members of the religious community who recognize their inability to maintain control over their sensual desires and formally leave the community to return to lay life before committing a sexual offense are not defeated, since they have withdrawn from the battlefield before the enemy can defeat them.[19]

Some Hindu Brahminical texts advocate abstention from sexual intercourse due to fear of the loss of semen—a potent but polluting substance—and out of the conviction that contact with the divine requires physical purity.[20] In what seems almost a parody of the Brahminical notion that a man's physical health is dependent upon retention of his semen, the Buddhist *Vinaya* records the case of a young monk in poor health who regains his vitality after he takes the advice of an elder monk and begins to masturbate and spill his semen on a daily basis. When his actions are brought to the attention of the Buddha, the Buddha rebukes him for failing to understand that Buddhist teachings are intended to curb passion and sensual pleasures.[21] For the Buddhist, living a chaste life involves more than just physical virginity; chastity involves restraining the mind as well as the body. In all cases of sexual misconduct, what is at issue for monks and nuns is not just control of their genital organs but, more importantly, control over a higher organ, the mind. Control over the mental organ is essential to Buddhist practice, since passion pollutes the mind and makes the experience of enlightenment impossible.

"Passion has been stilled," Obeyesekere says, referring to the Buddha's experience of enlightenment, "and the source of the passion—the penis—is symbolically castrated."[22] His association of what he regards as the dominant features of Theravāda sculpture of the Buddha—remoteness, serenity, asexuality—with symbolic castration is at odds with Buddhist tradition both iconographically and philosophically. The tradition of the thirty-two characteristic marks of a Buddha's body specifies that a Buddha's penis is drawn inwards or enclosed with a sheath. "The sheathed penis," Nancy Barnes suggests, "symbolizes that his genital virility is controlled and contained and is replaced by his oral 'virility.'" Noting that another of these marks, the long, broad tongue, is closely connected in the earliest textual references with the mark of the sheathed penis, she points out that the Buddha fathers sons and daughters "who are born of his mouth, that is, of the truth he teaches."[23] His procreative energy, in other words, has been "displaced upwards" to his tongue. Similarly, the nuns' procreative powers are also redirected towards the creation of spiritual daughters. "I heard her teaching," one nun says about another nun who influenced her decision to become a member of the Buddhist community, "then I cut off my hair, and I went forth" (Thig. 103).

The source of the passion that Buddhists combat is not the penis per se but rather the mind. The passion which the Buddha and his spiritual sons and daughters seek to still is an attitude of the mind and is conquered by the serenity which meditative training and practice impart. The philosophy of Buddhism emphasizes control over the mind because the mind influences the direction of all physical actions. The physical act of shaving the head places novice monks and nuns in the right direction and on the Buddha's path, but progress on this path depends on the control they have over the mind's tendency to seek out and pursue sensual desire. "It is quite an easy matter to cut one's hair," a contemporary nun reports; "it is changing the mind that is very difficult."[24]

SHAVEN HEADS AND THE COOLNESS OF NIRVANA

Both monks and nuns seek to liberate themselves from the cycle of birth, death, and rebirth. Buddhist views of this cycle and of the means of escaping from it differ sharply from the advice that Brahminical texts give to householders. According to some Brahminical texts, a son's performance of the appropriate funeral rites assures his father of one kind of immortality ("below the navel"), physical immortality. Another kind of immortality, however—spiritual immortality ("above the navel"), advocated in the Upanishadic texts—is lost through the birth of a son and the resultant ties to *samsara*.[25] This latter view is more in accord with the position of Buddhism, which regards Vedic rituals and the birth of sons as fetters that perpetuate bondage in the continuous cycle of birth, death, and rebirth. The Buddha's discourses, the majority of which record advice given to monks and nuns, stress that desire fuels this cycle and that sensual desire is one of its primary manifestations. Since lay life and the attendant procreative duties of householders are fertile ground for the cultivation of sensual desire, leaving home for the homeless life leads a monk or nun away from sensual desire and attachment to family and toward detachment from all desire.

The Buddha frequently warns monks about the dangers of sensual desire, and especially about the threat posed by women's seductive beauty. Hair fragrant with the scent of jasmine or sandalwood and soft to the touch forms part of this physical attraction, which binds men and women to one another and perpetuates their bondage in a world set ablaze with the fire of passion. To escape this all-consuming fire, monks and nuns must strip off the heavy adornments of lay life, shave their heads, put on identical shapeless robes, and then begin the process of personal transformation that culminates in the cool, tranquil, deathless state of nirvana. The nuns' verses in the *Therīgāthā* collection speak of their experience of enlightenment in terms of stilling and coolness: "desire is stilled" (Thig. 1); "the burning fever has been cut out; I have become cool" (Thig. 34).

The physical action of shaving hair off the head cools the body; the intention of turning the mind away from the blazing sensual objects of this world cools the mind. In these Buddhist texts a shaven head signifies also the cooling behavior of renunciation.

LOOSE HAIR AND RITES OF PASSAGE

Loose hair as well as a shaven head can signify a rite of separation. Loose, disheveled hair indicates a woman in mourning, separated from a close family member. It marks the passage from a sexually active state to an inactive state, lasting at least for the duration of the mourning period and becoming permanent in the case of widows who shave their heads. Before entering the Buddhist community, Vāsiṭṭhi says: "I wandered here and there with my hair disheveled, afflicted by grief for my son" (Thig. 133). Like a widow, Vāsiṭṭhi in becoming a nun and shaving her head communicates her adoption of a chaste life.

Changes in how the hair is treated also mark the passage from childhood into young womanhood. "No longer do they leave their locks disheveled," writes a poet whose works the Buddhist scholar Vidyākara included in his anthology of Sanskrit poetry, the *Subhāṣitaratnakoṣa*, but these young women now "study how to braid their hair . . . and knot their skirts."[26] The young women's hair braided with jasmine flowers and decorated with gold hairpins indicates their passage from the sexually inactive state of childhood into the sexually active state of adolescence.

In Sanskrit and vernacular poems, the untying of the hair knot is an action that precedes untying the knot that holds a women's sari together. The use of literary conventions—such as the fragrant and ornamented hair which signals the sexual attractiveness of a young women, and the loosening of her braided hair which signals her sexual receptiveness—can be found also in stories of the Buddha's previous births (*Jātaka*). In one of these stories Isisinga's practice of asceticism so disturbs the god Indra that he schemes to destroy this young ascetic's power. Indra informs a king whose land has become barren from lack of rain that he will release the fertilizing rains only after the king's daughter Nalinikā successfully seduces the young ascetic. Isisinga, who has never before seen a woman, asks the daughter (who is disguised as a male ascetic) what that lovely thing s/he has between her thighs is.[27] Has her "best member" (a term usually meaning head but here signifying penis) disappeared? Nalinikā explains that a fierce wild animal fell upon her, forcibly attacked her, and ripped it off. Ever since then the wound has been itching, but you, she says to Isisinga, can relieve this itch. He offers medicine for what he perceives as a deep, fresh, red wound; but instead of medicine she says, "I need you to rub against it and give me the greatest pleasure." When his father returns and finds his feverish son, Isisinga tells him about the beardless youth whose parted and braided hair was fragrant and ornamented with gold. "When he unbound those beautiful, sweet-smelling braids, their scent pervaded this ashram, like the scent of blue lotuses released by the wind." Then the handsome youth with the long, loose hair "embraced me with his soft arms and gave me pleasure." Isisinga's not-so-innocent father informs him that this was a female demon; and Isisinga, thoroughly frightened, resumes the chaste life of an ascetic meditator.[28]

In an alternative *Jātaka* version of this story, Indra sends a divine nymph, Alambusā, to seduce Isisinga. After attracting his interest, she pretends to run away. He catches hold of her long hair. A man's hands catching hold of a woman's hair, as another poem from Vidyākara's anthology makes clear, is the starting point for those hands to move slowly further down the contours of her body.[29] Caught by his hands, the nymph embraces him. Three years later, Isisinga remembers his deceased father's warnings about the dangers of women, unwraps himself from her arms, and resumes his chaste meditative practice.

In these *Jātaka* stories, it is the young, naive Isisinga who shares the psychoanalyst's perception that "the female body is marked by lack, that it is wounded, deficient, defined by the absence of the phallus."[30] The fear of women expressed by Isisinga's more worldly father does not center on the putatively deficient, wounded nature of the female body; rather, the fear, expressed also in the Buddha's warnings to his spiritual sons, lies instead in the dangerous power present in a women's physical beauty, in the scent of her fragrant hair and the soft touch of her embrace. The fear is of the power that sensual pleasure and passion possess to captivate a man's mind and deflect its energies away from the proper task of meditation.

LOOSE HAIR, MENSTRUATION, AND RITUAL SEXUALITY

When the hands that catch hold of a woman's hair are unwanted, the act becomes a sexual assault. The pulling of Draupadī's hair in the epic saga the *Mahābhārata* is considered a sexual assault, and her vow to leave her hair loose until she can wash it in the blood of her assailant is considered a reversed image of sexual revenge: purification by a ritual hair bath, not with water but with male blood.[31] Draupadī's loose, uncombed hair signifies her state of menstrual impurity. The blood flow of a menstruating woman makes her impure for three days; the prohibition against combing her hair makes a woman sexually unattractive to men. The traditional medical and legal texts (*dharmaśāstra*) further emphasize the dangers of sexual contact with women during their menstrual periods with the warning that if a menstruating woman makes love during the crucial three days, the child that results from this unfortunate union will be considered an outcaste or cursed.[32] Menstruating women themselves are treated during this time as if they were outcastes: physically separated from the rest of the family and reintegrated into the life of the household only after taking a purifying bath, washing their hair, and oiling and rebraiding its loose strands. For men the menstrual flow is defiling; for women, however, it is a purification and cleansing of the womb.[33]

This purifying function of menstrual blood is also associated with myths according to which the earth, the trees, and women each assume some of the evil that resulted from Indra killing a Brahmin; this evil assumes the form of "red secretions" from the earth, sap in the trees, and menstrual blood in women. In return, Indra grants that the plowed earth will heal again, cut trees will grow once more, and women may have sexual intercourse repeatedly.[34] The parallelism here is striking. In each case, things are split apart and wounded; a woman's genitals, from a male perspective, are, as the naive Isisinga observed, like a raw red wound.

In the context of menstruation, P. Hershman observes, the association between the genitals and the head and head hair is most explicit. A woman communicates the onset of her period to other household members by saying "I have to wash my head," informing them that she can no longer cook until she has taken a ritual bath. Her washed hair will then be re-knotted with the plaits pulled back to leave a central part. The reddening of a married woman's hair part, says Hershman, makes it stand as a symbol of the vagina. Female hair becomes symbolic of female sexuality, specifically associated with vaginal and menstrual blood. Male ideas concerning the impure and dangerous nature of female sexuality, he suggests, correlate well with restrictions placed on the way women treat their hair.[35] Hershman's analysis here exemplifies the male gaze, which eroticizes the female head and makes the woman's parted hair into a reflection of her parted genitals.

A woman's loose hair communicates to men her impure state and the danger involved should they wish to approach her sexually. Both menstruation and sexual intercourse involve the release of bodily fluids that are considered impure. But, as Frédérique Apffel Marglin points out, alongside these negative valuations of menstruation and sexual intercourse as rendering one impure, there is also a positive valuation: both are considered auspicious.[36] As opposed to the dangerous otherworldly celibacy of male ascetics such as Isisinga, female sexuality is "inherently auspicious, the source of the regenerative powers of women, of the earth, and, by metaphorical extension, of the cosmos."[37] Against the dominant discourse of the male gaze, which regards female sexuality as alluring but also as dangerous and polluting, Marglin celebrates the earthy vitality and auspicious life-giving power of female sexuality.

The long, loose hair characteristic of certain Hindu and Buddhist goddesses signifies their celibate (though not necessarily chaste) status. Poets describe the goddess Kālī as "the loose-haired charmer of the mind,"[38] the goddess whose "disheveled hair has world-charming beauty."[39] This loose hair flows around her body or up toward the sky, as in the case of the goddesses whose hair the *Kubjikāmatatantra* describes as "wild, flowing upwards" (*barbarordhaśiroruha*).[40] Loose hair is also a distinguishing feature of the Buddhist *ḍākinī*, the ideal sexual partner of the Tantric adept (*siddha*);[41] a *ḍākinī* may also be visualized with "hair streaming up from her head."[42] As with the goddess Kālī, although these *ḍākinīs* may appear terrifying, they also are protective, and a source of power and inspiration. Marglin rejects the belief that the power of these divine women is inherently dangerous and that the restraining force of the male transforms this dangerous female power into a beneficent force in a sexual/marital relationship. The danger, she argues, comes not from female sexuality but from the celibate state—a danger that is equally distributed among males and females. In any sexual relationship the female energy is auspicious, but, as she says, sexual union "tames" and softens the male as much as it does the female.[43]

The auspicious nature of female sexuality comes into play in the lyrics of Tantric practitioners. The songs of Kaṇha and other Tantric adepts, in contrast to the verses of monks and nuns which celebrate the joys of chastity and solitude, frequently celebrate the joys of union with a consort who is young, sexually attractive, and fertile. Of these consorts, low-caste washerwomen, who deal with the impurity of menstrual blood, are most often mentioned as the sexual partners of choice.[44] Some Tantric texts, in a reversal of practices proscribed by orthodox Brahmins, advocate sexual contact with a menstruating woman: "Bring a women while she is menstruating and at midnight worship your personal deity [*iṣṭadevatā*] within her genitals."[45] The form this worship may take involves what Marglin describes as "inverse sexual intercourse": instead of the woman receiving the male sexual fluid, the man ingests female sexual fluid.[46] The *Caṇḍamahāroṣaṇa Tantra* indicates that the male participant should use his tongue to consume blood and female semen from his female counterpart's vagina.[47] Menstruation and sexual intercourse are considered as heat-caused and heat-generating processes,[48] and in Tantric ritual intercourse the ingested menstrual blood combines with the retained semen to release a heated energy that leads to the experience of bliss. In a ritual act involving transformation through combining, the impure but auspicious processes of menstruation and sexual intercourse play a role in dissolving the dualistic distinctions of semen/blood, pure/impure, auspicious/inauspicious, high-caste/low-caste, male/female, self/other with which the mind normally operates. The sexual experience as described by the female partner in one of Vidyākara's favorite verses—"within his arms, I can't remember who he was or who I was, or what we did or how"[49]—comes to stand for the ultimate realization of nonduality. In the ideal sexual union depicted in Tantric texts, the simultaneous orgasm both partners experience, the blissful sensation of completely merging into one another resulting in a loss of self, represents the ultimate bliss that can be experienced by an enlightened mind.

Unlike the couples whose sensual experiences Vidyākara's anthology records, however, the erotic or sensual quality of Tantric practitioners' sexual encounters is downplayed. In interviews with female members of a Hindu Sahajiyā group, the majority claimed to have inherited the role of ritual assistant for male practitioners from their mothers; they entertained no lustful feelings for their partners.[50] Tantric practitioners, June McDaniels notes, have sex without sensuality; sensuality is reserved for "the goddess of mystery and danger (*yoginīs* and *ḍākinīs*), while physical women are merely spiritual batteries, or at best one-half of a synergetic system."[51] Despite the Tantric fascination with the creative powers of women and the idealized sensuality of the goddess, contemporary practitioners observe the traditional role of female subservience and male control of female sexuality.[52]

Hindu Tantric texts describing ritual sexual practices are usually written with the male participant in mind. He is encouraged to identify his semen with Śiva and the woman's menstrual flow with Śakti, to unite these two forces of creation and retain both of the fluids discharged during intercourse within his own body (regardless of whether the union is physical or mental) and thereby experience the natural state of blissful relaxation (*sahaja*).[53] Similarly, according to the Buddhist *Caṇḍamahāroṣaṇa Tantra,* the man should consider himself an unshakable (*acala*) Buddha and his sexual partner as the embodiment of perfect wisdom (*prajñāpāramitā*); each should regard the other with sexual desire but their minds must remain in focused concentration. Emphasis is placed upon his remaining still; motionless, he concentrates with his mind on the pleasure arising from their union. Then the two partners perform a long list of sexual postures, requiring in addition to mental concentration a supple and acrobatic body.[54] In the concluding chapter of this work, the goddess Prajñāpāramitā says she is to be honored in the form of all women; when a man makes love to his wife after meditating on her embodiment as perfect wisdom, enlightenment will come from that union.[55]

Despite this text's insistence on the exalted nature of a man's wife, however, I wonder whether its statements are not examples of the "upside-down" paradoxical language characteristic of the writings of both male and female Tantric practitioners, in which frogs swallow elephants, barren women give birth, and mice chase cats.[56] The force of this "upside-down" language comes from the unsettling contrast between ordinary life, in which cats chase mice, and an alternate reality in which the ordinary world and ordinary language are transformed. In the ideal world of the *Caṇḍamahāroṣaṇa Tantra,* men place a woman's sexual pleasure before their own, women eat first and men feast on their leavings—in contrast to the ordinary world of India, both past and present.

LIBERATED WOMEN AND THEIR LOOSE HAIR

The *Caṇḍamahāroṣaṇa Tantra* says "women are Buddha."[57] The sacred biographies of the few female Tantric practitioners whose life stories have
been preserved tell how these women became liberated from the cycle of
birth, death, and rebirth. Many of these women rejected conventional marriages. Some refused outright to marry. Mandāravā pulled her hair out to
make herself so unattractive that no man would want her.[58] Others left their
husbands and spent the remainder of their lives practicing meditation and
receiving and giving teachings. Lakṣmīnkarā, whose songs celebrate the
transformation of mind that allows frogs to swallow elephants, was born
into wealth but chose to pursue the life of an itinerant holy woman. She
cut her hair and escaped from her husband's palace, and for seven years
engaged in yoga and meditation until she attained spiritual powers (*siddhi*).
She spent the remainder of her life instructing sweepers and other low-
caste disciples.[59]

One of these women, Yeshe Tsogyel, is the subject of both sacred biography and liturgy. Her biography records that this eighth-century c.e. Tibetan woman was born with long hair that fell to her waist. At the age of
twelve she was married against her will to a king, who subsequently released
her so that she could become a consort of the Tantric adept Padmasam-
bhava. She subsequently bought the freedom from slavery of her consort
Atsara Sale with gold received from a man whose son she had brought back
to life. As in the case of the Buddha, her creative powers were "displaced
upwards": she let a drop of saliva pass from her mouth into the corpse's
mouth while she pointed her finger at his heart and whispered mantras in
his ears. Subsequently, for three years she practiced austerities until she was
close to death. At that point she received a vision of a naked woman, red
in color, from whose vagina she drank life-giving blood. Later, as Yeshe
Tsogyel sat in meditation, her sexual fantasies took the form of young men
who exposed their sexual organs and embraced her. By gaining control
over her sexual desire she made them vanish. Now enlightened, she began
to teach and to create spiritual sons and daughters. Her manner of teaching, like that of the Buddha, was adapted to the needs of those who sought
it. She spat into the mouths of celibate monks who sought her wisdom so
that they could defeat their non-Buddhist adversaries. To the lustful, she
gave her sexual parts. But she advised one of her spiritual daughters that
sexual activity without control is just fornication. After vanishing into rain-
bow light, she left her hair behind as a relic to be honored.[60]

Many of the episodes in this biography focus on the relationships Yeshe
Tsogyel forms with other men and women. Though she is Padmasambha-
va's consort, often she practices without him, in solitude or with other
consorts of her own. These relationships, Rita Gross says, "are not primarily

erotic encounters; they are primarily *dharmic* encounters to which there is a sexual aspect."[61] An understanding of the positive force of sexual attraction and a willingness to put it into practice exemplify the skillful means through which Yeshe Tsogyel and other Tantric practitioners bring Buddhist teachings to the unenlightened.

The biography focuses on Yeshe Tsogyel's spiritual life and the practices she perfected in becoming an enlightened person. She is considered a fully enlightened being, a Buddha, whose life story follows the pattern of renunciation, asceticism, enlightenment, and teaching familiar to the biographies of all Buddhas. Her biographer presents her as an already enlightened being who recognized that the time had come for her to appear in the form of a Tibetan woman and spread to the Tibetan people the teachings of Tantra. The liturgical texts invoke Yeshe Tsogyel as an embodiment of wisdom, a *ḍākinī*. The rituals and visualizations described in these texts endow the person who performs them with a means of entering into her enlightened mind. In the texts she is visualized as naked, blood-red in color, and with long, dark, flowing hair. In most paintings and woodblock prints her sexual organ, marking the entrance to her womb, is visible. This part of her body, as the liturgical texts indicate, represents the source of all beings: "This womb of the mother-consort [Yeshe Tsogyel] is reality; it is the source of all Buddhas, the basis of all coming and going; the place of the arising of all existents."[62] In contrast to western psychology, which views any inclination to reassociate with the maternal womb as regressive, in the Tantric liturgy, as Anne Klein states, the wish to renew one's association with the womb is not regressive but developmental: "It points to the birth of an understanding that fully recognizes the enduring source of existence, which is embodied as a female organ."[63] Through the performance of this liturgy, the practice of visualization associated with it, and the study of teachings preserved through the efforts of Yeshe Tsogyel, meditators come to realize that the wisdom she embodies is in fact embedded in themselves. Wisdom is the key that unlocks the potential all human beings have to become Buddhas; all have within themselves the womb that generates Buddhas (*tathāgatagarbha*).

Tantric texts and the life stories of Tantric practitioners indicate that the chaste behavior associated with the practice of physical austerities and meditation alternates with periods of ritual sexual activity. But in this ritual sexuality, firm control is maintained over the sexual organs and the physical and mental sensations that result from sexual contact. The body is still and motionless; the mind is concentrated. In these stories the power built up through the practice of yoga and chastity is further enhanced through ritual sexual relationships and its "heat" channeled upwards toward the center at the heart. This heated yet controlled force of sexuality is thus channeled toward the realization of Buddhahood.

The loose hair depicted in the portraits of these female Tantric practitioners symbolizes the power both of their celibate yogic practices and of the auspicious nature of female blood and sexuality. The unbound hair signifies also liberation and enlightenment: "To show that she has untied the knot which holds all things," *Cakrasamvara Tantra* says of the *ḍākinī* Vajravārāhī, "her hair is loose and flowing."[64]

CONCLUSION

Both a shaven head and loose hair are deviations from the norm of braided hair. Both symbols form part of a larger network of related concepts. The nun's shaven head is associated with notions of purity, chaste behavior, and cooling actions that involve mental control over the heated force of sexuality. In contrast to the nun's shaven head, the loose hair of the female Tantric adept is associated with ideas of impurity, the alternation of chastity and ritual sexual activity, and actions that involve mental control and transformation of the heated force of sexuality.

Obeyesekere argues that the primary psychological meaning of the symbol of a shaven head is castration; its further cultural meaning is chastity; its extended message is renunciation.[65] In fact, however, the shaven head does not evoke an emotional response—fear, revulsion, or anxiety—either among those who choose to shave their heads or among those who witness the action. Such a response might support Obeyesekere's claim that the unconscious meaning of shaving the head is castration; but there is no such response. Further, a claim of symbolic castration ought to work best in a situation where the severing occurs just once. Severed hair, by contrast, grows back again, and nuns bound by the restrictions of a disciplinary code shave their heads year after year on a monthly basis. Castration, then, is not the issue. Rather, hair is a secular symbol of sexual attractiveness, and the nun by shaving off her hair renders herself sexually unattractive and unavailable, thus removing herself as a potential threat to her male counterpart's spiritual practice.

In the context of an ordinary woman's alternating patterns of chastity and sexuality, loose hair communicates the enforced chastity that obtains while a woman menstruates. A woman may also unbind her hair as she prepares to give birth. In the context of secular love poetry, a woman's unbinding of her braided hair signals her sexual receptiveness. These secular meanings of loose hair, along with the religious meaning of loose hair—the ritual impurity associated with menstruation and childbirth—come into play in the ritual practices of Tantric adepts. Tantric texts and the practices they advocate reject Brahminical notions of ritual purity/impurity. They emphasize the auspicious nature of female sexuality. While the nun is a potential threat to the monk's spiritual development, the female Tantric practitioner is an essential complement to her male counter-part's practice. But in the ritual sexual practices referred to in these texts, the emphasis is placed on control over sexual desire. The loose, unre-strained hair of the Tantric practitioner does not bear out Leach's conten-tion that in ritual contexts loose hair correlates with unrestrained sexuality.

Returning to the questions Leach raises, the answer—on the basis of the Buddhist material examined here—is that hair symbolism does not have the same meanings everywhere and phallicism is not the fundamental principle involved. In both the spiritual practice of a nun and the spiritual practice of a Tantric adept, the fundamental principle involved is not con-trol of sexual organs but rather control over the mind through the disci-pline of meditation. The use of female sexual symbolism in such works as the ritual texts connected with Yeshe Tsogyel, moreover, suggests that "the erection of the phallus as privileged symbol" and the perception of man as complete and woman as deficient is not a universal fact of culture.[66]

NOTES

1. Leach 1958:148–55.

2. Obeyesekere 1981:38.

3. Obeyesekere 1981:13, 17, 19, 34, 36.

4. The origins of Tantric practice in India remain obscure. One Tantric move-ment, the Sahajayāna, dates its origins back to the eighth century C.E., when long-haired *siddhas* began to travel throughout India and into Tibet initiating carefully chosen disciples into the vehicle (*yāna*) of ritual, meditation, and sexual-yogic tech-niques that culminated in the bliss of enlightenment (*sahaja*).

5. Leach 1958:162.

6. The translations are mine, based on the edition of Oldenburg and Pischel (1966). Abbreviations: "Thag." = *Theragāthā;* "Thig." = *Therīgāthā.*

7. *Muṇḍaka-bandhakiniyo,* translated as "shaven-headed strumpet" by Horner 1969:178, 257, 275.

8. Lienhard 1975 discusses the stylistic similarities between Ambapālī's verses and secular love poems in Prakrit and Sanskrit. For a rhetorical analysis of the language Ambapālī uses to describe her physical transformation see also Richman 1988:148–49.

9. Rhys Davids and Norman 1989:142.

10. Tessa Bartholowmeuz, "Women under the Bo Tree," a talk given at the Uni-versity of Virginia, September 7, 1990.

11. Keyes 1986:73.

12. Wijayaratna 1990:40.

13. Obeyesekere 1981:43 records the following comment of a Sinhalese lay per-son: "These are not good monks, look at their hair."

14. Keyes 1986:85–87, 93.

15. Wilson 1979:87–88, 90.

16. Horner 1969:21–38.

17. Horner 1969:39–62. These same stories are summarized and discussed by Stevens 1990:32–39.

18. Hirakawa 1982:104–7; Horner 1969:53–54.

19. Wijayaratna 1990:93.

20. On these texts see Gonda 1985:284–314.

21. Horner 1969:92–96. The intentional emission of semen necessitates calling a meeting of the community, which then places the monk on probation.

22. Obeyesekere 1981:39.

23. Barnes 1987:259, n. 11.

24. Khandro 1989:71.

25. On these two types of immortality see O'Flaherty 1980:3–5.

26. Ingalls 1965:154.

27. Five verses of this *Jātaka* (vv. 13–17) were excised by the Victorian translator, H. T. Francis. My translation and summary of these verses are based on pp. 36–37 of J. Kashyap's 1959 edition of the *Jātakapāli*.

28. See O'Flaherty 1973:42–52 for additional versions of this story.

29. Ingalls 1965:255.

30. Du Bois 1988:3.

31. Hiltebeitel 1981:204–5.

32. Leslie 1989:283–85.

33. Hershman 1974:286: "Punjabi women see it [menstruation] as a necessary bodily process in order to purge themselves of pollution and make clean their wombs."

34. Leslie 1989:251; see also O'Flaherty 1976:57–58.

35. Hershman 1974:277, 280.

36. Marglin 1985:40.

37. Marglin 1985:54.

38. Goudriaan and Gupta 1981:179.

39. Kinsley 1975:151.

40. Goudriaan 1983:105.

41. The *Sādhanamāla* (425) describes the *ḍākinī* as having loose hair (*muktakeśa*). On various translations and interpretations of the *ḍākinī* see Willis 1989.

42. Allione 1984:xxix.

43. Marglin 1985:43, 47, 56–57.

44. Kvaerne 1977:113, 131, 150.

45. McDaniels 1989:132, 181–84.

46. Marglin 1982:310.

47. George 1974:22, 30, 56, 74–75.

48. Daniel 1984:125.

49. Ingalls 1965:203.

50. Ibid., 175.

51. McDaniels 1989:274.

52. Goudriaan and Gupta 1979:33–34, Brooks 1990:25,74.

53. Goudriaan and Gupta 1979:183.

54. George 1974:27–31, 67–77.

55. George 1974:33, 83.

56. The expression "upside-down language" comes from Hess 1983. The specific examples cited are from Shaw 1989:52–53.

57. George 1974:33: *striyo buddhah.*

58. Ray 1989:229.

59. See Robinson 1979:250–53.

60. This summary is based on Dowman 1984.

61. Gross 1989:24.

62. Klein 1985:131.

63. Ibid.

64. Dawa-Samdup 1919:28.

65. Obeyesekere 1981:45–46.

66. This is the same conclusion as that reached by du Bois on the basis of her study of Greek materials. Her analysis of the Medusa myth (87–91) differs radically from that of Freudians, for whom this myth is an important source in the development of theories about castration.

REFERENCES

Allione, Tsultrim
 1984   *Women of Wisdom.* London: Arkana Press.
Barnes, Nancy Schuster
 1987   "Buddhism." In *Women and World Religions,* ed. by Arvind Sharma, 105–33. Albany: State University of New York Press.
Brooks, Douglas Renfrew
 1990   *The Secret of the Three Cities: An Introduction to Hindu Sakta Tantrism.* Chicago: University of Chicago Press.
Daniel, E. Valentine
 1984   *Fluid Signs: Being a Person the Tamil Way.* Berkeley and Los Angeles: University of California Press.
Dawa-Samdup, Kazi, trans.
 1919   *Tantrik Texts.* London: Luzac & Co.
Dowman, Keith, trans.
 1984   *Sky Dancer: The Secret Life and Songs of the Lady Yeshe Tsogyel.* London: Routledge and Kegan Paul.
du Bois, Page
 1988   *Sowing the Body: Psychoanalysis and Ancient Representations of Women.* Chicago: University of Chicago Press.
George, Christopher, trans.
 1974   *The Caṇḍamahāroṣaṇa Tantra.* New Haven: American Oriental Society.
Gonda, Jan
 1985   *Change and Continuity in Indian Religion.* New Delhi: Munshiram Manoharlal.
Goudriaan, Teun
 1983   "Some Beliefs and Rituals Concerning Time and Death in the Kubji-kāmata." In *Selected Studies on Ritual in the Indian Religions,* ed. by Ria Kloppenborg, 92–117. Leiden: E. J. Brill.

Goudriaan, Teun, and Sanjukta Gupta
  1979   *Hindu Tantrism*. Leiden: E. J. Brill.
  1981   *Hindu Tantric and Sakta Literature*. Wiesbaden: Otto Harrassowitz.
Gross, Rita
  1989   "Yeshe Tsogyel: Enlightened Consort, Great Teacher, Female Role Model." In *Feminine Ground: Essays on Women and Tibet*, ed. by Janice D. Willis, 11–32. Ithaca, N.Y.: Snow Lion.
Hershman, P.
  1974   "Hair, Sex and Dirt." *Man: Journal of the Royal Anthropological Institute*, n.s., 9(2): 274–98.
Hess, Linda
  1983   "The Cow Is Sucking at the Calf's Teat: Kabir's Upside-Down Language." *History of Religions* 22(4):313–37.
Hiltebeitel, Alf
  1981   "Draupadi's Hair." *Puruṣārtha* 5:179–214.
Hirakawa, Akira, trans.
  1982   *Monastic Discipline for the Buddhist Nuns*. Patna: Jayaswal Research Institute.
Horner, I. B., trans.
  1969   *The Book of Discipline*. London: Pali Text Society.
Ingalls, Daniel H. H., trans.
  1965   *An Anthology of Sanskrit Court Poetry*. Cambridge: Harvard University Press.
Kashyap, J., ed.
  1959   *Jātakapāli*. Bihar: Pāli Publication Board.
Keyes, Charles F.
  1986   "Ambiguous Gender: Male Initiation in a Northern Thai Buddhist Society." In *Gender and Religion: On the Complexity of Symbols*, ed. by Caroline Walker Bynum, Stevan Harrell, and Paula Richman, 66–96. Boston: Beacon Press.
Khandro, Sangye
  1989   "Personal Development as a Nun." In *Sakyadhitā: Daughters of the Buddha*, ed. by Karma Lekshe Tsomo, 71–73. Ithaca, N.Y.: Snow Lion.
Kinsley, David R.
  1975   *The Sword and the Flute: Kālī and Kṛṣṇa, Dark Visions of the Terrible and the Sublime in Hindu Mythology*. Berkeley and Los Angeles: University of California Press.
Klein, Anne C.
  1985   "Primordial Purity and Everyday Life: Exalted Female Symbols and the Women of Tibet." In *Immaculate & Powerful: The Female in Sacred Image and Social Reality*, ed. by Clarissa Atkinson, Constance H. Buchanan, and Margaret Miles, 111–38. Boston: Beacon Press.
Kvaerne, Per, trans.
  1977   *An Anthology of Buddhist Tantric Songs*. Oslo: Universitetforlaget.
Leach, Edmund
  1958   "Magical Hair." *Man: Journal of the Royal Anthropological Institute* 88:147–68.

Leslie, I. Julia
    1989   *The Perfect Wife: The Orthodox Hindu Woman According to the Strīdharma-paddhati of Tryambakayajvan.* Delhi: Oxford University Press.
Lienhard, Siegfried
    1975   "Sur la structure poétique des Theratherīgāthā." *Journal Asiatique* 263:375–96.
McDaniels, June
    1989   *The Madness of Saints: Ecstatic Religion in Bengal.* Chicago: University of Chicago Press.
Marglin, Frédérique Apffel
    1982   "Types of Sexual Union and Their Implicit Meanings." In *The Divine Consort: Rādhā and the Goddesses of India,* ed. by John Stratton Hawley and Donna Marie Wulf, 298–315. Berkeley: Graduate Theological Union.
    1985   "Female Sexuality in the Hindu World." In *Immaculate & Powerful: The Female in Sacred Image and Social Reality,* ed. by Clarissa Atkinson, Constance H. Buchanan, and Margaret Miles, 39–60. Boston: Beacon Press.
Obeyesekere, Gananath
    1981   *Medusa's Hair: An Essay on Personal Symbols and Religious Experience.* Chicago: University of Chicago Press.
O'Flaherty, Wendy Doniger
    1973   *Asceticism and Eroticism in the Mythology of Śiva.* Oxford: Oxford University Press.
    1976   *The Origins of Evil in Hindu Mythology.* Berkeley and Los Angeles: University of California Press.
    1980   "Karma and Rebirth in the Vedas and Purāṇas." In *Karma and Rebirth in Classical Indian Traditions,* 3–37. Berkeley and Los Angeles: University of California Press.
Oldenburg, H., and R. Pischel, eds.
    1966   *The Thera and Therī Gāthā.* London: Pali Text Society.
Ray, Reginald
    1989   "Accomplished Women in Tantric Buddhism of Medieval India and Tibet." In *Unspoken Worlds: Women's Religious Lives in Non-Western Cultures,* ed. by Nancy Falk and Rita Gross, 227–42. Belmont, Calif.: Wadsworth Press.
Rhys Davids, C. A. F., and K. R. Norman, trans.
    1989   *Poems of Early Buddhist Nuns (Therīgāthā).* Oxford: Pali Text Society.
Richman, Paula
    1988   *Women, Branch Stories, and Religious Rhetoric in a Tamil Buddhist Text.* Syracuse, N.Y.: Maxwell School of Citizenship and Public Affairs, Syracuse University.
Robinson, James, trans.
    1979   *Buddha's Lions: The Lives of the Eighty-Four Siddhas.* Berkeley: Dharma Press.
Shaw, Miranda
    1989   "An Ecstatic Song by Lakṣmīṅkarā." In *Feminine Ground: Essays on Women and Tibet,* ed. by Janice D. Willis, 52–56. Ithaca, N.Y.: Snow Lion.

Stevens, John
   1990   *Lust for Enlightenment: Buddhism and Sex.* Boston: Shambhala.
Wijayaratna, Mohan
   1990   *Buddhist Monastic Life According to the Texts of the Theravāda Tradition.*
           Trans. Steven Collins. Cambridge: Cambridge University Press.
Willis, Janice D.
   1989   "Ḍākinī: Some Comments on Its Nature and Meaning." In *Feminine
           Ground: Essays on Women and Tibet,* ed. by Janice D. Willis, 57–75. Ithaca,
           N.Y.: Snow Lion.
Wilson, Frances
   1979   "The Nun." In *Women in Buddhism: Images of the Feminine in Mahāyāna
           Tradition,* by Diana Y. Paul with contributions by Frances Wilson, 77–
           105. Berkeley: Asian Humanities Press.

THREE

Untangling the Meanings of Hair
in Turkish Society

Carol Delaney

Hair is an object of intense elaboration and preoccupation in many societies; seemingly the most superficial part of the human body, its meanings
are nevertheless deeply rooted in culture. Hairstyles, and the practices
involved in hairstyling, convey messages about people's beliefs and commitments. How quick we are to make inferences and judgments about a
person's morality, sexual orientation, political persuasion, or religious sentiments when we see a particular hairstyle![1]

The meanings of hair are sometimes transcultural, but more often they
are culturally specific—and even then they depend on the range of varia-
tions that are permitted and expressed in the particular culture. Abstract
or general theories about hair are therefore not sufficient to interpret particular hairstyles or practices relating to hair; one must know quite a lot
about the culture in order to do so.

ISSUES ABOUT HAIR IN THE TURKISH CONTEXT

To the Western eye, the covering of women's heads in Turkey and other
Muslim countries is surely one of the most noticeable and provocative practices related to hair. Although this practice is often referred to as "veiling,"
which implies covering the face as well as the hair, what is usually meant is
the covering of women's hair with scarves of various kinds.[2] Westerners have
ambivalent responses to this practice, considering it both exotic and erotic
or, in a more negative vein, as evidence for the backwardness of Islam and
the oppression of women. Indigenous reformers have often accepted such
evaluations and spent considerable energy trying to get women to uncover.
This was surely a goal of Mustafa Kemal Atatürk, the founder and first
president of the Republic of Turkey.

The issue of headcovering goes back to the beginning of the Republic and is intimately intertwined with its history. Atatürk felt that in order for the defunct Ottoman Empire to be transformed into a modern, Western nation-state, people not only had to think differently but also to dress differently. The head was a prime target. He banned the male headgear called the "fez" and instituted the use of the brimmed hat. He encouraged women to uncover; he felt it was both a means to and a symbol of becoming modern and Western. He toured the country giving lectures on the topic, accompanied by his uncovered wife and female assistants. Headscarves were banned for civil service employees, including nurses and teachers, as well as for students in public schools and universities.

Today, however, there is a controversy raging among certain Turks in both Turkey and Europe with regard to a woman's *right* to wear a headscarf—to school or university, or when performing civil service jobs, that is, in the very places and contexts from which it had originally been banned.[3] For many, the headscarf is a symbol of allegiance to Islam. In Turkey that allegiance conflicts with nationalist ideals; the wearing of the headscarf can thus be interpreted as a potential threat to the secular national government. In Europe, in contrast, the headscarf can serve as a marker of both national and religious identity, at least among Sunni Turks.

The headscarf debate has been cast in terms of civil rights, and especially of freedom of religion. The issue has divided women (and men) in Turkey and Europe; it has also divided feminists among themselves both inside and outside of Turkey. In my view, however, the debate is miscast; the emphasis on the political and religious dimensions of the headscarf has left the meanings of the body, sex, and gender in place. The contemporary debate, and Western analyses of it, ignore such elementary questions as: (1) Why covering? (2) Why is it *women's* heads that are covered? (3) Why is covering a symbol of Muslim and/or Turkish identity? and (4) Why are women's heads the site of political and religious conflict? The issue cannot be reduced to an either/or question—either women have the right to wear headscarves or they don't—because the meanings of hair in Turkish society are in fact very complex.

In Turkish society hair is an emotionally charged symbol with different meanings that depend on gender, age, class, political commitments, and religious sentiments. All of these factors can become entangled in any given context. I do not intend to approach the headscarf debate head on because I believe that the covering of women's heads cannot be understood in isolation from a whole range of meanings and practices related to hair in Turkish society. In order to understand the meaning of women's hair and its covering, it is necessary to analyze women's hair in relation to men's hair, head hair in relation to body hair, and the different hair-related practices over the human life cycle. An ethnographic perspective becomes indispensable. Drawing upon my fieldwork in Turkey,[4] I attempt to untangle some of the sexual, political, and religious meanings of hair in Turkish society while weaving in and out of theoretical discussion of the topic. With this background, I will return at the end to the debate about headscarves.

ETHNOGRAPHIC EVIDENCE

My own hair became a subject of immediate concern as I sought permission to live in a particular village in central Anatolia in order to conduct my anthropological research. I was told that it would be difficult for villagers to accept me if I did not cover my hair. I did not want my presence to be a continual irritant, so I adopted the headscarf. I also wore the baggy, comfortable trousers called *şalvar*, and the rubbers used for footwear which are easy to slip off and on as one enters and exits a house. When I put on the villagers' clothes, I also put on a new social body and became, in their words, *tam köylü*—a complete villager.

The significance of hair was further impressed upon me during my first few days in the village. Before it was decided that I could live in a house by myself, I was the guest of a family preparing for the wedding of their daughter, whom I shall call Ayşe. I was not the only guest: relatives who lived outside the village had returned for the wedding festivities. Since the whole village is included in a wedding—an event which spans several days—it is a major undertaking. I became an extra pair of hands instead of an extra burden; thus my introduction to village life was much more as a participant than as an observer. At Ayşe's request I became her *sağdıç*, her helper and confidante, and was intimately involved in the details of the process that transformed her into a bride. Hair was very much a part of this process.

One of my first tasks was to help Ayşe pluck out her underarm hair. This was part of the customary practice of removing all body hair, a custom that applies to both men and women and not only at the time of a wedding. Men and women alike are expected to keep body hair removed throughout their adult lives, although women are expected to comply more strictly. While the practice of removing body hair has a long history in Turkish society, many men of the urban Westernized elite do not comply, and some may even be unaware of the history or the practice. A visit to a *hamam* (public bathhouse) would acquaint them with it.

Saturday morning of the wedding weekend began with a ritually prescribed bath that took place in the laundry house among Ayşe's female friends. No one takes a bath alone—I would help her and she would help me. Ayşe advised me to take my bath first so the other women would not see me *keçi gibi*—like a goat. It was a reference to pubic hair, but the association was redolent of animality and the wanton sexuality that goats symbolize. Was the removal of pubic hair an attempt to remove these associations?

It is expected that men are to control the sexuality of "their" women (wives, sisters, daughters) as well as that of their animals. One of the sites of control is hair. It is a male prerogative to initiate sex; they also decide when the animals will be bred and oversee the process. Men also shear the hair of goats and the wool of sheep and give it to the women, who then transform it into socially useful products. Wool is used to stuff mattresses and quilts, and goat hair is spun and knitted into socks and sweaters. The word for knitting (*örmek*) is also used for the braiding of women's hair.

Ayşe washed my head hair and I hers. We used soap rather than shampoo even though I offered the latter.[5] Her hair was long and luxuriant, for it had not been cut since puberty. Long hair is both the glory and the symbol of womanhood, and yet the saying *saçı uzun, aklı kısa* (long hair, short intelligence or wisdom) implies that women lack something men have. Simultaneously, what women are thought to have, a loose and rampant sexuality, must now be tamed and brought under further control. This is symbolized by braiding the hair for the wedding.[6] After the bath and hair washing we went to the house of a relative where her female friends had gathered for dancing and the ritual of hair braiding.

Braids are considered an essential part of the bride's costume, and the braiding party an essential part of the wedding ceremonies. These braids are not simply two plaits but consist of from twenty to thirty narrow braids, each woven with silver tinsel. It is necessary for the braids to reach the bride's feet, but since a girl's hair is rarely that long, black yarn is woven in to make up the difference. At the end of one of the braids a blue bead is attached. This implies that the braids are an object of desire; the blue bead is there to ward off the evil eye of those who would covet them.

The hair braiding was accompanied by stories, jokes, and remembrances, each woman weaving her story and memories into a braid. The process was clearly an ordeal for Ayşe and she cried intermittently. The hair combing was rough and no doubt it sometimes hurt. More painful, perhaps, was the awareness that the multistranded playful relationships among these women would soon be woven into an orderly pattern through marriage. Their relationships would be permanently changed, as she too was being permanently changed into a bride, wife, and daughter-in-law, and would soon be a mother and eventually a mother-in-law herself.

Saturday evening is the traditional time for festivity and celebration, although women and men celebrate separately. *Kına gecesi*, henna night, as it is called, ends with the application of henna on the bride's hands and feet; a small amount is taken to the groom's house and smeared in a complementary way on his palms. But the night begins with the bride, replete with braids, wedding dress, and veil, being introduced to all the guests and dancing a number of rounds with her friends. The erotic and gendered meanings of hair were dramatized at one wedding. Even in the dim light, one could feel something stirring the huge crowd of women: a "man" was present. It was even more surprising to me since "he" looked exactly like a fellow student at the University of Chicago! It turned out to be a woman, who had not only dressed like a man but had pulled her hair back so that it seemed short and had attached a mustache. The contrast with the other women was striking.

Sunday morning the bride, again in her wedding dress and heavily veiled, was taken to the groom's house, where she would sit "in state" all day to be viewed by his relatives and friends. However, the right to lift the veil was his alone and would be done in the privacy of their room.

Theoretically, her braids would be kept for forty days after the wedding, at which time they would be cut; in practice they would be cut sooner, indicating that the number forty should be taken symbolically and not literally.[7] "Forty days" symbolizes a transitional period that is both auspicious and dangerous, and the number is employed on a number of occasions: for example, the forty days of gestation before the soul opens, the forty days after birth when life is held in the balance, and the forty days after death when the fate of the soul is being decided (after which a commemorative service called a *mevlud* is held). Forty days after the wedding, the bride is expected to be initiated into her new role and duties.[8]

My own intense and immediate initiation into some of the practices related to hair thus sensitized me and made me curious. Over the next twenty months I was able to observe and ask questions about the treatment and meaning of hair in a variety of contexts. Why all this attention to hair, and what did it mean? I have since learned that I am not the only one to have noticed. One Muslim scholar notes that "there is an undeniable fetishism of hair in Islam, the significance of which is both sexual and religious."[9] In Islam the relation between sexuality and religion is very strong; hair is but one symbol of this relation.

The sexual significance of hair, of course, is of no surprise to those familiar with the debate between Berg, Leach, and Obeyesekere discussed in the Introduction to this volume. What may not be so clear is that the debate has tended to revolve around three intertwined issues: (1) the relation between public expression and private motivation, (2) the use of sexuality for religious/ritual ends, and (3) the phallic character of hair. Leach contests the assumption of the *direction* from private, personal motivation to public expression and takes a Durkheimian position that "public ritual symbols are given potency by society and not by individuals."[10] His position does not preclude public symbols from being internalized and having personal meaning; it only contests an intrapsychic source for them. Secondly, most of the theorists have been concerned primarily with the religious uses into which the sexual significance of hair is channeled, rather than with the relationship between secular and religious meanings and practices.

Thus Obeyesekere, like Leach, discusses the meanings of hair in relation to Hindu ascetics and Buddhist monks—those who either let their hair go and become matted (supposedly indicating their letting go of sexuality), or who cut or shave their hair (to indicate a cutting off of sexual life for religious ends). He wants to show that these hair practices represent two different kinds of asceticism and therefore different motivations, and also that not just anyone takes up an ascetic mode of life.

Each of these theorists appears to endorse the view that sexuality is phallic by definition. Thus Leach fully agrees with Berg that "when head hair becomes the focus of ritual attention this is very commonly because the head is being used as a symbol for the phallus and head hair as a symbol for semen";[11] for Leach the bone of contention is not so much whether sexuality is phallic but whether the phallic origin of the symbolism is repressed.[12]

Are these scholars, however, implying that the head is *always* a symbol for the phallus, even for women, or that *only* men's heads are the object of ritual attention? Although Obeyesekere chooses to concentrate on the ways six female Hindu ascetics treated their hair, he nonetheless interprets the sexual significance of their hair in phallic terms. For example, the matted locks that emerge from a woman's head are thought to represent the sublated penis of the god.[13]

But how does such a framework help us to understand the covering and binding of women's hair? And what would it make of a Turkish married woman whose hair cutting signified just the opposite of sexual renunciation—her initiation *into* sexual life? I cannot go so far as Hallpike, who asserts that "there is no frequent association of head hair and male genitals"; but I do go a long way in following his suggestion that the "symbolism is 'about' the world, rather than 'about' the subconscious . . . for it makes it possible to evaluate different explanations of a particular piece of symbolism in terms of how well they fit the facts."[14] The "world" of Turks includes a strong connection between sex and hair symbolism, but the meaning is specific to each gender. To understand the gendered meaning of hair, we need to understand something about the meanings of gender.

An understanding of the significance of hair also demands consideration of the relation between the religious and secular uses and meanings of hair—that is, how the meanings of hair are engaged and construed by ordinary people in their ordinary life contexts, whether secular, ritual, or specifically religious. The relation between the sacred and the secular needs to be studied empirically to see if the two domains are separate and mutually exclusive or intimately entwined.[15] In Turkey, at least, I suggest that the meaning of hair is *simultaneously* religious and sexual, and that these meanings have political implications.

MEANINGS OF GENDER

In Turkish society, as in many others (including our own), the meanings of male and female are commonly felt to derive from their role in procreation. Yet understandings of this process vary cross-culturally as well as historically; the meanings are not naturally given but are culturally informed,[16] and within Turkish culture can vary somewhat between educated city people and villagers. Nevertheless, there are significant commonalities. I have discussed the Turkish material at length elsewhere;[17] here I can give only an intimation.

The man begets, the woman gives birth. The male is thought to provide the generative, creative spark of life which bestows specific identity upon persons and which, if renewed in each generation of males, is theoretically eternal. The production of semen, therefore, signifies more than a sexual or physiological process; it is endowed with creativity and agency and is associated with divine activity.[18] The ancient notion that semen originates in the brain[19] is alive and well in rural Turkey. The pride that is attributed to the male organ of generation is also conferred on men's heads or, more accurately, the two are seen as intimately connected.

The definition of maleness is not confined to the body; it overflows its physical meaning and becomes generalized. For example, seminal production is also associated with intellectual production, as expressed quite explicitly in the notion of the "seminal idea," a generative, creative idea. Men can produce brain children as well as physical ones; they can inseminate minds as well as bodies, establish intellectual lineages as well as biological ones.[20]

In contrast, women are imagined primarily *as* bodies, and as providing the material that nourishes and sustains life. They thus become defined by and even more restricted to their physical roles. Male genitals are associated with the creative divine element and become a source of pride, whereas female genitals are thought to lack that element and are, therefore, felt to be a source of shame.[21] Unlike the penis, which receives a great deal of attention especially throughout childhood, female genitals are strictly taboo and are rarely mentioned. A woman's honor consists in keeping them under wraps, so to speak, keeping them for the use of only one man. These specific meanings, I suggest, are displaced to the female head, where they become integrally related to the symbolism of hair.

Girls and boys, in rural Turkey at least, are relatively neuter as children. As infants both are fully swaddled with their heads covered, and as toddlers they are dressed in the same kind of pants and tops. Both are given the freedom to run in and out of people's houses. Nevertheless, gender differences soon become focused on hair. Around the age of two a baby boy's hair is cut short and will be regularly trimmed. After that even playing with a headscarf can call upon his head a string of shaming comments. For example, an older sister teased her baby brother who had put on the head-scarf, "Now you've become a girl." Their mother got angry and shouted at him, "You are male, you are male, take that off." Although both boys and girls are indulged and spoiled, girls seem to be more spoiled and less tame. Their hair, too, is free and often tangled. Hallpike's notion that unruly hair can symbolize the state of being outside society is useful here; while girls are not exactly outside society, they will not enter it to the same extent that boys will. Thus Hallpike's view that hair cutting indicates entrance into society applies only partially and only to boys. Boys are expected to show by their demeanor their recognition, and thus internalization, of their more exalted status. They are being groomed to enter into the public so-ciety of men, whereas girls will soon be confined to the private world of the home. More convincing perhaps is Firth's suggestion that hair cutting, rather than indicating a relation between the inside and the outside of society, may symbolize a transition from one type of social control to an-other.[22] Boys begin to learn that they must control themselves, whereas girls will be controlled externally.

Upon entering school, boys have their heads almost shaved; the same occurs when they enter the army or, for that matter, prison. Thus hair cutting does seem to signify entrance into a disciplined regime. Girls may or may not have their hair cut when entering school; it is believed that girls cannot become quite so disciplined.[23] Nevertheless, even though children do have their hair cut occasionally they do not really become social beings until puberty and not fully adult until marriage. Since women must always be under the mantle of some man, it could be argued that they never really achieve full adult status at all.[24]

For boys there is a transitional stage before puberty. Sometime before the age of twelve, and generally after the age of five, boys are circumcised. They become socially gendered beings by the removal of a bodily cover-ing—the "veil of the penis"[25]—while girls become socially gendered when they are "veiled" by the headscarf. Girls cover the site of their shame; boys reveal the locus of their pride. The boy's penis is displayed during the circumcision ceremonies, and it is the object of much attention.[26] There-after the sight of the genitals is taboo and they are covered by clothes.[27]

The genitals are clearly the site of gender; but since they must be hidden, their meanings are displaced to the head, where they can be publicly dis-played. And while the head can symbolize the genitals it is not just a symbol of the phallus. As different meanings are attributed to the genitals of each gender, so too are the heads of men and women treated differently.

Puberty is the time when gender meanings become inscribed in bodily practices, and in Turkey practices relating to hair are quite prominent. The abstract notion of puberty as mere sexual maturity gives no indication of its specific cultural meanings, nor of the differences in meaning for girls and boys, nor finally of any implications beyond the physiological. For a boy, puberty is demonstrated by the ability to ejaculate and is interpreted as a sign that he can produce living "seed." Puberty is also exhibited by the emergence of both pubic and facial hair, an event that further associates the genitals with the head. Pubic hair should be neither seen nor mentioned and in Turkey, as noted, it is often removed. Nevertheless, the mustache sprouting above a boy's mouth is the emblem he can display to proudly proclaim his virility.

Women remove their pubic hair and cover their head hair. The fact that the removal of pubic hair is discussed in terms of cleanliness suggests that it carries meanings of dirt and dank sexuality, with cloying tendrils that entrap men. Women's sexuality is not allowed to run rampant or to be displayed; instead it is covered up and kept under strict control. Women's hair, it would seem, comes to symbolize the physical entanglements by which men are ensnared, and thus must be kept out of sight. Women's sexuality is meant for men's pleasure, and while men are meant to enjoy sex they should not become enmeshed in it. They are supposed to keep their emotional distance and keep their minds free.[28] The headscarf and other coverings are meant to facilitate this repose.

The sight of women's head hair, especially the hair of unrelated women, is felt to trigger uncontrollable sexual desire in men, perhaps because of the connection between head hair and the female genitals. As several men told me: "A woman's hair is the ruination of families." They meant not only that a woman with uncovered hair will arouse a married man and cause him to commit adultery at least in his mind, but also that even within the house too much loose hair creates disturbance. Perhaps hair also evokes the image of *Sirat,* the bridge over which the souls of the dead must walk. It is said to be the thickness of a single strand of hair; it slices the wicked like a razor and they fall into hell, but for the righteous it widens out into a path leading to heaven. The more pious men avowed that for every strand of hair that a woman shows, she is said to burn one day in hell.[29] This theme is reiterated in Muslim scholarly texts; one such text suggests that this may be why images of the Muslim hell are full of women.[30] Women's hair is a highly charged symbol of the power of female sexuality; men's attempts to control the latter may be symbolized by their attempts to control the former.

Women's hair and heads are covered in a number of ways (see figures 1 and 2) and there are a number of terms used to refer to these coverings—there is no one single canonical form of headcovering nor one cover term. The most common term is *çarsaf* (literally, bed linens), which can function almost as a generic term but also refers to a large outer scarf that covers the upper body. *Yemeni* refers to the small, square, pastel-colored printed gauze scarves that women trim with beads and tatting. These can be tied

Figure 1. Three styles of head covering. (Photos by author)

Figure 2. A group of women having a tea party outdoors. (Photo by author)

in back or draped under the chin and tucked into the sides so that the face is surrounded. *Yemeni* were worn at all times regardless of what other coverings might be added; in our village they were worn even in the house, though they might be more loosely tied, and even allegedly to bed! In other villages I have heard that some women may remove the scarves at home among family. When a woman goes out into the street or visiting, she will add a larger, printed cotton scarf called a *yasmak* over the *yemeni*. Often the pattern of these scarves is specific to a particular region (for our region see figure 1, top left), and although there are a number of ways to drape them, they should cover not only the hair but also the shoulders and breasts. However, see figure 2 and note the outer scarves in the tree! In winter, a large woolen square called an *atkı* is used. Villagers also used the term *dülbent* for a plain white scarf with or without trimming, and *başörtü* for a Western-type printed "silk" square that is tied like a kerchief under the chin. Normally this would be used for trips to the city. This style of scarf, though of plainer cloth, is what is meant by *türban*. As a Turkish word, it is quite a new term: in neither village, town, nor city did I hear the word, nor is it in my 1979 edition of the Redhouse Turkish dictionary. *Türban* refers to the headcovering favored by the urban Islamic groups; but the recency of the word underscores the fact that this so-called Islamic headcovering is not a traditional type of covering but is, instead, a relatively new phenomenon.

Small girls in the village played at covering themselves, but the headscarf became obligatory at puberty. Puberty for a girl is signaled by menstruation—an indication that she is sexually open, that she is fertile. Her fertility, like that of the soil, must be enclosed in order that a man may know that the seed sowed there belongs to him. When a woman puts on the headscarf, she is referred to as *kapalı*—"covered, closed." A woman who goes about bareheaded is referred to as *açık,* "open"; this implies that she is available and open to the advances of men.

The headscarf is a sign that everyone can read, and it says, "I am a proper woman, I am under the protective mantle of my father." He is guarantor of her sexuality until he transfers it to her husband upon marriage. By means of the headcovering a woman indicates that her fertile field is not free for the planting; it has boundaries and belongs to some man. These boundaries, like those of a field, cannot be transgressed without dire consequences.

Regardless of the actual physiological onset of puberty, for girls its social recognition[31] is at the end of primary school when they are about twelve years old—and at this time they must cover. Schools are state-supported and secular, and during the time I was in Turkey neither female teachers nor students were permitted to wear headscarves.[32] Indeed, the wearing of headscarves is not just a violation of the dress code but might almost be considered as treason. Such behavior could easily be interpreted as expressing a commitment to Islam that takes precedence over the allegiance expected toward the secular state that Atatürk worked so hard to establish. Currently, school attendance is obligatory only until the end of primary school, or fifth grade. Since most village girls do not attend school beyond primary level, the law banning headscarves in school was acceptable to most villagers. The conflict between religious custom and sentiment, on the one hand, and nationalist ideology and allegiance, on the other, was thereby accommodated. Some of the meanings of sexuality and hair covering emerge in the case of girls who wish to continue school beyond the fifth grade. Since a father's permission is necessary for a girl to continue in school, a girl who wished to do so would first have to convince her father to support her in this struggle and consent to her abandonment of the headscarf; in going to school she would have to flout custom.

The few fathers I knew who did give permission for their daughters to attend middle school were called "Communists." This had nothing to do with what was being taught in school but had much to do with "covering." Because these girls would be mingling freely with boys without the curtain of protection between them, it was as if their bodily boundaries were being compromised; metaphorically, it was as if they were common land.

Formerly, the uncovered female head was associated with the loose immorality of the West; during the time I was there, people would invoke an association either with the West or with the Communist world, depending on circumstances. In either case, however, uncovering was interpreted as a capitulation to the material world, something antithetical to submission to the religious order of Islam. At the same time, it must be noted that women of the urban elite classes have long been oriented toward the West and many have been educated in the West. Women from these classes do go uncovered and have done so for some time. Atatürk considered Westernization a necessary aspect of modernization, and a major sign of modernity was, for him, uncovered women. In today's climate of antagonism to the West, however, some of these women have begun to adopt the *türban*.

There is one kind of hair that has yet to be addressed. Although we have briefly touched upon the meaning of the mustache, we have not yet broached the topic of the beard. Since children, women, and eunuchs are beardless, the beard is surely a salient symbol of masculinity;[33] but such an observation does not take us very far. While the beard can distinguish between age groups, and between men and women, it can also distinguish between different groups of men.[34] What sort of masculinity, then, does it symbolize? In traditional Islam, the beard is "a mark of authority and piety."[35] Traditionally in Turkey it is only older men, especially those who have made the hajj (pilgrimage to Mecca), who are permitted to let their beards grow. A man who has made the hajj has completed the five conditions of faith, and having fulfilled his pious duties can legitimately wear a beard.

In Mecca, as men and women enter the sacred precinct, they are required to abstain from sexual activity for the period of the hajj. But since women's sexuality is at the command of men, the injunction is really directed to men. The symbolic association between sexuality, religion, and hair is further strengthened by the fact that during the hajj men let their hair and beards grow, like the ascetics so much discussed in the anthropological literature about hair. Hair grooming would imply that their minds were still focused on worldly things when they should be focused on God. After the hajj rituals and the sacrifice commemorating Abraham's ordeal have been completed, the hajj proper comes to an end and the pilgrims reenter the mundane world. Men cut their hair and shave their facial hair, women cut off a lock of hair. In this context hair cutting does not symbolize a cutting off of sexuality or a commitment to celibacy—in fact, just the reverse. It does mean, however, a renewal of commitment to a socially pre-scribed control and use of sexuality. The theoretical implications of this hair behavior make it clear that while hair cutting may stand cross-culturally in some symbolic relation to sexuality, the actual meaning of that relation cannot be deduced from universal "facts," but must be empirically inves-tigated in specific cultural contexts.

Upon returning home from Mecca, with life's purpose fulfilled, the male pilgrims may again let their beards grow. Their minds, now, should be turned to religious matters, so they should neither devote too much atten-tion to the care of the beard nor ignore it to the extent that it becomes disheveled.[36] A properly kept beard implies not only the authority con-ferred by age and religion, but also the wisdom to strike a balance in the use of that authority. For these reasons, the older men in the village I studied considered it their prerogative to wear a beard, and they perceived a young man with a beard as both sacrilegious and rebellious. The older men interpreted such behavior as a direct threat to their authority.

Not surprisingly, no youth in our village had a beard. And yet things are not so simple. In other Muslim countries, for example, the beard has be-come a sign of affiliation with some of the new conservative, "fundamen-talist" Muslim groups.[37] For some young men, therefore, the beard can be a sign of their own piety and the authority that goes with religious obser-vance. This phenomenon is not so prevalent in Turkey, where a bearded youth is more often assumed to be a member of a leftist, Marxist group. In either case, however, a young man wearing a beard is seen as a threat to authority.

The dress code that prohibits female university students from wearing headscarves also prohibits male university students from wearing beards; both are interpreted as threats to the authority of the secular state. In the university context a beard is interpreted as a symbol of leftist tendencies, a symbol of those who sabotage the order of the state. In this instance, the secular state seems ironically to have appropriated the mantle of the sa-cred.[38] A Turkish friend of mine confided that every time he returns to Turkey he shaves off his beard because he wants to avoid the consequences of its social meanings. Not only beards, but "during the 1970s mustaches in Turkey became a symbolic badge of political identity."[39] Certain styles of mustaches were classified as "leftist"—especially those that were bushy and turned down at the sides of the mouth. This style was known as *Stalin bıyığı* (Stalin mustache). In contrast, those with the edges curled up recalled the style of the Ottomans and were, at least in the 1960s, emblematic of the "rightist" nationalists. Mustaches are occasionally tolerated in the army, but they are not approved. In any case, they must be thin and neither cover the upper lip nor extend beyond it. Beards, however, are not permitted.

Because the significance of hair in Turkey is at once sexual, religious, and political, it becomes entwined in different ways in different contexts for different people. Men, clearly, have their own issues and problems with hair that are different from those that affect women. But the meaning of women's headcovering is not unrelated; it is neither an isolated phenomenon nor uniform in meaning. For rural women the meaning is different from what it is for urban women, and urban women are hardly unified over this issue. The meaning of the headscarf is also different depending on whether the context is Europe or Turkey, and different for the Alevi minority as opposed to the Sunni majority. Class differences may be involved, but class is not the decisive indicator. The issue is a significant one primarily for those women who wish to make a self-conscious statement about their religious sentiments and commitments. Whether urban women express their reasons for covering as emancipation from the male gaze, as devotion to Islam, or, more politically, as resistance to the West, the sexual, religious, and political meanings cannot be separated.

THE HEADSCARF DEBATE

The foregoing discussion should make it clear that the headscarf debate is far more complicated than it has hitherto been portrayed. Because the debate has been so narrowly focused on the political issues of individual rights and freedom of religion, there has been no examination of the cultural logic or rationale behind the differential meanings and values of male and female bodies, of sexuality, and of gender.

A number of women are protesting the law that prohibits them from wearing the headscarf to schools, especially to the universities. They argue that they have a right to do so and that the abrogation of this right is a restriction of the freedom of religion and an infringement of individual rights.[40] Framed in this way, the issue has ironically united some elements on the left with those on the conservative right. But other female students ask: "If I support their right to wear Islamic scarves, will they tolerate my mini-skirt?"[41] The ironies of the debate have been obscured by this rhetoric, for those who demand the right to wear the scarf are using what are essentially Western liberal arguments to protest *against* the West. Their portrait of the West highlights stereotypic images of women as loose, immoral, and scantily clad beings. Neither they nor their Western sympathizers have stopped to ask just whose vision/version of Western women is being invoked. Why is there so little awareness that these images have been painted primarily by men, both in Muslim countries and in the West? And correlatively, why has there been no counterprotest from Western women, many of whom are well aware that these images of womanhood are further fetishized and exploited by the advertising that is necessary to increase the demand for all kinds of commodities that are integral to Western economies? What these Muslim women do not seem to realize is that the vision of women they reject is also one which many Western women struggle against. But for Western women to counter these stereotypic and damaging images by covering themselves and adopting something equivalent to "Islamic dress" would imply that at some level they themselves accept the stereotypes.[42]

Another factor overlooked in the debate is its urban character. It is carried on by young women who have considerable freedom to express and exercise their choices. Of course, if allegations prove true that some of these women are being paid by Islamic "fundamentalists" to wear *türban*s to the universities, their credibility and freedom of expression will be undermined. In any case, these women do not speak for the greater numbers of women who are less free to express their choices, caught as they are in networks of small-town and village pressures from family and friends. Even among the urban elite, this pressure exists. It can be subtle and is more reflective of a woman's background and peer group; only sometimes is it overt. But in villages, the sentiment and weight of the entire community comes down on women's heads. The women demanding the right to wear the headscarf and their Western supporters rarely consider how their actions may affect the thousands of women who are not privy to the debate.

The argument in favor of covering and "Islamic dress," known in the Arab world as *hijab,* is that it removes women from being perceived as erotic and sexual objects.[43] No doubt it does indeed provide this kind of shelter. At the same time, however, one could just as easily argue that covering advertises the entire body as an erotic object. This indeed seems to be behind the notion of covering at least for certain Muslims. "Key concepts relating to the Islamic ideology of female modesty are contained in the words ʿawra, fitna, and zina. That is, the entire body of a woman (except her face and hands) is to be treated as pudenda; it is a vulnerable, weak object that must be covered to avoid embarrassment and shame. Even the voice of a woman is ʿawra and should not be heard."[44] Clearly, a closed mouth is analogous to a closed vagina, as Eilberg-Schwartz suggests (this volume); for a woman to speak openly is almost equivalent to exposing herself. Not only is the equation between the female head, in this case the mouth, and the genitals reinforced, the equation has specific gendered meaning. As men call things into being with their "seed," so too do they have the power to call things into being with the word. It is their prerogative to initiate conversation (as well as sex) and to define the situation, including what is to count as "true" Islam. This does not mean that women do not speak; the cultural wisdom, however, is that their words carry no weight, that they are not generative or definitive. These ideas are not unique to Turkey; they are familiar to Christians in Paul's command: "Let a woman learn in all submissiveness. I permit no woman to teach or have authority over men; she is to keep silent" (1 Tim. 2:11–12). Curiously, this passage occurs immediately after a demand that women not adorn themselves with jewels and braided hair! Women, at least in some circles, *are* speaking out; but they struggle against a cultural and religious tradition that has discouraged them, and their encroachment on male power threatens the social order sanctioned by that tradition.

CONCLUSION

Notions of gender are deeply entangled with meanings of hair in Turkish society. Neither the women who call for their right to wear the headscarf nor their Western sympathizers seem to realize that whether women wear the scarf or not, whether we are covered or uncovered, we are still being defined by our bodies in ways that men are not. The polarization between covering or not covering not only divides women but in the process obscures the much larger issue: how to transform the meanings of the female body and sexuality. And urban Muslim women, I suggest, are doing exactly what they accuse some of their Western sisters of doing: presuming to speak for those who do not have a voice and who have never had a choice whether or not to cover their hair.

NOTES

An abbreviated version of this paper was presented at the annual meeting of the American Ethnological Society, Atlanta, Georgia (April 1990), and at the Universities of Oslo and Bergen, Norway (June 1990), and the American Academy of Religion, New Orleans, Louisiana (November 1990). A slightly modified version appeared in the *Anthropological Quarterly* 67(4): 159–72, 1994. I have benefited greatly from conversations with Howard Eilberg-Schwartz, whose interests and enthusiasms overlap with mine. I would also like to thank Eser Ayanoğlu, Hamit Fişek, Akile Gürsoy-Tezcan, and June Starr for their sensitive readings and helpful comments.

1. For example, anyone who was a teenager in the United States in the 1950s can recall the response of parents and "straights" to the male hairstyle called a DA. DA did not mean District Attorney; it was not a lawful hairstyle but rather a flippant tail (Duck's Ass) turned on authority. Firth 1973 has an excellent discussion of public reaction to long-haired youths in the 1960s; comparing with the Tikopia, he makes it clear that the meaning is culturally specific. More recently the same sort of response has been transferred to people with punk-style hair or skinheads. Blacks make statements by straightening their hair or wearing an Afro, weaving it into cornrows or letting it mat into dreadlocks. As Hebdige 1979 has shown for youth groups in Britain, hairstyles can index an entire system of meaning.

2. The large number of books that include "veil" in their title, whether written by Middle Easterners or Westerners—for example *Veiled Sentiments, Beyond the Veil,*

Behind the Veil in Arabia—would seem to cater to and perpetuate the exoticization of the Other. What is often forgotten by Westerners is the fact that until fairly recently women in the West wore hats when they went out publicly and always covered their heads upon entering church. This custom is attributed to Paul's statement: "A man ought not to cover his head since he is the image and glory of God, but woman is the glory of man" (1 Cor. 11:7).

3. For an excellent discussion of this issue in Turkey see Olson 1985; and for similar discussion in Germany, Mandel 1989.

4. My research in Turkey was conducted between September 1979 and June 1982, twenty months of which were spent in a village in central Anatolia. A full account of that work can be found in Delaney 1991. Additional observations come from return visits in 1986 and 1992.

5. Berg (1951) suggests that massaging the head during hair washing may have sexual connotations and that the white froth of shampoo can be associated with semen. I do not know whether any such association was made by the villagers, but their feeling that using shampoo was somehow sinful may relate to this. The relation between head hair and sexuality was, however, involved in villagers' reactions against the practice among urban Turkish women of going to beauty salons to have their hair cut, and therefore touched, by men.

6. Compare Firth (1973:273) for discussion of the meaning of braids among certain American college girls in the 1950s.

7. The number forty is very prevalent in Turkey and Islam, as well as in a number of other traditions. One need only think of the forty days and forty nights that Noah's ark was tossed upon the flood, or the forty days Jesus spent in the wilderness. See also Brandes 1987.

8. Hirschon 1978.

9. Bouhdiba 1985:35.

10. Leach 1958:159.

11. Leach 1958:157.

12. Leach 1958:155.

13. Obeyesekere 1981:33.

14. Hallpike 1969:263.

15. Such anthropological studies are rare; most have focused on the hair practices of monks and other religious people, and the meaning of hair has been construed as sexual, specifically phallic. Hershman 1974 is a partial exception. He discusses everyday practices related to hair among Hindus and Sikhs. He faults Hallpike (1969) for his lack of a "theory to explain why hair in particular is chosen to symbolize social control," and feels "inclined towards the Freudian position that the subconscious symbolism of hair is sexual" (291). Yet when it comes to specific ceremonies such as the Punjabi mourning rites, he says, "it does not necessarily follow that the symbolism of hair will also be sexual" (ibid.).

16. Even scientific theory is itself a product of particular social, historical, and cultural circumstances; it has changed drastically over the centuries, and is unevenly disseminated throughout the world. This is especially true of contemporary genetic theory. This theory has only become widely known in Western culture during the last seventy years or so; not only has it failed to dislodge some of the older images

and ideas, which often crop up in ordinary conversation, but it is itself suffused with some of them.

17. For a fuller account of my theoretical approach to notions of procreation and their significance, see Delaney 1986, 1987, and 1991.

18. These notions are hardly unique to the village in Turkey where I did my fieldwork; they have a long history in the West as well. They are explicitly stated by Aristotle and are implicit in the Bible, both of which have had a profound effect on Western notions of gender. The similarity between the Western and the Turkish conceptions may relate to the fact that Islam has itself been heavily influenced by both Aristotle and the Bible; but this does not mean that villagers today are familiar with those texts.

19. This notion can be traced to Aristotle, for example in his *Generation of Animals,* but may not have originated with him. See also Onians 1951:109–11. My own feeling is that this belief is also related to the story in which Zeus "gives birth" to Athena from his head. (Little known is the fact that he first devoured her pregnant mother, Metis, wisest of all the gods.)

20. It is perhaps no coincidence that schools established to study the sacred text, the seminal word of God (*logos spermatikos*), were called seminaries. See also Eilberg-Schwartz 1990, chapter 9.

21. Delaney 1987, 1991, Hoffman-Ladd 1987, Marcus 1984, 1992.

22. Firth 1973.

23. After reading a draft of this paper, a Turkish friend wrote to me about the following practice: "With the custom of taking young girls as *besleme* for househelp (which means that the girl will then begin to live in the new household), one of the first things usually done to the young girl is to have her change her name, and also to cut her hair really short. There is a hygienic explanation often given to the hair cutting (the girl comes into a middle or upper class family from a rural or working class environment, and it is assumed she may carry *bit* [lice]), but I think the hair cutting must also have identity implications for the girl in question."

24. A divorced woman would usually return to her father's house, while a widow would remain in the home of her dead husband and come under the protection and control of his father or brothers. Although several women in the village left their husbands for periods of time, they were eventually reunited; there were no divorced women in the village and no divorce occurred while I was there. (Cf. Starr 1985 for the very different situation in the area around Bodrum.) Urban, highly educated women told me how difficult it was to live alone after a divorce because they were presumed to be sexually promiscuous. While women in Turkey have many rights equal to men, a man still determines domicile and must give permission for his daughter or wife to work. Legal rights, in any case, do not guarantee social equity; this is as true in the United States as in Turkey.

25. Boddy 1988:5.

26. Orga 1950, Pierce 1964, Roper 1974.

27. Nevertheless, some Turkish men, particularly in urban areas, continue to draw attention to the genitals by wearing tight pants and/or by touching the genital area as they strut down the street. I do not know whether this behavior is almost unconscious, since it goes unnoticed by most Turks, or whether it is done specifically to provoke foreign women. It was an aspect of my own urban experience, and a

number of foreign women have mentioned it to me as well. It was not, however, my experience in the village.

28. Sabbah 1984:117.

29. Firth 1973:267–68 suggests that the power of even a single strand of female hair to move men is a theme not unique to Turkey or Islam but also contained in the literature of the West.

30. Smith and Haddad 1975.

31. A concept suggested by Van Gennep 1909.

32. Since that time, because of the protests of some women and their male supporters about their right to wear the headscarf, a number of conflicting laws have been passed. Apparently the government permitted headcovering in universities by a special bill passed in 1988; but then President Evren annulled the bill through the *Anayasa Makemesi* (Constitutional Court) in 1989. Meanwhile, Turkey's Higher Education Council lifted the headscarf ban in December 1989, with the approval of the then-new president, Turgut Özal. Now universities are caught between the Constitutional Court and the Higher Education Council, and each university seems to be making its own decision on the matter. See *The Turkish Times,* January 17, 1990.

33. Firth 1973:285.

34. For example, a beard can serve to distinguish between priests and other men and even between different kinds of priests. But such meanings cannot be known *a priori.* "In Eastern Christianity beards have traditionally been held appropriate for priests, but this has not been the view of the Western church, where there has been considerable divergence of opinion" as well as custom (Firth 1973:285). Firth goes on to suggest that the wearing of beards by Eastern Orthodox Christian priests may have the connotation that they are more manly but also of lower status, since they are also permitted to have wives. Yet even if Western priests go beardless and are unmarried, and even if it is accepted that they are of higher and more sacred status, an uncomfortable contradiction looms: on this view a higher, more sacred status would seem to be closer to femininity than to masculinity, and this appears to fly in the face of all the cultural evidence.

35. Gaffney 1982:56.

36. See the treatise by Al-Makki (d. 996), 1978:101.

37. Gaffney 1982.

38. Toprak 1981, Delaney 1991.

39. Starr 1992:xviii–xix.

40. The cold-blooded murder of two young Algerian women for not wearing the veil (*New York Times,* March 31, 1994) is the latest evidence that the issue is hardly one of individual rights.

41. *The Turkish Times,* December 14, 1989.

42. It is also ironic, if not tragic, that as the sociopolitical boundaries and walls dividing peoples of the world are coming down, the sexual barriers between men and women as well as those creating divisions among women are going up. For forty years, between 1939 and 1979, the *chador* was officially outlawed in Iran. For a similar amount of time, though beginning and ending a few years later, a wall (the Iron Curtain) divided East and West. And just as peace in the Middle East seems on the verge of becoming a real possibility, uncovered Palestinian women in the

West Bank and Gaza are being harassed by paint-slinging, name-calling male youths who police the streets. These youths are calling for them to adopt the head covering and even the face veil in order "to keep our morals and traditions intact" (*New York Times,* August 22, 1991). Not only is this a reassertion of male dominance, it is also a way to keep the divisions between Muslims and Jews inviolate.

43. Sherif 1987.

44. Hoffman-Ladd 1987:43. She also defines the words `*awra* as weak spot, pudenda, *fitna* as temptation, chaos, discord, and *zina* as adornment, beauty. The *zina* "that may be shown in public is the face and hands, whereas the hidden zina is the rest of the body" (29). She makes a very interesting and convincing argument that what is today considered Islamic dress or *hijab* is actually contemporary and not at all traditional Islamic dress. She also discusses how women who wear *hijab* are in fact perceived as a threatening and therefore somewhat aggressive presence in modern Egyptian society—a perception at odds with the very rationale for wearing it!

REFERENCES

Al-Makki, Abu Talib
 1978 "The Beard." *The Muslim World* 68(2): 100–110.
Aristotle
 1979 *Generation of Animals.* Trans. A. L. Peck. Cambridge: Harvard University Press.
Berg, Charles
 1951 *The Unconscious Significance of Hair.* London: George Allen and Unwin.
Boddy, Janice
 1988 "Spirits and Selves in Northern Sudan: The Cultural Therapeutics of Possession and Trance". *American Ethnologist* 15(1): 4–27.
Bouhdiba, Abdelwahab
 1985 *Sexuality in Islam.* London: Routledge and Kegan Paul. [Previously published in French, 1975.]
Brandes, Stanley
 1987 [1985] *Forty: The Age and the Symbol.* Knoxville: University of Tennessee Press.
Delaney, Carol
 1986 "The Meaning of Paternity and the Virgin Birth Debate." *Man* 21(3): 494–513.
 1987 "Seeds of Honor, Fields of Shame." In *Honor and Shame and the Unity of the Mediterranean,* ed. by David Gilmore, 35–48. Washington, D.C.: American Anthropological Association.
 1991 *The Seed and the Soil: Gender and Cosmology in Turkish Village Society.* Berkeley and Los Angeles: University of California Press.
Eilberg-Schwartz, Howard
 1990 *The Savage in Judaism: An Anthropology of Israelite Religion and Ancient Judaism.* Bloomington: Indiana University Press.
Firth, Raymond
 1973 *Symbols: Public and Private.* Ithaca: Cornell University Press.

Gaffney, Patrick
   1982   "Shaykh, Khutba and Masjid: The Role of the Local Islamic Preacher in Upper Egypt." Ph.D. dissertation, University of Chicago.
Hallpike, C. R.
   1969   "Social Hair." *Man* 4:256–64.
Hebdige, Dick
   1979   *Subculture: The Meaning of Style.* London: Methuen.
Hershman, P.
   1974   "Hair, Sex and Dirt." *Man,* n.s., 9(2): 274–98.
Hirschon, Renee
   1978   "Open Body/Closed Space." In *Defining Females: The Nature of Women in Society,* ed. by Shirley Ardener, 66–88. New York: John Wiley and Sons.
Hoffman-Ladd, Valerie
   1987   "Polemics on the Modesty and Segregation of Women in Contemporary Egypt." *International Journal of Middle East Studies* 19:23–50.
Leach, Edmund
   1958   "Magical Hair." *Man: Journal of the Royal Anthropological Society* 88:147–68.
Mandel, Ruth
   1989   "Turkish Headscarves and the 'Foreigner Problem.'" *The New German Critique* 46:27–46.
Marcus, Julie
   1984   "Islam, Women and Pollution in Turkey." *Journal of the Anthropological Association of Oxford* 15(3): 204–18.
   1992   *A World of Difference: Islam and Gender Hierarchy in Turkey.* London: Zed Press.
Obeyesekere, Gananath
   1981   *Medusa's Hair: An Essay on Personal Symbols and Religious Experience.* Chicago: University of Chicago Press.
Olson, Emelie
   1985   "Muslim Identity and Secularism in Contemporary Turkey: 'The Headscarf Dispute.'" *Anthropological Quarterly* 58(4): 161–71.
Onians, R. B.
   1951   *The Origins of European Thought.* Cambridge: Cambridge University Press.
Orga, Irfan
   1950   *Portrait of a Turkish Family.* New York: Macmillan.
Pierce, Joe
   1964   *Life in a Turkish Village.* New York: Holt, Rinehart and Winston.
Roper, Joyce
   1974   *The Women of Nar.* London: Faber and Faber.
Sabbah, Fatna
   1984   *Woman in the Muslim Unconscious.* Trans. Mary Jo Lakeland. New York: Pergamon Press.
Sherif, Mostafa Hashem
   1987   "What is Ḥijāb?" *The Muslim World* 77(3–4): 151–63.

Smith, J., and Y. Haddad
  1975   "Women in the Afterlife: The Islamic View as Seen from the Quran and Hadith." *Journal of the American Academy of Religion* 18:39–50.
Starr, June
  1985   "Folk Law in Official Courts of Turkey." In *People's Law and Folk Law,* ed. by A. Allott and G. R. Woodman, 123–41. Dordrecht: Foris.
  1992   *Law as Metaphor: From Islamic Courts to the Palace of Justice.* Albany: State University of New York Press.
Toprak, Binnaz
  1981   *Islam and Political Development in Turkey.* Leiden: E. J. Brill.
Van Gennep, Arnold
  1960 [1909] *The Rites of Passage.* Chicago: University of Chicago Press.

—⊶⊷⊶—

FOUR

The Gendered Grammar of Ancient Mediterranean Hair

Molly Myerowitz Levine

For you, Cleis, I have no gay headband, and know not whence one shall come . . .
SAPPHO (FRAG. 98, LOBEL-PAGE)

This essay represents one way to cut the deck of the vast amount of data that has come my way in the process of writing a book on ancient Greek, Roman, and Jewish hair. The evidence for ancient Mediterranean hair is dauntingly complex and intertwined: the hair laws, rituals, and practices of real people as deduced from legal, historical, and iconographic evidence; myths and stories that encode cultural significances of hair; and literary texts which self-consciously manipulate historical practices and cultural meanings of hair. Ultimately, these many different types of evidence may be taken together to distill a kind of grammar for the ancient Mediterranean language of hair. By grammar I mean a consistent system which accommodates, organizes, and governs the various significances of hair so as to articulate some larger cultural sense. Native speakers unconsciously absorb the rules of a grammar together with its vocabulary. A grammar not only informs the way in which speakers use the elements of a language, in this case the language of hair; it also molds and limits what can and cannot be articulated. Considerations of space limit the following discussion to only a sampling of the types of evidence, with emphasis on some ways in which cultural meanings of the masculine and feminine are both produced by and produce a gendered grammar of hair.

   In my discussion, I shall use the traditional societies of the ancient Greeks, Romans, and Jews (including those modern-day Orthodox Jews who, defining themselves as traditional, claim in a self-conscious effort to have either preserved or elaborated upon ancient Jewish practices) to examine briefly this gendered grammar which has hair as its vocabulary. A flexible grammar, but never a rigid algebra, as Eustathius, the twelfth-century commentator on Homer, well knew, when he read hair in Homer's *Iliad* as a variable sign for praise or blame depending on context: Homer's

Achaean warriors at Troy wear their hair long (*karē komoōntes*) like the mane of a lion (*leōn khaitēn*) to terrorize the enemy, but Paris skulking in the bedroom of Helen to avoid battle wears his fair hair as a sign of his effeminacy (*ēukomos gunē*) and therefore as a sign of his shame (Eust. 381.30, ad *Iliad* 3.55; Van der Valk 1971:602).

Why do I juxtapose Jewish traditions with those of the Greco-Roman world? Partly, it must be readily admitted, because these are the cultures I know something about. I have had a vested interest in Jewish hair since the time of my own marriage, when I was expected to cover my hair to signify my new status as matron. Above all, I juxtapose these traditions because it is increasingly clear to me that any study of any one of these cultures must always take into account their common Mediterranean context. In the case of hair, the message from antiquity is garbled, with ancient Greek, Roman, and Jewish sources sounding like static-muffled voices over a transatlantic phone line. Often the message makes sense only when the cultures are heard in tandem, as they supplement each other to fill in the missing gaps in our conversation with Mediterranean antiquity. Whether speaking a language of argument or agreement, these peoples, in close physical contact during various historical periods, share a common cultural grammar, at least as far as hair is concerned. Thus, much of the confusion about hair codes—Greek, Roman, and Jewish—can be clarified by references from one culture to another. As it happens, a picture is worth a thousand words in explaining what I mean.

B'NAI-BRAK, ISRAEL, CIRCA 1990

The scenes in figures 1 and 2 more or less capture what I saw a few summers back while strolling along Rabbi Akiva Street, the main drag of what the newspapers like to call the ultraorthodox city of B'nai-Brak in Israel. This is an area where for religious reasons most of the women are wigged or scarved and almost all of the men wear some form of head covering. As I passed one of the many fashionable wig stores agleam with glass and chrome, I paused at a particularly opulent display, only to do a double-take when I noticed that in addition to the dazzling variety of wig styles, the styrofoam heads were all sporting dark sunglasses. A local friend explained that the self-styled B'nai-Brak "Modesty Brigade" had objected to this abundance of hair displayed on the public thoroughfare as a potentially dangerous erotic distraction for the men of the town.[1] They had demanded that the shopkeeper cover her wigs with scarves to hide all that hair. When the shopowner protested that she was in the business of selling wigs and not scarves, a rare compromise was reached. The hair could remain if the (painted) eyes were dimmed. (Note that the holes in the noses serve to deflect the charge of exhibiting graven images.) I was impressed by the

Figure 1. Display at wig store on Rabbi Akiva Street, B'nai-Brak, ca. 1990.
(Photo by author)

Figure 2. Close-up of display at Rabbi Akiva Street wig store.
(Photo by author)

very healthy instincts of the parties concerned, and even more impressed
by the lesson it taught me about the common grammar of ancient Mediterranean hair upon which the compromise rested. Without ever having
read those lines of Aeschylus that tell of "the melting shafts of the eyes'
glances, the heart-biting blossom of love" (*Agamemnon* 742–43) or Euripides' "Eros, Eros that drips desire from the eyes, awakening sweet rapture
in the soul of those whom he would defeat" (*Hippolytus* 525–27; cf. Achilles
Tatius 1.4.4), the Modesty Brigade of B'nai-Brak circa 1990 knew very well
that to dim the (albeit nonexistent) eyes of the female heads in that store-
front would afford some measure of compensation for the erotic allure of
all that feminine hair.

The cultural and historical chasm between the wigged and covered heads of the twentieth-century females of Jewish B'nai-Brak and the masculine manes of the fifth-century B.C.E. Spartan soldiers who died fighting valiantly at Thermopylae may well seem unbridgeable until we recall the following curious anecdote from the Greek historian Herodotus.

It was 480 B.C.E. in the month of August when Leonidas, the Spartan king, brought his small contingent of three hundred Spartan warriors to meet the invading Persian army at the pass of Thermopylae. A mounted spy sent ahead by the Persian king Xerxes observed the outer guard of Spartans, "some of them engaged in gymnastic exercises, others combing their hair" (Hdt. 7.208). The amazed scout returned to report to his great king all he had seen, but Xerxes, as Herodotus tells it, "had no means of interpreting the truth (*sumbalesthai*), namely, that the Spartans were preparing to kill or be killed according to their power. To Xerxes, what they did seemed laughable." Damaratus, the great king's perspicacious advisor, offered this interpretation: "These men have come to fight with us for the pass and it is for this that they are now making ready. It is their custom (*nomos*) whenever they are about to risk their lives, to groom their heads" (Hdt. 7.209). Xerxes ignored his advisor's interpretation, and waited in vain for the Spartans to flee.

Only after the carefully combed Spartans had died to the last man at Thermopylae, I would imagine, did Xerxes come to understand that for Spartan warriors to groom their hair before battle was no laughing matter, and far more than a matter of wanting to die, as one modern Greek historian trivializes, "with their heads tidy" (Burn 1966:178). The ancient biographer Plutarch was closer to the truth when he remarked of the Spartans:

> In time of war, too, they relaxed the severity of the young men's discipline, and permitted them to beautify their hair and ornament their arms and clothing, rejoicing to see them, like horses, prance and neigh for the contest. Therefore they wore their hair long as soon as they ceased to be youths, and particularly in times of danger they took pains to have it glossy and well-combed, remembering a certain saying of Lycurgus, that a fine head of hair made the handsome more comely still, and the ugly more terrible. (Plut. *Vitae Lycurgus* 22.1; Perrin 1914:275)[2]

As Xerxes learned the hard way, hair is serious business.

THE LANGUAGE OF HAIR

Perhaps the most arresting, dramatic, and universal bearer of our nonverbal messages, hair—by its presence and absence—is, at the same time, so commonplace that we tend to take for granted its interwoven significances. The appearance of our hair transmits many complex and intertwined messages about ourselves to the world. In turn, these messages rebound upon ourselves, facilitating our definition of self in relation to society.[3]

In the polyglot grammar of the modern "open market," meaning often gets blurred. The cultural and political significances of hair are refracted by the dizzyingly ephemeral and often internally inconsistent codes of fashion, itself a kind of secular religion of innovation. Significance is more accessible in traditional societies, by which I mean societies that insist self-consciously on the preservation intact of systems of meaning assumed to be "original," often with creation myth or revealed text as a point of reference. Thus ancient and/or traditional societies offer an accessible, consistent, coherent, and relatively closed set of practices which reveal not merely the significances of hair, but the cultural grammar which produces meaning through hair.

"Meaning" or "significance," as I use the terms here, is not to be confused with "cause" or "reason." The reason which a society or individual ascribes to a particular hair custom (if a reason is ever sought)—whether historical etiology or self-conscious rationalization—is not necessarily identical with the significance of that custom as part of a coherent and internally valid, ahistorical system of generating meaning (Leach 1958). Or, to put it another way, significance (what the practice means), forms and patterns of action (what we do), and the personality of individual actors (who we are / how we feel) all mesh to weave—in the "ideal" traditional society—a seamless cultural fabric. Individuals within such societies may or may not be happily oblivious to the role of hair customs or fashions in generating cultural meaning; they may practice such customs for purely personal, psychological satisfaction.[4] Nonetheless, individual actors through their individual acts participate in a larger grammar, a system of collective signification, which, *inter alia,* is used to make symbolic statements regarding women's place in the larger social order and cultural scheme. In practice, whenever stories are told and acts are performed, members of a group manipulate and transform hair as if it were a word in a sentence, instinctually conforming to a dynamic but firm set of rules, a grammar that paradoxically enables transformation even as it suppresses true change.

Herodotus's Spartans at Thermopylae, who have come to symbolize the Western martial ideal of manhood, were no different from generic modern males, for whom, as the mother or sister of any adolescent male can attest, hair is of obsessive concern. Historically, however, men probably have attended even more to women's hair than to their own. Again, we may invoke the Spartans by way of example. Writing of Spartan marriage customs, Plutarch tells us that after the bride had been carried off by her future husband, "the so-called bride's-maid took her [the bride] in charge, sheared her hair off close to the skin, dressed her in a man's cloak and sandals, and laid her down on a pallet, alone, without light" (*Vitae Lycurgus* 15.3). As

Jean-Pierre Vernant reminds us, beyond rites of inversion, the bride's shorn hair is the structural opposite of the flowing locks of the Spartan warrior. As the long hair of the young hoplite warrior preserves the primordial fury that will terrorize the enemy, so the shaven head of the bride extirpates every trace of the martial, masculine, and wild from her new matrimonial state (Vernant 1991:120).

DAPHNE'S STORY

A familiar Ovidian scene from Book One of the *Metamorphoses* (452–567) offers a Roman version of the gendered grammar of hair. This very first mythological metamorphosis of Ovid's poem on changing forms tells of the transformation of Daphne from woman to laurel tree. In Ovid's version, the story is explicitly an etiological tale of Apollo's association with the laurel wreath, the sign of Roman victory. Implicitly it is a foundation myth for Roman courtship and marriage, a story of Apollo's first love (*primus amor*, 452) from *illo tempore*—the time which Eliade has described as that creative era of beginnings[5]—when the god had already triumphed over the monster Python, but not yet over any woman. "There was no laurel yet and Apollo would garland his long and lovely hair from any tree" (450–51); for Daphne, Apollo's first love, had not yet been transformed into the god's own laurel.

Apollo, god of the unshorn hair, destined to be crowned in laurel leaves, pursues Daphne, the nymph of lawless locks (*sine lege capillos*, 477)—whose hair, disarrayed in flight (*inornatos capillos*, 497), places her metaphorically in the company of bird and beast (505–7), even as it incites the god to imagine her combed in his honor (*quid, si comantur?* 497).

> He sees the loose disorder of her hair
> And thinks what if it were neat and elegant!
> He sees her eyes shining like stars, her lips—
> But looking's not enough!—her fingers, hands,
> Her wrists, her half-bare arms—how exquisite!
> And sure her hidden charms are best! But she
> Flies swifter than the lightfoot wind nor stops
> To hear him calling: "Stay, sweet nymph! Oh stay!
> I am no foe to fear. Lambs flee from wolves
> And hinds from lions, and the fluttering doves
> From eagles; every creature flees its foes.
> But love spurs my pursuit."
>
> (*Met.* 1.497–507; Melville 1986:16)

In contrast to the overeager Apollo, Daphne is reluctant to abandon her unmarried state and become a wife:

Many would woo her; she, rejecting all,
Manless, aloof, ranged through the untrodden woods
Nor cared what love, what marriage rites might mean.
Often her father said, "My dearest daughter,
It is my due to have a son-in-law."
Often her father said, "It is my due,
Child of my heart, to be given grandchildren."
She hated like a crime the bond of wedlock,
And, bashful blushes tingeing her fair cheeks,
With coaxing arms embraced him and replied:
"My dear, dear father grant I may enjoy
Virginity for ever; this Diana
Was granted by her father."
                    (*Met.* 1.478–87; Melville 1986:15)

In the chase the virgin's hair streams free (*et levis inpulsos retro dabat aura capillos,* 529), as the god in hot pursuit breathes upon her streaming hair (*imminet et crinem sparsum cervicibus adflat,* 542). After capture, her hair becomes the leaves (*in frondem crines,* 550) that are the sign of male victory (560–65). The god's hair will never be shorn (*utque meum intonsis caput est iuvenale capillis,* 564), but Daphne's leaves will be cut again and again, conveniently evergreen, a source of perpetual leafy honors (*perpetuos frondis honores,* 565; *Tristia* 3.1.45) for masculine victories. Mute in the prison of the new roots of her ever-fertile, vegetable reality, Daphne's last word is an enigmatic rustle of the leafy locks on her head (*adnuit utque caput visa est agitasse cacumen,* 567):

And still Apollo loved her; on the trunk
He placed his hand and felt beneath the bark
Her heart still beating, held in his embrace
Her branches, pressed his kisses on the wood;
Yet from his kisses still the wood recoiled.
"My bride," he said, "since you can never be,
At least, sweet laurel, you shall be my tree.
My lyre, my locks, my quiver you shall wreathe;
You shall attend the conquering lords of Rome
When joy shouts triumph and the Capitol
Welcomes the long procession; you shall stand
Beside Augustus' gates, sure sentinel
On either side, guarding the oak between.
My brow is ever young, my locks unshorn;
So keep your leaves' proud glory ever green."
Thus spoke the god; the laurel in assent
Inclined her new-made branches and bent down,
Or seemed to bend, her head, her leafy crown.
                    (*Met.* 1.553–67; Melville 1986:17–18)

From Apollo's point of view, this is the story of the god's abortive trans-formation from adolescent ephebe into (would-be) husband. For this nar-rative is more than a typical Ovidian seduction/rape scene. (The language of *conubia* is conspicuous by its presence here and its absence from other Ovidian narratives of Apollo's love affairs.)[6] Ovid's Apollo has marriage on his mind: "Apollo loves Daphne on sight and desires marriage" (*cupit co-nubia*, 490). After Daphne's transformation, the god laments the loss of Daphne as his "wife" (*coniunx*, 557), settling for what might seem second best and taking possession of Daphne as his tree. By conflating the etiology of the laurel wreath as the sign of Roman triumph with Apollo's conquest of a prospective wife, Ovid equates masculine political and military triumph with the triumph over and transformation of a reluctant woman in mar-riage.

In fact, nowhere in myth does the god Apollo successfully negotiate and complete the passage from adolescent male to mature man—nor should he. Apollo's role in Greek myth and cult is to be forever unmarried, to remain the eternal ephebe, a mythologem (to borrow and adapt Kerenyi's [1969] term) of that moment in time whose all-too-brief passage is marked for mortal males by the shearing of hair. Apollo is forever the young man poised on the brink of maturity, a time that the Greeks saw as the apex of masculine perfection. Unlike the hair of mortal men, Apollo's hair will never be cut.[7] Nor will he ever marry. At the conclusion of the story the god's hair is crowned and exalted in laurel, but he has no wife and will have no children from Daphne (from the archaic point of view children are the whole point of marriage—*liberorum procreandorum causa;* recall the plaints of Daphne's father, Peneus, *Met.* 1.478–87, quoted above). As an immortal, the god is not troubled by the mortal project of continuity through progeny, the acquisition of "the child who resembles the father." In the ideal world of myth, the god's possession of the woman can be absolute, uncompromising: Daphne is his, all hair and no head, without eyes, her voice reduced to the rustle of leaves, her very head (*caput*) trans-formed to a treetop (*cacumen*, 567). Increased by his triumph, yet undi-minished by the changes wrought by time—the passage from unmarried ephebe to married man with its implications of mortality—the victorious Apollo can take complete possession of the fertile woman (who only ap-pears to escape), while remaining himself untransformed and unreduced in a patriarchal dream of marriage: Apollo, "forever beautiful and forever young" (Callimachus *Apollo* 36).

Daphne, on the other hand, whose free-flowing hair had earlier marked her free and unmarried status (477),[8] has undergone a complete and ab-solute transformation from virgin to wife, again without the compromises necessitated by physical reality and the need for living progeny. Despite her timely transformation, Daphne does not "get away" from Apollo. On the contrary, her "marriage" to Apollo is more complete and absolute than had she become his bride in actual fact. Her hair has been transposed to his head.

There are many morals to this story of Daphne's metamorphosis; most apt for our purpose here is this: For a man to marry a woman is for him to transform her, not for him to transform himself. Hair is the sign of this feminine transformation in marriage. In historic traditional marriage women's hair changes, men's hair does not. To marry a woman is thus both literally and symbolically to transform her hair.

WHY HAIR?

As a signifier, hair operates both metonymically and metaphorically. In its metonymic mode hair stands for the "whole person." As such, hair is useful for rituals implying movement and exchange, passage and negotiation, changes in status. Each such event occurs in time and tells a diachronic story with a beginning, middle, and end. In its metaphoric mode, hair signifies nature in an ahistorical synchronic dialectic with culture. Both the metonymic and the metaphoric functions of hair are simultaneously operative in hair codes. Hair serves as both metonym and metaphor particularly in the case of adolescent rites of passage. These transformations, which are enacted as ritual deaths by the metonymic cutting of hair, enable the adolescent's rebirth into a higher cultural order: for the adolescent male, the transformation from boy to male warrior and citizen; for the female at menarche, transformation from girl to mother. The one-time act of hair cutting that marks the death of the old social self is followed by a permanent change in hairstyle or hair treatment that metaphorically signifies the new cultural status quo. In order to decode the gendered cultural grammar of hair, one first must understand hair in myth and custom as a signifier which operates along both metonymic and metaphoric axes.

METONYMIC HAIR

By metonymic hair, I mean hair standing in a metonymic/synecdochic relation (*pars pro toto*) to our physical selves.[9] *Capillus,* the Latin word for hair, is itself a diminutive meaning "little head"; the etymology demonstrates hair's function as a metonym for the entire person. As Petronius's drunken Eumolpus punningly puts it, when your hair goes, "you've already lost part of your life/head" (*capitis perisse partem; Satyricon* 109). Particularly important for ritual is the fact that hair is the only prominent feature of the body (fingernails and toenails are too small and transparent to be of comparable visual significance) which is at the same time capable of painless amputation, infinite manipulation, and endless regeneration, what anthropologists would call "a wasting asset" (Firth 1973:263). That is to say, if ritual is a game, then hair is the stuff *par excellence* of game-playing, allowing us always "to have our cake and eat it, too" as we modify, elaborate, and backtrack *ad infinitum*. Because hair can serve as an overdetermined and ambiguous symbol, it can create tragic significance, as it does in what is perhaps the most famous and complex hair scene in Western literature, the prologue to Aeschylus's *Libation Bearers*. In this scene a son's act of maturation simultaneously entails his total identification with his dead father. Orestes, now matured, returns home to cut two locks of hair at the tomb of his father, Agamemnon: the first, the nurturant (*threptērion*) lock to the river Inachus; the second, the lock of mourning (*penthētērion*) for the slain Agamemnon (*Libation Bearers* 6–7). On another level, as a purely ritual act, the operation is, of course, painless and the lost hair will regenerate. This physical fact enables the mourner to act out metonymically the ambivalent human response to death, both to die with the dead and to separate from the dead. It also demonstrates the ultimate and essential pragmatism of ritual, perhaps its most humanly endearing quality.

Furthermore, the absence of hair is most prominent in babies and old men, those chronologically closest to the margins of life. Ritual baldness itself mimics the liminal states of infancy or advanced age, thus anticipating transitions to new and different modes of existence.[10]

Finally, even if we "die" metonymically when we cut our hair, none of us wants to die for a fact. Here, too, hair by its very nature provides a kind of reassurance that the passage from living to nonliving may be simply yet another transition from one mode of existence to another, however unknown and forbidding. For hair may instantiate a *tertium quid* between the stark poles of life and death. Because of its peculiar physical properties, hair is perceived to be simultaneously both alive and dead. Like the dead, hair feels no pain; yet at the same time hair is emphatically, dramatically alive, as alone among the parts of the human body it continues to grow noticeably throughout maturity. In death, too, hair exhibits similarly paradoxical qualities. Unlike the rest of our bodies, hair does not rapidly decompose, but seems to survive. The Victorians kept their dead alive with hair broaches, and conversely, the ever-lengthening hair of corpses moldering in the grave is the stock-in-trade of popular superstition. The latter has a classical precedent in the myth of Attis, whose hair, thanks to Zeus, continued to grow after his death.[11] Jews, too, acknowledge this ambivalent, intermediate quality of hair by classing hair (together with fingernails, toenails, and teeth) as a body part which, when detached from the polluted dead body, somehow escapes from the ritually impure state of the corpse into the ritually pure state of the living (Talmud *Niddah* 55A; cf. *Nazir* 51A). Thus hair itself, by virtue of its physical properties, can suggest a state of life in death or death in life. Hair can imply an intermediate stage between the two poles, a state which is neither dead nor alive, but at the same time similar to and different from both: similar enough to reassure, different enough to be credible.

It is this confluence of attributes—hair's metonymic relation to the whole person, its painless malleability, baldness as evocative of liminality, and hair's intermediary quality of being at the same time neither fully dead nor fully alive—that explains the widespread use of hair in many rites. These include not only rites of passage, which enact symbolic death while pointing to subsequent rebirth (enabling, in Greek literature especially, the very common convergence of motifs of marriage/sacrifice/death),[12] but also mourning rites, where we both unite with and separate from the dead by dying while not really dying; purification rites, involving symbolic rebirth; and votive offerings, which play at death while allowing real life to continue, as in an act of *do ut des* we offer ourselves (or a part of ourselves, the best part, the first fruits) in return for whatever it is that we want from God or the gods.[13] And, since the liminality of the passage from adolescence to adulthood is particularly fraught with danger, hair may be doubly determined especially for the adolescent ephebe or bride as a means both of initiating the passage and of redemption from its dangers.[14]

METAPHORIC HAIR

Thus hair, as we have seen, may function as a metonymic sign for the whole body, speaking a language of death while hinting at possible renewal and enabling change or exchange or process. Yet, as in Ovid's story of Daphne, hair is also used to speak exclusively about life and the living, seen synchronically as a state of being. Here, hair stands primarily in a metaphoric relation to those various qualities that are associated with the head and the sexual organs, often interchangeably. This association is clearly connected to the ancient privileging of the head (where human hair growth is, in fact, most visible) as a site of generation.[15]

That the hair of both men and women signifies the natural part of human existence was axiomatic in Mediterranean antiquity. The Roman philosopher Seneca (1st century C.E.), for example, saw men's hair streaming down—shaken out "just as noble animals shake out a mane" and, significantly, untouched by the hand of a woman—as the mark of a bygone era before culture, when men were closer to animals (Sen. *Quaestiones Naturales* 1.17.1).

Read metaphorically, hair can be used to enunciate a dialectic between nature and the norms and restraints of culture.[16] Thus Genesis sets the struggle for Isaac's patrimony between the naturally hairy Esau (Gen. 25:25) and the smooth-skinned Jacob (Gen. 27:11), who cunningly makes himself hairy when necessary by assuming the hide of an animal (Gen. 27:16). The Biblical narrative uses hair to indicate a desirable middle point between no hair and too much hair, between no nature and too much nature. It is this "hair" equilibrium, worked out in the narrative, which overrides moralist apologetics and ensures that Jacob will rightfully tame and rule other men as he does the animals in his flock (Gen. 27:29, cf. 30:25–43). It is the destiny of Esau, marked by his abundant hair as more "natural" than his relatively hairless brother, to be ruled, however fitfully (Gen. 27:40), in accordance with the divine plan that ordains that all nature be ruled by human beings (Gen. 1:28).

Hair serves as an especially congenial locus for the signification of this dialectic between nature and culture, again because of its peculiar physical properties. Hair is, first and foremost, eminently natural: it grows of itself and is part of our physical selves. Yet hair can exist independently of the body as a cultural product: wigs, toupees, fur coats, lionskins. Furthermore, unlike other parts of the body, hair is often more serviceable when pruned, trimmed, or tied up in some way so as (at a minimum) to allow for comfortable vision. This is to say that even in its most natural state, hair seems especially to demand the attentions of culture. In addition, unlike other parts of the body—which when treated by culture are generally merely covered or concealed—hairstyles and customs usually require that we be conscious simultaneously of both the hair itself (nature) and the style of its treatment (culture). In other words, hair can be seen equally as body (nature) and as costume or cosmetic (culture). According to Apuleius, a second-century C.E. Latin author whose interest in hair has been described as "obsessive,"

> hair is the most important visible part of the body and as such first attracts our attention. It naturally covers the head with the bright beauty that clothes give the other limbs. . . . To conclude, such is the dignity of hair that no woman, although dressed in gold, fine fabrics, jewels, all other cosmetical apparatus, could be described, unless she had arranged her hair, as dressed at all. (Apuleius *Metamorphoses* 2.8–9, passim)[17]

Thus hair, seen as conjoining nature and culture, is an apt, almost inevitable, choice as a *locus* for the statement of social attitudes regarding the proper or desired relationship between nature and culture.

All cultures work out an equilibrium point between too much hair and too little hair as an expression of a viable compromise between nature and culture. Men can be too hairy or too smooth-skinned, and the balance shifts over time according to the particular cultural desideratum. In the beginning, still in the state of nature, there was always, at least in human imagination, lots of hair. Long unbound hair serves as a sign of a state of nature prior to the intrusion of culture, whether in the context of first-century Romans looking back on their shaggy (*incompti*), unbarbered (*intonsi*) ancestors[18] or of fifth-century B.C.E. Athenians recounting the heroic exploits of Homer's long-haired Achaeans at Troy, or singing of the untamed young virgins of Sparta who "like fillies . . . bound with quick steps all along the river Eurotas, raising up the dust; and their hair is tossed like those of the bacchants who brandish the thyrsus and frolic about" (Aristophanes *Lysistrata* 1308–13). When culture enters, hair is transformed.

It is when hair is a metaphor for nature that its grammar is gendered. Whatever the balance point of a viable cultural equilibrium between too much and too little hair, the hair scale is calibrated very differently for men than it is for women. Seneca's primordial men preen their hair like Herodotus's Spartans at Thermopylae, the former in a dream of uncorrupted pristine nature, the latter doomed to live out forever the moment of youthful masculine perfection frozen in heroic death. The only Biblical commands regarding men's hair are prohibitions against cutting it (Lev. 19:27, Deut. 14:1, cf. Lev. 21:5).

Men are reluctant to tame their own hair because they are reluctant to tame their own natures, and the primary significance of hair is the natural, specifically the virile and generative, part of man. Hair in the Midrash is like a tree or a forest; so too in classical thought from Homer on, where hair and foliage share the same name: *komē* in Greek, *coma* in Latin.[19] Trees, forests, and foliage are remarkable primarily for their markedly visible growth. Thus to prune one's hair is to impose the limits of culture on one's nature. In the case of men's hair, the generative vitality which is its root meaning expands to include such social desiderata as heroic strength and political power. Homeric representations of male divinities with potent flowing locks—Zeus of thundering, ambrosial locks (Hom. *Il.* 1.527–30; cf. *Hymn. Hom.* 1.13–15, Ovid *Metamorphoses* 1.177–80); the dark-haired *kuanokhaitēs* Poseidon (Hom. *Il.* 13.563, 14.390, 15.174, 201, 20.144, *Od.* 3.6, 9.528, 536, Hesiod *Theogony* 278, *Hymn. Hom.* 22.6, Lucian *De sacrificiis* 11.7); Hades (*Hymn. Hom.* 2.347, with Richardson 1974: 266 ad loc.; cf. Euripides *Alcestis* 439: *melagkhaitēs* "black-haired"); and Dionysus, whose glossy hair evokes the gleaming manes of horses[20]—are icons to an archaic Greek dream of expanded, unfettered virility. The streaming locks of Homer's "long-haired" (*karē komoōntes*)[21] Achaeans encode an identification of masculine hair with martial strength rooted in natural virility, specifically the vitality of youth.

"They represent him forever a youth," remarks the satirist Lucian of Apollo (*De sacrificiis* 11). On their voyage of adventure, the young Argonauts invoke the god: "Youth still beardless, still rejoicing in your locks. Be gracious. Lord, may your hair forever be uncut, forever be unharmed. For so it is right" (Apollonius Rhodius *Argonautica* 2.708–9; cf. 676–77). For it is Apollo, *akersekomēs,* of the unshorn hair, whose perennially flowing locks serve as the quintessential Greek icon of the moment of youthful masculine perfection and potency undiminished by time.[22]

Bound by their physiology to the mortal cycle of reproduction, women and their hair undergo transformations over time which are relatively easily accepted and seen as inevitable, because necessary for human survival and continuity. Men can die, frozen at their prime, but women must survive, grow old, and wither to ensure the birth of the next generation of men. At Delos, before marriage both bride and groom dedicated hair to the Hyperborean maidens—hers wound about a spindle, his around a green stick (Herodotus 4.34). Physiologically more distant from the process of reproduction, men can and do play with the fantasy of immortal vitality. Thus in myth and reality alike, men's hair can be allowed unproblematically to flow uncut and uncovered.

WOMEN WHO THREATEN MEN'S HAIR

The oldest Near Eastern myth tells of a man whose state of pristine nature is marked by hair which is shaggy and "luxuriant as a woman's." This is Enkidu, the Mesopotamian epic hero whose encounter with a courtesan leaves him depleted and alienated from nature; she remains unchanged (*Gilgamesh*, Tab. I 86–88; Kovacs 1985:6). When intimations of mortality and diminution intrude on visions of male agelessness, myths tell of men's hair being threatened with cutting. The thread of a man's life is both spun and snipped by the feminine Fates. Women use their sexual allure to seduce men into the process of reproduction. And once enmeshed within the human cycle of begetting and becoming, men must abandon eternity. Men's sexual need for women—which entails relinquishing the dream of individual immortality in exchange for genetic perpetuity—is projected onto the feminine figure of the seductress; woman is transformed from object to subject. Masculine virility encoded in hair extraordinary for its length or its color may, in legend and myth, be threatened directly by the sexuality of the female. Seductresses—all aggressive, sly, and treacherous—cut men's hair.

Delilah enervates Samson, with the hero's hair in this story serving as the sign of both his martial strength and his sexual vulnerability.[23] Samson's Greek counterpart, the often unmanned Heracles, is swallowed by a sea monster where "on a flameless hearth [he] sheds the hair of his head to the ground." His hair loss is the consequence of his engulfment "in the steam of a cauldron" (the creature's stomach). This myth thinly disguises the fear of entrapment by a female in a story of the hero's fight to escape from the belly of a sea monster.[24]

Crazed with love for the Cretan Minos, Scylla betrays her own father, Nisus, when she robs him of the purple lock that guarantees his royal power (Apollodorus *Bibliotheca* 3.15.8, Ovid *Metamorphoses* 8.1–151, Aeschylus *Libation Bearers* 612–22, Hyginus *Fabulae* 198, 242, Pausanias 1.19.4, 2.34.7,

Propertius 3.19.21–28, Vergil *Georgics* 1.404–9 [cf. 2.60], *Ciris*). In what amounts to a doublet of this story, Comaetho is driven by desire for Amphitryon, her lover and her father's enemy. To help her lover, Comaetho despoils her father of his political power by plucking a golden lock from his head.

> Now, so long as Pterelaus lived, he [Amphitryon] could not take Taphos; but when Comaetho, daughter of Pterelaus, falling in love with Amphitryon, pulled out the golden hair from her father's head, Pterelaus died, and Amphitryon subjugated all the islands. He slew Comaetho, and sailed with the booty to Thebes. (Apollodorus *Bibliotheca* 2.4.7; Frazer 1921, vol. 1, 173)

In all of these stories, men who lose their hair because of the sexuality of a woman gain nothing thereby and lose everything. Entrapped by female sexuality, men lose their masculine ability to fight and win, to maintain and wield political power. The converse was the case, as we have seen, in Apollo's "courtship" of Daphne, a masculine success story culminating in an ideal "marriage" where the male keeps his own hair, and indeed increases his head with the female's "foliage." From the male point of view, Apollo wins all. Never doomed to forgo his timeless moment of ephebic triumph for the cycle of reproduction, Apollo assumes Daphne's hair—her evergreen fertility—and transforms it into the sign of men's political and military victories.

WOMEN'S HAIR: IN THE BEGINNING

Like men, women, too, initially wear their hair fair and flowing as a mark of fertility and sexuality. The hair of goddesses and mortal women in the heroic age of Greek epic is singled out as the object of an exceptionally rich vocabulary of epithets. Goddesses such as Rhea (Hesiod *Theogony* 625, 634, *Hymn. Hom.* 2.60, 75, 442), Demeter (*Hymn. Hom.* 2.1, 297, 315 with Richardson 1974:137 ad 1, *Hymn. Hom.* 13.1, Hesiod frag. 280.20 [Merkelbach and West 1967]), Hera (Hom. *Il.* 10.5), and Athena (Hom. *Il.* 6.92, 273, 303) are rich-haired or fair-haired: *ēukomos, eukomos*. The same epithet is also frequently found applied to minor goddesses and heroines conspicuous for their maternity, such as Leto, mother of Apollo (Hom. *Il.* 1.36, 19.413, *Od.* 11.318, *Hymn. Hom.* 3.178, 27.21); Thetis, mother of Achilles (Hom. *Il.* 4.512, 16.860); Danae, mother of Perseus (Hesiod *Scutum* 216); and Niobe, the *mater dolorosa* of Greek mythology (Hom. *Il.* 24.601). It is also used by Hesiod (eighth/seventh century B.C.E.) both for the sea goddess Tethys (Hes. frag. 343.4 [Merkelbach and West 1967]), perhaps alluding to the tradition that she was the mother of the gods (Hom. *Il.* 14.200–207), and for the Oceanid Doris, mother of fifty daughters (Hes. *Theogony* 241). The fair hair of generic maidens (Hes. frag. 10[a] 32 [Merkelbach and West 1967]), nymphs (*Hymn. Hom.* 26.3), and mothers (Hom. *Il.* 24.466) is also described with the epithet *eukomos*.

The epithet, however, is not limited to those epic women conspicuous for maternity and fertility. The word *eukomos* is, in fact, most frequently used of Helen, who in epic instantiates feminine sexuality;[25] it is also found with such nonmaternal, explicitly sexual and/or threatening female figures as Calypso (Hom. *Od.* 8.452, 12.389), the Harpies (Hes. *Theogony* 267), and most tellingly Medusa (Hes. frag. 37.21 [Merkelbach and West 1967]). In virtually every instance the epithet for fair or rich hair exists exclusively within a context circumscribed by maternity or sexuality; it appears in formulaic expressions such as "whom the fair/rich-haired nymphs nurtured" (*Hymn. Hom.* 26.3), "whom fair/rich-haired Leto bore" (Hom. *Il.* 1.36), or "[Paris] husband of fair/rich-haired Helen" (Hom. *Il.* 7.355 = 8.82).[26]

In all cases, women's hair in Greek epic retains its primary association with generative vitality, though in contrast to masculine hair epithets, predictably, the association does not extend into the masculine realms of politics and war. The epic praise of feminine hair suggests that for women, too, there was a time located by memory or imagination in the heroic past (the mythic analogue of youth, when virgins' hair is allowed to flow free) when feminine generative vitality was seen as a desirable ideal.

For the women of epic, rich, fair hair is a positive attribute. The same quality of luxuriant hair, however, may assume a negative valence in contexts where female fertility and/or sexuality are viewed with suspicion and disparagement. When uncontrolled by men, female sexuality is seen as a potential threat. Women who pose this threat to men are often pictured with an abundance of untamed hair. Thus Medusa, the erstwhile maid of lovely locks, is transformed into a snakey-haired monster, to be decapitated by the hero Perseus in an act that Philip Slater has described as "maternal desexualization."[27] A lock of her disembodied hair will put an enemy to flight (Apollodorus *Bibliotheca* 2.7.3; Pausanias 8.47.5). Or, in another example, the Maenads who head for the wilds with streaming hair are, like their leader Dionysus of the flowing locks, an expression—often threatening to male authority—of revolt against the strictures of culture through reversion to a state of rampant, unfettered nature.[28] When female sexuality is perceived as threatening to the male, fair female hair turns ugly, transformed from rich and abundant to rampant and wild. In the ideal world of myth the final solution is to remove woman's hair and head altogether.

MEDUSA'S HAIR AND THE IDEAL OF PATRIARCHAL MARRIAGE

In a golden age women may wear their fair hair freely as a mark of fertility and sexuality, but, as Vernant has elegantly argued for the case of the Greeks, patriarchal marriage requires only female fertility, not sexuality, in the service of its descent lines. In fact, active female sexuality can only be seen as a threat to the purity of patrimony, since it implies the potential of corruption through adultery.[29] Accordingly, female sexuality within marriage is often seen (to a greater or lesser degree) as antithetical to fertility. Thus rampant hair as a sign of unfettered sexuality is, in the Talmud, a curse laid on womankind. As a result of the transgression of Eve, "a woman grows her hair like Lilith, urinates like a domestic animal [in a crouching position], and becomes a pillow for her husband [sex object]." Lilith herself is identified as a sexually voracious she-devil, mother of demons, and, significantly, as the thief of legitimate children.[30]

Patriarchy attempts to overcome the threat of female sexuality by splitting off women's sexuality from fertility within marriage. In myth, female sexuality can be eliminated and fertility can function on its own within an "ideal" patriarchal marriage, represented by a scenario in which a woman's threatening hair and head are removed altogether. This ideal marriage is nicely realized in Hesiod's version of the Medusa myth:

> And again, Ceto bare to Phorcys the fair-cheeked Graiae, sisters grey from birth: and both deathless gods and men who walk on earth call them Graiae, Pemphredo well-clad, and saffron-robed Enyo, and the Gorgons who dwell beyond glorious Ocean in the frontier land towards Night where are the clear-voiced Hesperides, Sthenno, and Euryale, and Medusa who suffered a woeful fate: she was mortal, but the [other] two were undying and grew not old. With her lay the Dark-haired One in a soft meadow amid spring flowers. And when Perseus cut off her head, there sprang forth great Chrysaor and the horse Pegasus who is so called because he was born near the springs [*pegae*] of Ocean; and that other, because he held a golden blade [*aor*] in his hands. (Hes. *Theogony* 270–83; Evelyn-White 1914:99–101)[31]

In all versions of the myth Medusa loses not only her fair hair but ultimately her entire head. In a marvelous feat of mythic displacement, she is left with a gaping hole where her head and hair had once been. This headless hole becomes the fertile chasm from which progeny spring. In this sense, Medusa's fate is not much different from that of Daphne transformed to the evergreen laurel tree. Voiceless but fertile, the headless Medusa encodes the patriarchal ideal of maternity without sexuality. In Hesiod's *Theogony*—our earliest source for this myth—the story of the mortal maiden whose bad luck it was to attract the attention of the darkmaned Poseidon stops here.[32]

Like Daphne, the sexual Medusa herself disappears after conquest. No seductive hair, no singing voice, no human head.[33] Only Medusa's conspicuous fertility remains after her rape by the Dark-haired One (*kuanokhaitēs*, *Th.* 288) on a soft meadow of spring flowers. Poseidon, the dark-haired god (otherwise unnamed in the text), leaves the encounter untransformed;

Medusa, as a result of the rape, ultimately loses hair and head; children are born. The ideal story—as Hesiod tells it.

But splitting off the female head brings with it the potential danger of negative female sexuality unmoored from its compensatory positive aspect of fertility. The head may roam disembodied as the distillation of the female threat. This patriarchal nightmare is expressed in other, more popular versions of the Medusa story, such as Ovid's, which focus on the transformation of Medusa's hair to threatening snakes; this aspect of the myth uses hair to encode both the lure and the threat of female sexuality to patriarchy. Drawing on a tradition which casts Medusa as a rival of Athena (although she is, in fact, a doublet of Athena),[34] Ovid's Medusa owes her troubles to the beautiful hair that attracted the god Poseidon and led him to rape her in Athena's temple:

> Her beauty was far-famed, the jealous hope
> Of many a suitor, and of all her charms
> Her hair was loveliest; so I was told
> By one who claimed to have seen her. She, it's said,
> Was violated in Minerva's shrine
> By Ocean's lord. Jove's daughter turned away
> And covered with her shield her virgin eyes,
> And then for fitting punishment transformed
> The Gorgon's lovely hair to loathsome snakes.
>   (Ovid *Met.* 4.794–801; Melville 1986:98)

Transformed from golden to serpentine, Medusa's head, once unmoored, becomes a reincarnated, infinitely more potent version of the pure female threat. Like the roaming demonic Lilith or the Furies who rise from the corpse of the slain Clytemnestra, the disembodied head of Medusa exacts endless vengeance of men.[35]

In the versions of both Hesiod and Ovid, Poseidon rapes Medusa and disappears, leaving the ephebic hero Perseus to play midwife by severing Medusa's head. Even in myth, the splitting off of female sexuality from female fertility is not so unproblematic as Hesiod's truncated version makes it sound. Perseus, a mortal hero, is no Apollo, although Perseus, too, is an ephebe faced with the task of subduing both the monster and the woman.[36] For Apollo, the two were split: first the Pytho, then Daphne. Perseus must confront both in the single person of the Gorgon Medusa.[37] Like Apollo with his Daphne, Perseus transforms Medusa and enables female fertility. But Perseus's conquest of the female head is less successful than that of his divine counterpart. As Ovid tells it, "in order to terrorize and numb her enemies, Athena still wears the snakes she made upon her breast" (*Met.* 4.802–3). Unlike the transformed, treed, and silenced nodding head of Daphne, the decapitated Medusa continues to threaten men with her gaze and snakey locks, now securely nestled on Athena's breast.

The second-century C.E. Greek traveloguer Pausanias offers a telling footnote to the Medusa story when he reports a tradition from Argos that Perseus, slayer of the Gorgon, named his own daughter Gorgophone, "voice of Gorgo." Gorgophone's grave, he relates, is to be seen beside the monument of the slain Gorgon Medusa (now euhemerized into a warlike African princess) in Argos.[38] Significantly, Pausanias ascribes the etiology of her ominous-sounding name to the fact that Gorgophone was the first woman to marry a second time, "since she took a new husband upon the death of her first husband rather than live as a widow, as wives before her were wont to do." In other words, Pausanias associates her Gorgon name with her sexual independence. Distilled in the disembodied head as the pure threat of feminine sexuality, Medusa is reborn in the flesh as Perseus's own daughter. The patriarchal decapitation of the female engenders its own problematic consequence: kill the sexual wife and she is reborn as the sexual daughter. In the case of Gorgophone the sexual threat of the daughter is conspicuously marked: she, first of all women, independently transfers her sexuality from a first husband to a second. Unlike the perpetually ephebic divine Apollo, the all-too-mortal ephebe Perseus will live on to marry, to grow up and grow old, and to father a daughter who is Medusa *rediviva*.

Medusa's story has a better ending—from the patriarchal point of view—as Hesiod tells it.

WOMEN'S HAIR IN THE REAL WORLD: SOME PATRIARCHAL DILEMMAS, PARADOXES, AND SOLUTIONS

Untrammeled by the constraints of physical or historical reality, myth is free to construct extreme and absolute models as neat and easy resolutions to the paradoxes of culture. In the world of myth, Daphne can be treed for Apollo's triumph and Medusa decapitated and yet still fertile. But ritual and custom, operative in the arena of historical and physical reality, must construct particularistic and imperfect solutions, making do with partial gestures toward ideological absolutes. The styrofoam sunglassed and wigged heads on Rabbi Akiva Street gaze blankly through their plate glass window, icons of both the extent and the limit of men's transformation of the real hair of real women. Unlike their mythological counterparts, the wigs and the women who wear them are anchored within the cycle of historical time and human biology. I conclude this essay with a glance at some actual customs of virgins, brides, and wives in which practice counterpoints myth to enunciate the cultural grammar of hair.

VIRGINS' HAIR

Female sexuality is tolerated, if not encouraged, in traditional patriarchal societies for only that brief and evanescent period immediately prior to marriage. At this time public display of hair serves as a sexual stimulus and thus as an incentive and inducement for men to marry. Marriage enables propagation along properly regulated descent lines. Thus almost universally the hair of young girls is "untamed," left flowing and free like that of Ovid's virginal Daphne—*pace* Paul, Tertullian, and many others, in an ascetic line continuing today in some contemporary Rabbinic responsa that would cover even virgins' hair.[39]

Whatever headcoverings unmarried girls do wear—Homer's virginal Nausicaa leaves her home wearing a *krēdemnon,* literally a headband or binder (Hom. *Od.* 6.100), Ovid's Daphne has a fillet (*Met.* 1.477), the Biblical Rebecca wears a veil (Gen. 24:36–37)—only take on cultural significance at the age when marriage is a possibility, i.e., at the cessation of childhood, the time when girls would normally marry in Jewish and Greco-Roman antiquity.[40] Rebecca veils herself only after identifying the mysterious man on the horizon as Isaac, her betrothed, in a narrative that uses the act of head covering to point to the marriage that is destined to follow. According to the Talmud, "Men sometimes cover, sometimes uncover their heads, but women always cover their heads, and minors never cover their heads" (*Nedarim* 30B). When girls cease being minors, they become brides, and the first culturally invested covering of the hair for girls of marriageable age is what initiates this transformation. The transformation is completed through marriage ceremonies in which the veiled bride is uncovered by her husband; then, once married, her hair is covered for all time against the eyes of all others. This first unveiling for or by a man—the ritual analogue of the surrender of her virginity—completes her transformation into a wife. The covered hair of the wife publicly proclaims her new status.

BRIDES: TO MARRY IS TO COVER/UNCOVER/COVER

Greek, Roman, and Jewish marriage rituals variously manipulate and emphasize the elements of head covering and uncovering to mark the transformation of the female in marriage (see figures 3 and 4). When virgin becomes wife, wedding rituals find precedents for covering and uncovering the bride's hair in mythical stories of a "first marriage." A fragment of Pherecydes, a sixth-century B.C.E. cosmogonist, suggests that the transformation of the universe from chaos occurs with a wedding ceremony at which Zeus (Zas) produces a cloth, decorated with earth and ocean, for a chthonic goddess:

> His halls they make for him, many and vast. And when they had accomplished all these, and the furniture and manservants and maidservants and everything else necessary, when everything was ready, they hold the wedding. And on the third day of the wedding Zas makes a great and fair cloth and on it he decorates Ge and Ogenos and the halls of Ogenos . . . "for wishing [or some

Figure 3. Ancient Greek bride, ca. 320–310 B.C.E. Aphrodite makes an offering of a jewel box to the fully covered bride. Peitho (Persuasion) whispers into the bride's ear and chucks her chin in a gesture of encouragement while a diminutive Eros hovers above. (Skyphoid Pyxis, Moscow, Pushkin Museum 510; *LICM* II.1, 1569)

such word] marriages to be yours, I honour you with this. Hail to you, and be my consort." And this they say was the first Anacalypteria: from this the custom arose both for gods and for men. And she replies, receiving from him the cloth . . . (Diels-Kranz 1951:7 B 2; Kirk and Raven 1963:60 #54)

For Pherecydes, the key to the transformation of chaos to civilization may lie in the covering of the female head.[41] However, the fragment quoted above is adduced as a primordial precedent for the first *anakaluptēria*, a

Figure 4. Modern Jewish bride follows the wedding customs of a *haredi* (ultraorthodox) community in Israel. The seated, fully veiled bride is aided and encouraged by the older women who flank her. (Photo by Uriel Da'el)

ritual act of uncovering, rather than of covering. To cover a woman is only partly to marry her. In order to complete the marriage the veiled woman must then be unveiled by her new husband. Hesiod's earlier, more popular version of the "first marriage" supplies some of the missing gaps in the Greek story of woman's transformation in marriage.

Pandora, the first bride, is decked out by the gods and brought to the unwitting Epimetheus in Zeus's act of vengeance and reprisal for Prometheus's theft of fire for the benefit of mortals. The story is told by Hesiod in both the *Theogony* and *Works and Days*. In both versions the narrative lingers on the "decking out" scene, which becomes a paradigm for the traditional adornment of the bride at human weddings.[42] In the *Theogony* the description of the adornment of the first bride focuses particularly on her headdress:

> Forthwith he made an evil thing for men as the price of fire; for the very famous Limping God formed of earth the likeness of a shy maiden as the son of Cronos willed. And the goddess bright-eyed Athene girded and clothed her with silvery raiment, and down from her head she spread with her hands a broidered veil, a wonder to see; and she, Pallas Athene, put about her head

lovely garlands, flowers of new-grown herbs. Also she put upon her head a crown of gold which the very famous Limping God made himself and worked with his own hands as a favour to Zeus his father. On it was much curious work, wonderful to see; for of the many creatures which the land and sea rear up, he put most upon it, wonderful things, like living beings with voices: and great beauty shone out from it. But when he had made the beautiful evil to be the price for the blessing, he brought her out, delighting in the finery which the bright-eyed daughter of a mighty father had given her, to the place where the other gods and men were. And wonder took hold of the deathless gods and mortal men when they saw that which was sheer guile, not to be withstood by men. (Hes. *Th.* 570–89; Evelyn-White 1914:121–23)

The point of the elaborate covering of this first bride's head is the perilous act of uncovering that will follow. When she is brought to her new home, Epimetheus will uncover her, and she in an act of displacement will uncover the fabulous jar of human misery.

Hesiod's description of the first bride to be brought to a man's house provides a mythic prototype for covering the bride's head. It also points to the perilous act of uncovering, enacted ritually in the *anakaluptēria*, the central act of the Greek wedding ceremony, when the "strictly veiled bride" (*panu akribōs egkekalummenē,* Lucian *Symposium* 8) is publicly uncovered after her journey by cart to the groom's house. The *anakaluptēria* occurs at the moment in the Greek wedding when the bride raises her veil before her bridegroom and the men of his household. This uncovering ceremony in which the bride unveils herself before her new husband in the reassuring presence of a company of men is in fact the act of marriage for the bride. The unveiling symbolizes her willingness and consent; henceforth she is married. The moment is the ritual analogue of the surrender of her virginity. Gifts given to the bride at this point (also called *anakaluptēria*), which are in a special sense her personal property, ritually compensate for the loss of her virginity.[43]

The Greek focus on uncovering confronts the paradox of the veil: the invisible woman may deceive, for her very veil represents the danger of unknowability. The covered woman is "sheer guile and beguilement, not to be withstood by men" (Hes. *Th.* 589), and who because she is veiled may not be what she seems.[44] Only after the bridegroom sees beneath the veil for the first time can he know what it conceals. However it may have been experienced by the bride, the *anakaluptēria* was created by and for men—"in order that she may be seen by the men";[45] the act derives from and responds to male interests (Sissa 1990:95). The ancient Greek bride unveiled ritually and in public in order to indicate consent and to enable public support for the groom as he confronted the paradox of the veiled woman at the marriage ceremony, experienced as the mythical "first time" of a man's real-life marriage story.

Roman marriage ceremonies also seem to privilege head covering. Indeed, the Latin word *nubere* "to marry" literally means "to veil oneself," and according to the *Oxford Latin Dictionary* (s.v. *nubo*) is probably cognate with *nubes* (cloud). For a woman to become married (*nubere*) is for her ritually to cover/cloud her head.

Ancient lexicographers agree in locating the root meaning of the marriage ceremony in the act of covering the bride's head. Varro, the second-century B.C.E. Roman scholar, derives *nuptiae* (wedding) and *nuptus* (wedlock) from *nuptus* (veiling), which he defines as *opertio* (the act of covering) and associates with the word *nubes* (cloud) (Varro *De Lingua Latina* 5.72). The eighth-century C.E. lexicographer Paulus (epitomizing Festus [second century C.E.], who himself epitomized the Augustan scholar Verrius Flaccus's *De significatu verborum*) also derives the word *nuptiae* from a word which means to veil the head: "*obnubit*: he covers the head; whence marriages [*nuptiae*], too, derive their name from the act of covering [*opertio*] the head" (Paulus, s.v. *obnubit*; Lindsay 1913:201). Festus himself suggests one derivation of the word *nuptiae* (marriage ceremony) from the fact that the bride's head is covered (*obnubere*) with a *flammeum*, a flame-colored veil.[46] Prior to assuming the veil, the bride's hair was arranged in six locks (*sex crines*) and bound by woolen fillets (*vittae*), an arrangement that Festus and most others read as a sign of chastity.[47]

For the Romans the act of uncovering focuses particularly on the bride's hair per se, and takes on peculiarly violent and martial symbolism in the marriage custom of parting the veiled and braided bride's hair with a bent spearhook, the *hasta recurva* or *hasta caelibaris* which "combs the hair of the virgin" (Ovid *Fasti* 2.560). Although the etiology of this custom may have puzzled later Romans (as evidenced by the lexicographer Festus's plenitude of alternative explanations), it unambiguously dramatizes marriage as the sexual invasion and parting of the female by the martial Roman phallus.[48]

It is difficult to disentangle the place of hair covering/uncovering in the ancient Jewish wedding ceremony. The reason for this is paradoxical: the act of covering is so central to Jewish marriage that as a living tradition it has grown overdetermined. The wedding canopy (*huppah*), the central symbol of the modern Jewish ritual, is etymologically rooted in "to cover." The canopy itself is both the relic of a special chamber where in Talmudic times the marriage was consummated and a symbol of the transfer of the bride to the "cover" of the groom's house in patrilocal marriage.[49] Similarly, the Hebrew word for bride or daughter-in-law, *kalah*, is itself derived from a Semitic root meaning "to cover." To cover the bride's head and face with a veil is the act of marriage; to cover her beneath her father-in-law's roof is to incorporate her into the patrilocal family.[50] The two acts of covering are homologous.

To cover, for Jews, is symbolically to assert ownership or mastery, to set apart and claim as one's own. Biblical evidence, often metaphoric, seems to indicate that for a woman to go under the "cover" of a man was itself an act of marriage; the Biblical Ruth's effort to put herself under the robe of Boaz is understood as a technical act of espousal (Ruth 3:9 with Talmud *Kidushin* 18B).[51] As for the covering of the head specifically, Epstein argues persuasively that in Biblical times to veil the bride's head held legal significance as an act of marriage. In Talmudic times, after the legal significance of to veil = to marry was superseded, head covering retained its original force as a legal requirement for the married woman, and still was perceived as so central to the act of marriage that, according to the Talmud, to uncover the wife's head is tantamount to an act of divorce terminating a common-law marriage among non-Jews.[52] As in the Bible, the covered bride is understood in Rabbinic sources as a symbol of marriage.[53] Finally, more than one Rabbinic source equates the head covering of the bride to the *huppah* itself (Abudraham 1963:357; cf. Mildola, *Huppat Hatanim*, p. 41).

The Jewish bride in Talmudic times was veiled and elaborately crowned, her hair arranged and covered.[54] Symbolically set apart and consecrated, she may be seen as corresponding to the sacrificial victim, whose status as sanctified and set apart from the flux of the profane is also marked by covering its head. Greeks wreathe and garland the heads of both brides and sacrificial victims; Jews cover the heads of their brides and lay hands on the head of the sacrificial animal.[55]

Finally, the Jewish ritual of *badeken,* in some ways homologous to the Greek *anakaluptēria,* specifically focuses on the public covering/uncovering of the bride's head by the groom. This ceremony, which plays only a minor role in traditional Jewish weddings, today is enacted as a ritual of covering. The groom, escorted by his attendants, is taken to the bride, where he lowers the veil over her face. The *badeken* takes place before the woman is led (in a procession corresponding to the passage of the Greek and Roman bride to her husband's house) to the wedding canopy, a symbol of the groom's marital chamber, where, in an act of incorporation, the bride circles the groom three times.[56]

Popular etiology, insisting on the *badeken* as an act of covering, derives the custom from the precedent of Rebecca, who veiled herself when she first glimpsed her future husband Isaac (Gen. 24:65). This etiology is reinforced by the traditional response of the onlookers to the *badeken,* using the words of the blessing bestowed upon Rebecca by her brother: "Our sister, be thou the mother of thousands of ten thousands" (Gen. 24:60).[57] But the prototype of Rebecca fails to convince. The Biblical Rebecca covered herself; in contrast, the *badeken* ceremony consists of the groom first raising and then lowering the veil over a passive bride. Probably more relevant to the *badeken* is the intent behind Rebecca's act of covering: to signify her acceptance of Isaac as her husband.

Another folk tradition ascribes the custom to the marriage of the Biblical Jacob; he assumed that he was marrying his chosen, Rachel, only to discover after he had taken his bride to his tent that the veiled woman given to him was not Rachel but her sister Leah (Gen. 30:21–30). By this etiology, the *badeken* must be construed as an act of exposure rather than concealment. Leah stayed covered to imply consent to a marriage which in fact ran counter to Jacob's desire; had Jacob uncovered her prior to the ceremony, the marriage would not have happened. In contrast to the Greek ritual of the *anakaluptēria,* in which male and female interests are conflated in the act of uncovering, these Biblical etiologies maintain a distinction between male and female interests. In the Biblical stories the woman's desire to marry is expressed in acts of covering and concealment; the male interest lies solely in exposure.

Thus the seemingly antithetical pair of folk traditions, the Greek *anakaluptēria* and the Jewish *badeken,* neatly conjoin two separate aspects of the bride's veil: concealment and exposure. Like the *anakaluptēria,* the point of the *badeken* ceremony may once have been for the groom publicly to view the bride for the first time and, in the supportive company of witnesses, to penetrate the mystery of the covered woman in a public ritual corresponding to the private *yihud,* the cloistering of the pair in the marriage chamber. Indeed, the earliest sources for the *badeken* take the ritual as a ceremony of uncovering the head of an invisible veiled bride, an act sometimes performed by surrogates.[58] According to at least one Rabbinic authority, there is no valid wedding without this ritual.[59] The striking homology between the Jewish *badeken* and the Greek *anakaluptēria* suggests that in ancient times uncovering was as central an act in the Jewish marriage ceremony as covering is today. Both acts focus on the head and hair of the bride.

WIVES

Since decapitation is a workable expedient only in myth, the universal sign of the transformation of virgin to wife among Greeks, Romans, and Jews early becomes hair—bound, tamed, braided, or covered, the token of matronly modesty and chastity. The social tolerance of female sexuality usually ends with marriage in patriarchal societies that value and need wives primarily for reproduction. Once children have become a reality, the generative vitality once signified by hair can be dispensed with; the significance of hair can be narrowed to pure sexuality, now divorced from fertility and antithetical to marriage. Accordingly, the ideals and realities regarding the taming or covering of hair are, as a system, more archaic, widespread, and internally consistent for married women than for any other group of people.

In Greek epic, married women cover their hair, often with the *krēdemnon,* a flowing headdress traditionally associated with married women or with an unmarried woman in the presence of her betrothed. As Nagler has shown, this headcovering, together with attendants or chaperones, forms the core of a formulaic cluster betokening female chastity that is manipulated to great effect in the epics. In Homer's *Iliad* (22.460–73), Aphrodite gives Andromache headgear including a *krēdemnon* on the day of her wedding, as emblems of her married state. Andromache sheds these when she sees her husband's slain body being dragged by Achilles' horses away from the city toward the ships of the Greeks; on the same occasion Hecuba, mother of Hector, throws off her *kaluptrē* (headcover or veil) at the sight of her slain son (*Il.* 22.406). The *krēdemnon,* held so as to veil the cheeks, betokens the sexual fidelity of Penelope (*Od.* 1.331–34; cf. 1.207–10, 16.413–16, 21.63–65). For a woman to remove the *krēdemnon* is a gesture of seduction. Conversely, when the *krēdemnon* is torn or ripped it may betoken sexual violation, as when, in the *Homeric Hymn* (2.40–42), Demeter shreds her *krēdemnon* in grief at the rape of Persephone.[60]

On the stage of classical Athens, Euripides has the distraught Phaedra, a wife torn between the exigencies of her own desire and her obligations to her husband, express her sexual conflict in terms of the covering and uncovering of her hair. In her repressed desire to throw off sexual restraint, Phaedra begs for her hat to be removed and her hair to fall free; almost immediately, her sense of shame demands that her hair again be covered.[61]

Writing in the first century B.C.E., Varro (*De Lingua Latina* 5.130) implies that matrons in the Republic went about with their hair covered and controlled by a *lanea* (woolen headband), *reticulum* (net cap), or *capital* (headband). The most striking marker for the matron remained the *tutulus,* a cone-shaped headdress of hair piled up and bound atop the head, which, Varro claims, was worn universally by Roman matrons in ancient times and was replicated in the bride's headdress. For Varro, the word *tutulus* signified protection: "The headdress was so named either from the fact that the headdress was for the purpose of protecting the hair or because that which is highest in the city, the Citadel, is called the safest (*tutissimum*)."[62] Like the city of Rome itself, the ideal Roman matron must be literally impregnable to invaders.

By the end of the Roman Republic, fashion had triumphed over tradition, enabling aristocratic Roman women freely to adopt a dazzling succession of hairstyles and headdresses.[63] Fashion trends notwithstanding, the ideal of the covered head as a sign of chastity persisted at Rome. Writing at the end of the first century B.C.E., the Roman poet Ovid can still invoke the *vittae, insigne pudoris*—the doubled fillets transferred from the bride's headdress—to serve as a universally recognized sign of the matron's chastity.[64] Throughout the Empire, even for aristocratic matrons, the covered head persists as an ideal, and for lower-class women, probably as a reality.[65] At moments of high social tension, tradition reasserts itself even among the permissive: the hair of all women is covered in the way attributed to earlier times on occasions of marriage, sacrifice, and mourning.[66] Priestesses, women set apart by the community as living icons of Roman ideals, still move among their more permissive sisters with distinctive hair coverings assumed to reflect the ancient norm. Vestals maintain the ancient hairdo worn otherwise only by brides on their wedding day.[67] The *flaminica,* wife of the priest of Jupiter, a kind of ritual "ur-matron" of the state, always wears the peculiar and deliberately anachronistic bride's headdress, including *tutulus* and *flammeum* (veil), with the special addition of a twig from a fruitful tree.[68] Writing in the first century c.e., Valerius Maximus can still raise the case of a patrician of some two hundred years earlier as an ideological exemplum of grim yet praiseworthy severity: he divorced his wife because she had gone out bareheaded.

> He dismissed his wife because he had learned that she had gone about publicly with an uncovered head, in a brusque but very rational statement: "The law restricts you to my eyes alone for validation of your beauty. . . . A further glimpse of you, invited by unnecessary provocation, is, of necessity, to be associated with suspicion and culpability."[69]

For jaded Romans of the upper classes this story may have had a quaint ring, but the ideal persisted. As Ramsay MacMullen has argued, lower-class Roman women throughout the imperial period, at least in the Eastern provinces, continued to conform in practice to the persistent ideal of covered hair for married women.[70]

At about the same time in Palestine, at the beginning of the common era, headcoverings for Jewish matrons had come increasingly to be the norm not only by custom but by law. According to a circa second-century c.e. Mishnah, a woman who enters the public arena with *rosh parua* (literally, a disheveled head) has violated *dat yehudit,* normative Jewish practice — selectively applied to women only. As a consequence, she is subject not merely to divorce, but divorce without payment of the sum specified for damages in her *ketuba* (marriage contract).[71] Jewish women from Biblical times on probably bound or covered their hair in some way after marriage, since the wife suspected of adultery, called the *sotah* (errant woman), undergoes, according to the Bible, a ceremony of testing in which the preliminary ritual is the dishevelment of her hair (Num. 5:11–31). The unbound or uncovered hair of the *sotah,* together with the further ceremonial dishevelment of her clothing (a Mishnaic addition), signifies her "loose," sexually suspect state.[72] Indeed, the immense body of Rabbinic legislation regarding the covering of married women's hair all derives from the disheveled hair of the hapless *sotah*.[73] In Rabbinic texts, covered hair is the hallmark of female chastity in marriage. The chaste wife covers her hair, hides her flesh, and silences her voice (Talmud *Berachot* 24A; cf. Eisenstein 1915:162).[74] She removes her sexuality from public display, reserving it strictly for the husband to whom she bears legitimate children.

Nor is this curb on female sexuality restricted to the public arena. As in the mythic case of the decapitated yet fertile Medusa, restrictions on real women's sexuality tend to gravitate toward an ideal of asexual fertility within marriage itself. Apparently untroubled by the fact that "if you despoil the most outstandingly beautiful woman of her hair . . . were she Venus herself . . . bald, she would not be able to seduce even her own husband" (Apuleius *Metamorphoses* 2.8), Jews are drawn toward an ideal of the asexual wife that recalls the Greek ideal of the virtuous, industrious, and sexually neuter "bee woman."[75] So in the oft-quoted Talmudic anecdote, Kimhit, who bore seven sons of whom all were high priests (including two who were priests on the same day), is marked as a supremely virtuous woman by her exceptional fertility. Attributing her fertility to her exceptional modesty, the Talmud reports Kimhit's claim that "even the beams of her house had never glimpsed a lock of her hair." In other words, even within the private sphere her sexuality was covered. That the chaste Kimhit was not exceptional is shown by the response of the Rabbis: "They said to her: There were many who did likewise and yet did not succeed."[76]

WHAT HAVE WE DONE? SOME GREEK, ROMAN, AND JEWISH ETIOLOGIES OF WOMEN'S HEADCOVERINGS

Patriarchal culture is understandably hesitant to tame the potent locks of the men who fight its battles and make its laws.[77] For men to cover the head, therefore, becomes a dramatic gesture betokening submission to divine authority.[78] Only at prayer and at sacrifice did aristocratic Roman men lift the toga over their heads in the gesture known from portraits as the *capite velato*.[79] Major representatives of the community before the gods were expected to be in a perpetual state of sanctity. The Roman priests called *flamines* (especially the priest of Jupiter, the *flamen dialis*) were forbidden to "be in the open air without a cap"; their heads were always kept covered with the *apex*, a distinctive skullcap fitted with an olivewood spike.[80] Traditional Judaism, too, which today universally covers the male head, apparently began to do so only after the Middle Ages and with a gradualness that betokens instinctive reluctance to cover men's hair. In Biblical and Talmudic times, headcovering for men seems to have been reserved for special occasions or extraordinary persons.[81] Aside from such exceptional cases, headcovering as a general practice in the ancient Mediterranean was more common for the physically and politically powerless: slaves and, of course, women.[82] For the free men of Mediterranean antiquity to cover the hair remained a voluntary act, either symbolic or purely utilitarian, as both Plutarch and the Talmud attest. Plutarch's comment (*Moralia* 267, *Quaestiones Romanae* 14) that "it is more common for women to go into the public place covered up, and for men to go uncovered" provides a striking parallel to the Talmudic observation that "men sometimes cover, sometimes uncover their heads, but women always cover their heads, and minors never cover their heads" (*Nedarim* 30B; cf. Talmud *Niddah* 31B, *Sotah* 11B; Midrash *Genesis Rabba* 17.8.2, *Exodus Rabba* 71.14).

Men with visible hair and married women with invisible hair form the normative landscape of the ancient Mediterranean. This distinction in practice engenders new etiologies: difference begets hierarchy. Men, who in patriarchy are the ones reading the signs and assigning the meanings, inevitably will be on top. However initially intended or read, the covered hair of the married woman can be and is transformed into a sign of women's moral inferiority. Women must have done something to provoke cultural restraints more stringent than those of free men. The covered hair of women easily lends itself to explanations which locate this difference in sin. The covered head of the bride evokes the covered head of the mourner or criminal.[83]

According to the Midrash, God himself participated in Eve's glorious bridal, arranging the plaits of her hair (Midrash *Genesis Rabba* 18.1 with Gen. 2:22; cf. Talmud *Eruvin* 18A, *Berachot* 61A, *Shabbat* 95A, *Niddah* 45B). However, the same Midrash includes a voice that explains the covered hair of the Jewish wife as a mark of "original sin." The covered hair of the wife is assimilated to her other biological and cultural differences and with these is read both as a sign of the "first wife's" betrayal of the "first husband" and as a testimony to every wife's social and moral inferiority.

> "Why does the man go forth with an uncovered head and the woman's head is covered?" [R. Yehoshua] told them: "As one who committed a sin and is ashamed in public, so the woman goes forth with a covered head." . . . "Why was the commandment of menstruation given to woman?" "Because she spilled the blood of the first man [Adam], she was given the commandment of menstruation." . . . "And why was she given the commandment of lighting the Sabbath candles?" "Because she extinguished the soul of Adam, therefore she was given the commandment of lighting the Sabbath candles."[84]

The inner contradiction within the Midrash suggests the implicit paradox of the headcovering of the wife. To cover a woman's head is to call attention to her hair even while concealing it. The elaborate headdress of real married women may simultaneously exalt and disparage.

The hair of Hesiod's mythical first woman is crowned with headgear as glorious as the midrashic Eve's. Not only concealed by an intricate veil (*daidaleēn kaluptrēn*), Pandora is crowned with a fabulous golden crown (*stephanēn khruseēn*) worked with all the marvelous creatures born on land and sea (Hesiod *Theogony* 574–75, 578–84). Despite the misogynist context, Hesiod's first woman keeps her fabulous crown as the sign of abundant, lifegiving female fertility.[85] In the same way, the *stephanē* that crowns the heads of goddesses in Greek epic extends the generative vitality of feminine hair to the headdress that covers it, with epithets such as *eustephanos* "well-crowned,"[86] *khrusostephanos* "gold-crowned" (*Hymn. Hom.* 6.1, of Aphrodite), and *kallistephanos* "fair-crowned" (*Hymn. Hom.* 2.295, of Demeter).

The golden *stephanē* of Aphrodite (*Hymn. Hom.* 6.7), like the turreted crowns of Minoan goddesses and of fertility goddesses such as Cybele, instantiates the magnetism of feminine hair. It further expands the sign of female generative vitality from the hair to its covering in precisely the same way that kings' crowns, victors' wreaths, and radiate crowns all mark and expand male generative vitality. For real human beings, male and female alike, the covering can extend the hair, which itself is seen as an extension of the head where generative vitality is centered.[87]

Like the *stephanē* of Aphrodite, even the *krēdemnon*, the Homeric sign of matronly modesty, can reveal as well as conceal. In preparation for her seduction of Zeus, after combing and plaiting her hair, Hera "shining among the goddesses veiled herself with a lovely fresh *krēdemnon*, bright as the sun" (Hom. *Il.* 14.184–85).[88] In epic, the positive allure of the *krēdemnon* is further enhanced by its description as *liparos,* a word whose base meaning is "fat" or "greasy": when used of the soil it implies fertility; when used of the human body or skin it is usually understood as sleek or healthy.[89] When used of the headdress traditionally associated with wives, it suggests abundant feminine fertility.[90] Thus the epithet *liparokrēdemnos,* "having a gleaming *krēdemnon*," is used of Hecate, a goddess particularly identified with abundance, increase, and fertility (*Hymn. Hom.* 2.438; cf. Hesiod *Theogony* 440–52); of Rhea, another mother goddess (*Hymn. Hom.* 2.459); of the Nymphs and Charites who adorn Aphrodite in a ritual scene of adornment prior to seduction (*Cypria* frag. 5.3 [Allen 1965]); and of the Nereid Charis, when as the wife of Hephaestus she greets Thetis (Hom. *Il.* 18.382).

The gleaming headdress reiterates feminine fertility with its doubled association of wetness or moisture and its privileging of the head, the traditional site of generation.[91] The Homerid invites the goddess Hestia to enter with "liquid oil dripping ever from your locks" (*Hymn. Hom.* 24.3). In the same way, the gleaming *krēdemnon* can suggest exceptional fertility in its capacity as a headcovering infused with generative moisture.

At its extreme, the paradox of the wife's covered head is instantiated in the gleaming headdress (*lipara krēdemna*) of Penelope, in Homer's *Odyssey* a sign of sexual magnetism and fertility but also of modesty in a wife who is at the same time a bride (Hom. *Od.* 1.334 = 16.416 = 21.65).[92] Penelope's veil shimmers, her headdress betokening chastity even as its sheen betokens fertility and sexual allure.[93] The *Odyssey* uses the headcovering to mark Penelope as the most desirable of wives. So, too, the headcoverings of historical Greek wives can be construed as a positive sign.

But, as in the case of the Jewish etiology for the wife's covered head, Penelope's attractive headdress finds its only etiology in a Greek story of feminine betrayal. According to this tradition, Penelope was the first woman to abandon father for husband in patrilocal marriage; in shame, she covered her head. Thus the veil of all wives can be referred to the veil of Penelope, with the Greek version of a wife's "original sin" located in the act of betrayal demanded of women by patrilocality. The same culture that compels a bride to abandon one man (her father) for another (her husband) explains the wife's covered head as the sign of her shame for this act:

> The image of Modesty [*Aidōs* = Shame], some thirty stades distant from the city, they say was dedicated by Icarius, the following being the reason for making it. When Icarius gave Penelope in marriage to Odysseus, he tried to make Odysseus himself settle in Lacedaemon, but failing in the attempt, he next besought his daughter to remain behind, and when she was setting forth to Ithaca he followed the chariot, begging her to stay. Odysseus endured it for a time, but at last he bade Penelope either to accompany him willingly, or else, if she preferred her father, to go back to Lacedaemon. They say that she made no reply, but covered herself with a veil [*egkalupsamenēs*] in reply to the question, so that Icarius, realising that she wished to depart with Odysseus, let her go, and dedicated an image of Modesty [*Aidōs*]; for Penelope, they say, had reached this point of the road when she veiled [*egkalupsasthai*] herself. (Pausanias 3.20.10–11)[94]

As in most Greek stories of a woman's desertion of father for husband (e.g., the stories of Scylla, Comaetho, Ariadne, Medea), so even Homer's faithful Penelope is not rewarded in all traditions for her anguished submission to patrilocality. Betrayal is seen as endemic to feminine sexuality. So we can read a final chapter in which an adulterous Penelope is evicted by Odysseus from his house and sent back home to Sparta, apparently only to be evicted from her paternal home as well: "The Mantinean story about Penelope says that Odysseus convicted her of bringing paramours to his home, and being cast out by him she went away at first to Lacedaemon, but afterwards she removed from Sparta to Mantineia where she died" (Pausanias 8.12.6; Jones 1977, 3:407).

Romans, too, report traditions that associate the bride's veil with the act of betrayal mandated for brides by patrilocality. Commenting on the custom of veiling or covering the bride's head, the lexicographer Festus observes that the act of covering the bride's head—and the verb naming the act (*obnubere*) — is identical to the act of covering performed on the head of a parricide.[95] Here, too, the covered head of the bride is assimilated to shame and guilt: like the parricide, the wife is guilty of repudiating the bond with the father.

The golden-crowned and veiled Aphrodite is the eternal bride. The veil that covers her hair instantiates the paradox of sexual mystery, the crown on her head, the glory of generative potency. On her wedding day, every bride in the ancient Mediterranean is this Aphrodite.

Yet a quite different Aphrodite also provides the paradigm for wives. In marriage, her name is changed, her feet are chained, and her veil takes on new meaning:

A little farther on is a small hill, on which is an ancient temple with a wooden image of Aphrodite armed. This is the only temple I know that has an upper story built upon it. It is a sanctuary of Morpho, a surname of Aphrodite, who sits wearing a veil [*kaluptran*] with fetters on her feet. The story is that the fetters were put on her by Tyndareus, who symbolized by the bonds the faithfulness of wives to their husbands. The other account, that Tyndareus punished the goddess with fetters because he thought that from Aphrodite had come the shame [*oneidē*] of his daughters, I will not admit for a moment. For it were surely altogether silly to expect to punish the goddess by making a cedar figure and naming it Aphrodite. (Pausanias 3.15.10–11; Jones and Ormerod 1977, 2:95–97)

Not quite as silly, perhaps, as Pausanias, the author of this passage, seems to think; Tyndareus was not the last man to punish one woman for the crimes of another. No longer embodying mystery but shame, the wife's veil has been assimilated to fetters. For all wives, the paradigms are the notorious daughters of Tyndareus, Helen and Clytemnestra, whose "uncovered" sexuality brought destruction and shame to men. As a result, Aphrodite's shimmering veil is assigned a new meaning: no longer a barrier against the gaze of men, but a blinder for women's eyes. Thus every woman's headcovering is in marriage reread: no longer a sign of mysterious sexuality and proud fertility, but of shame—collective, retroactive, proleptic, and prophylactic. Like the sunglassed heads in the shop window on Rabbi Akiva Street, or the blindfolded brides in some actual Jewish weddings, the ideal wife must be not only covered but eyeless. No hair, no eyes, hardly a head.

Thus hair codes speak their gendered grammar. Over time, men in patriarchal societies have tamed women's hair with relative nonchalance and ease: women are veiled, wigged, blinded, beheaded, and fettered. Men have had greater difficulty in dealing with their own hair and their own nature. Or as Paul put it (1 Cor. 11:7, 10): "A man ought not to cover his head, since he is the image and glory of God; but woman is the glory of man. . . . That is why a woman ought to have a veil on her head."[96] The gendered grammar of ancient Mediterranean hair was conceived in patriarchy. Its syntax requires that the hair of every woman begin as a sign of crowning glory and end as a statement of shame.

NOTES

Everyone knows something about hair, and my friends and colleagues all have generously shared their knowledge with me. Thus my list of acknowledgments has grown too long for any more than an enormous collective thank you. Special thanks to Mary Decker, Don Lateiner, Rachel Kitzinger, Jorgen Mejer, Victoria Pedrick, Edie Reichman, Alex Sens, Rabbi Reuven Stein, and Alex Tulin. I am grateful to the Department of Classics at Vassar College for giving me a year of extraordinary moral and material support for research as Blegen Fellow in 1990–1991, and to Howard University for a Faculty Research Fellowship for the summers of 1991– 1992. This study is dedicated to Moti Manovitz, who so generously shared the view through his window into the landscape of his scholarship and street.

Classical authors and works are cited according to the abbreviations at the beginning of the *Oxford Classical Dictionary* and *The Greek-English Lexicon* of Liddell and Scott. References to the Talmud are to the Babylonian Talmud unless otherwise indicated. Translations are by the author unless otherwise noted.

Due to constraints of space, many topics deserving fuller discussion have had to be reduced in this essay to a string of cryptic citations or notes. For fuller treatment of these, I can only refer the curious reader to my forthcoming book on ancient Mediterranean hair codes.

1. On hair customs and polemics in contemporary *haredi* (ultraorthodox) communities in Israel, see Levy 1989:72–82, 120–36.

2. See also Xenophon *Rep. Lac.* 11.3; Plutarch *Vit. Lys.* 1, *Mor.* 188E, 228F; Philostratus *VA* 3.15; Herodotus 1.82.8. Long hair for mature men seems to have remained the custom in Sparta long after it went out of fashion in Athens. Within the fifth-century B.C.E. Athenian context, the Spartans' long hair became invested with various, often contradictory, political meanings. See Aristotle *Rhet.* 1367a 29–31; Aristophanes *Av.* 1282, *Lys.* 1072 with discussion in Dover 1978:78; Ehrhardt 1971; Vernant 1991:66–67, cf. 118–20; David 1992. Further sources on Spartan hair in Daremberg-Saglio, s.v. *coma,* 1360, *barba,* 668; Bekker 1889:453–54.

3. See Corson 1980, Cooper 1971:91–119. Hair treatments and styles have taken on especially complex political significance for contemporary African-Americans in the United States; Nelson 1987.

4. Obeyesekere 1981:45. See also Leach 1958 (cf. Hallpike 1987:154), who argues against the unswervingly Freudian position of Berg (1951). Psychological and anthropological approaches, according to Leach, are neither inherently contradictory nor mutually exclusive; each gives a partial answer.

5. For discussion of this aspect of mythmaking, see Eliade 1959, 1960.

6. An examination of formal marriage terminology (*coniugium, conubium, coniunx*) in the *Metamorphoses* reveals this as the passage with the highest frequency (3x) of such language. In *Met. 7.69*, the poet draws a clear distinction between *coniugium* and furtive love; he seems to respect this distinction in his reservation of formal

marriage terminology for "legal" marriage throughout the poem. See, e.g., *Met.* 1.395 (Deucalion and Pyrrha), 6.428 (Procne and Tereus), 7.60, 69 (Medea and Jason), 9.259, 14.592 (Juno and Jove), 10.618, 621 (Atalanta and Hippomenes). Contra Bömer 1969 (ad *coniunx, Met.* 1.557).

7. Unshorn hair is the essence of literary and iconographic depictions of Apollo in sources from Homer (eighth century B.C.E.) through the sixth century C.E., as signified by the traditional epithet for Apollo, "of uncut hair" (*akersekomēs, akeirekomēs*): e.g., Hom. *Il.* 20.39; Hesiod frag. 60.3 (Merkelbach and West 1967); *Hymn. Hom.* 3.134, cf. 450; Pindar *Pyth.* 3.14, *Isthm.* 1.7; Diodorus Siculus 8.29.1; Pausanias 5.22.3 (quoting an inscription); Lucian *Alex.* 36; Flavius Philostratus *Her.* 1.725, *Ep.* 16.24; Philostr. Maior *Imag.* 2.19.3; Philostr. Jun. *Imag.* 885.16; Nonnus 10.207; *Anthologia Graeca* 2.1.266 (Christodorus). Roman poets also emphasize this aspect of the god, who is described as *intonsus* (uncut), e.g., Horace *Carm.* 1.21.2, *Epod.* 15.9; Ovid *Met.* 1.564, 3.421, *Tr.* 3.1.60; Tibullus 1.4.37–38, 2.3.11–13, 2.5.121, 3.4.27. Cf. discussion in Nisbet and Hubbard 1975:255–56, n.2.

Walter Burkert derives one component of the prehistory of Apollo worship from the *apellai*, tribal or phratry gatherings of Dorian northwest Greece which were the occasion for the enrollment of young members into the tribe and included the ephebic initiation ritual of hair cutting. Thus Apollo comes to instantiate the ephebe "on the threshold of manhood, but still with the long hair of the boy," Burkert 1985:144–45; cf. Burkert 1975. The god's ephebic status is also emphasized by the absence of a beard, Cicero *Nat. D.* 1.30 (83); cf. Josephus *Ap.* 2.242, Callimachus *Ap.* 36–37, Apollonius Rhodius *Argon.* 2.708–9. For iconography of Apollo with flowing locks see, e.g., Callistratus *Stat.* 10 434K (3) (on statue of Paean, identified with Apollo) and Baumeister 1889, s.v. Apollo.

8. Freely flowing hair bound only by a single fillet is the mark of an unmarried Roman woman. Cf. Ovid *Met.* 2.413, and remarks below on virgins' hair.

9. Cf. Wilken 1886, Redfield 1975:182. On metonymic/metaphoric modes in modern linguistic theory, see Jakobson 1990:115–32; in ancient rhetorical theory, see Quintilian *Inst.* 8.6.

10. On liminality with respect to hair, see Redfield 1975:181–82.

11. On the Victorian custom see Cooper 1971:29–30. For Attis, see Arnobius *Adv. Nat.* 5.7 ad fin. and 5.14 ad fin.; cf. Rose 1959:170, Weinrich 1924/1925:9.

12. For discussion see Foley 1982, Redfield 1982.

13. On votive hair offerings see Burkert 1985:70 with n. 29, Rouse 1902:240–49.

14. In both cases, hair offerings are common. On hair offerings by Greek youths and brides, see, e.g., Herodotus 4.34, Callimachus 4.296–99; cf. Pausanias 1.43.4 (youths and maidens on Delos); Paus. 1.43.4 (brides in Megara); Euripides *Hipp.* 1423–30, Paus. 2.32, Lucian *Syr. D.* 60 (brides at Troezen); Statius *Theb.* 2.253–56 (brides in Larissa); Plutarch *Mor.* 772B *Amat. narr.* 1 (brides in Boeotia); Plut. *Vit. Thes.* 5, Theophrastus *Char.* 21.3, Athenaeus 13.605a–b (youths at Delphi). Among the Romans, there is abundant evidence particularly for the *depositio barbae*, the dedication of the first beard by young men, e.g., Dio Cassius 48.34.3; Suetonius *Calig.* 10, *Nero* 12; Petronius *Satyr.* 29; Juvenal 8.166.

15. The Athenian herm, a boundary stone marked by a bearded head and erect phallus, is probably the most widespread ancient iconographic sign of the connection between male head, hair, and phallus. According to Aristotle, the brain contains

the greatest concentration of fluid in the body and this fact accounts for the relative thickness of the hair on the head, since hair absorbs the moisture of the brain (*Gen. An.* 782b 9–11). Semen, consisting of water and *pneuma*, an airy substance (*Gen. An.* 736a 1–24), originates in the brain. Sexual intercourse drains semen from the brain, depriving the head of both heat and moisture, and predisposes men to baldness (*Gen. An.* 783b 27–784a 12). Thus Freudian theory, which sees the head as a phallic symbol with hair symbolizing semen, and haircutting as symbolic castration, can find support in the Greek conception of semen as originating in cerebrospinal fluid; cf. Berg 1951, Hallpike 1969 and 1987:154. On the connection of the head with the production of semen, see Onians 1951:108–13 with copious references; Giacomelli 1980. For the parallel association of head hair and semen among the Punjabis of India, see Hallpike 1987:154.

16. Cf. Hallpike 1987:154.

17. On Apuleius's obsessive interest in hair, see Englert and Long 1973. See, too, Ovid's instructions on hairstyles in *Ars Amatoria* 3.133–68 for a view of hair as an especially rich locus for the attentions and activity of culture.

18. Horace *Carm.* 1.12.41 with Nisbet and Hubbard 1975 *ad loc.*, 2.15.11; Varro *Rust.* 2.11.10; Juvenal 5.30, 16.31 with Mayor 1901 *ad loc.*; Cicero *Cael.* 14(33).25 with Austin 1960 *ad loc.*; Vergil *Aen.* 6.809; cf. Servius ad *Aen.* 12.100.

19. On hair as foliage in the Midrash, see Eisenstein 1915:406. On the derivation of the Hebrew word for hair from a Semitic root for foliage, with examples of this usage in Hebrew sources, see Ben-Yehuda 1959:7596 n.4 and 7598, s.v. *śa'ar.* For the Greek use of *komē* and its compounds for foliage, see e.g., Hom. *Od.* 23.195; Euripides *Hipp.* 210, *Bacch.* 1055. For Latin *coma* and its compounds for foliage, see Catullus 4.12; Vergil *Aen.* 2.629; Horace *Carm.* 1.21.5, 4.3.11, 4.7.2; Vergil *Georgics* 4.122, *Aen.* 12.413; Pliny *HN* 13.59; cf. Onians 1951:231 n.1.

20. Dionysus is marked by his beautiful, dark, wavy hair, *kalai . . . etheirai kuaneai* (*Hymn. Hom.* 7.4–5; cf. Euripides *Bacch.* 150, 235–36, 239–41, 455–56, 493; Callistratus 8 431K 20 [3]), with the word for hair, *etheira*, being that generally used in Homer for the plumes of heroic horses (Liddell and Scott 1968, s.v. *etheira*). The epithet *kuanokhaitēs* (dark-haired) used of Poseidon and Hades is also used in epic of horses (Hom. *Il.* 20.224; Hesiod *Sc.* 120; Pausanias 8.25.8, quoting the epic *Thebais* [= frag. 4, Allen 1965]). For a historical instance of the association of horses' manes and heroic hair, see Herodotus's description of an Ethiopian battle helmet which consisted of the head of a dead horse (Hdt. 7.70).

The changing iconography of Dionysus varies in respect to hair; Baumeister 1889, s.v. Dionysus. In archaic and earlier classical art the god is shown with much hair and bearded, embodying a dignified, virile ideal. Later the god is depicted with long hair but without a beard. This feminizes the god, assimilating him to a more liminal, "ephebic" type.

21. The epithet occurs 26 times of the Achaeans in the *Iliad*, e.g., *Il.* 2.323, 443, 4.261, 13.312. Cf. *akrokomoi* "top-knotted" of the Thracians (*Il.* 4.533), *opithen komoōntes* "hair streaming back" of the Abantes (*Il.* 2.542), a hairstyle variously interpreted as protection from the grasp of the enemy (Strabo 10.465) or as the sign of a heightened rush of power in battle; cf. Kirk 1986:204–5 ad *Il.* 2.542. Note the contrast between Homer's long-haired heroes and the thin-haired, unheroic Thersites (*Il.* 2.219).

On the long hair of Homeric warriors, see Krause 1858:66–67, Bremer 1911:7–12, Bremer 1912:2109–12, Marinatos 1967:B2–3, Kirk 1986:271–72 ad *Il.* 3.43, Heubeck, West, and Hainsworth 1988 ad *Od.* 1.90. On identification of hair with heroic vitality, see Sommer 1912a:2105 and 1912b, 7–9, Schredelseker 1913:22–48, Kötting 1986:178–81.

22. On the related issue of the equation of hair with virile power in the Greco-Roman obsession with hairlessness as a prerequisite for the pathic member of a homosexual pair, see Boswell 1980:29 n. 55; cf. 76–77. For discussion of hair as an indicator of gender identity in the physiognomical corpus, see Gleason 1990.

23. For the story of Samson and Delilah, see Judg. 16:4–31 with Bal's discussion (1987:37–67). Note that Samson's hair has seven plaits (Judg. 16:13) and the number 7 appears repeatedly in the story. This has been related to the Mesopotamian idea of the hero's strength being symbolized by six or seven locks of hair (Kötting 1986:178).

24. Lycophron *Alex.* 36–37. Elsewhere Heracles, repeatedly defeated by women, is portrayed as devastated, seated indoors like a woman, with his head *veiled* like a woman (Diodorus Siculus 4.11.2; Euripides *HF* 1214–15, 1159, 1198, 1205 as cited in Loraux 1990:28 n. 31). For an excellent discussion of Heracles' emasculation in myth, see Loraux 1990.

25. Hesiod *Op.* 165, frags. 199.2, 200.2, 11, 204.43, 55 (Merkelbach and West 1967); Hom. *Il.* 3.329, 7.355, 8.82, 9.339, 11.369, 505, 13.766; *Cypria* 11 (Evelyn-White 1914 = Plutarch *Vit. Thes.* 32.7.6); *Certamen* 312 (Allen 1965).

26. For other instances of the epithet *ēukomos/eukomos*, cf. Aiolis: Hes. frag. 10(a) 103 (Merkelbach and West 1967); Briseis: Hom. *Il.* 2.689; Pero: Hes. frag. 37.8 (Merkelbach and West 1967); Charites: Pindar *Pyth.* 5.45; Muses: Pindar *Ol.* 6.91; Gorge: Hes. frag. 25.17 (Merkelbach and West 1967); Selene: Epimenides frag. 2.4 (Diels-Kranz 1951).

Other epithets marking women's hair include *khrusoplokamos* "with golden plaits" (*Hymm. Hom.* 3.205, of Leto); *euplokamos* "with fair plaits" (Hom. *Il.* 11.623, of Hecamede, a mortal woman; *Hymn. Hom.* 4.4, 18.7, of Maia, mother of Hermes; *Hymn. Hom.* 31.6, of Selene); *kalliplokamos* "fair-plaited" (Hom. *Il.* 14.326, of Demeter; 18.592, of Ariadne); *euplokamides* "fair-plaited" (Hom. *Od.* 2.119, of heroines Tyro and Alcmene); *kallikomos* "fair-haired" (Hesiod *Theogony* 915, of Mnemosyne; *Cypria* 7.2 [Allen 1965], of Nemesis, mother of Helen).

27. On the sexual significance of Medusa's snakey locks and her decapitation by the Greek hero Perseus, see Slater 1968:17–20, 308–36, passim and Barnes 1974:10–11, summarizing the theories of Freud (1950 [1922]) and Ferenczi (1952 [1923]) in which Medusa's hair symbolizes genitalia. Barnes argues for an existential interpretation which concentrates on Medusa's gaze rather than her hair.

28. For the traditional depiction of Maenads with long flowing hair, see e.g., Euripides *Bacch.* 695, 757–8, 864–65, 930; Callistratus 2.K.423.20 (3). The flowing hair of Bacchants is emphasized in the conventional iconography of Maenads with heads tilted back in ecstasy. On the significance of hair in Euripides' *Bacchae*, see Segal 1982:174–77.

Note, too, that the conventional hairiness of the satyrs often depicted as companions of the Maenads is (together with rampant potency) emblematic of nostalgia for a fantasy state of nature; see discussion in Lissarrague 1990. In the case of the male satyrs, hairiness is a Greek dream; in the case of the wild-haired Maenads, hairiness is a nightmare.

29. See J.-P. Vernant's introduction to Detienne 1977: i–xxxv. Cf. Carson 1990, especially 149–53 on the antithesis between work (procreation) and play (eroticism) and on the role of marriage, which limits female sexuality to procreation.

30. Talmud *Eruvin* 100B; cf. *Niddah* 24B, *Shabbat* 151B. The Talmud quotes a dissenting opinion which argues that these three "curses" are in fact praise rather than blame.

For Lilith as the mother of demons, see Talmud *Bava Batra* 73A; as the strangler of newborn infants, see Midrash *Numbers Rabba* 16.25, *Zohar* 1.19b. For discussion of Lilith as succubus, child-slayer, killer of child-bearing women, injurer of newborn babies (boys until circumcision, girls until twenty days of age), and thief of men's sperm (she excites men in their sleep and steals their sperm to manufacture demon children), see Patai 1978:180–225; Scholem 1972.

31. For other versions of the Medusa story, see Hesiod *Th.* 270–83, *Scut.* 216–37; Pindar *Pyth.* 10.44–48, 12.11–24, *Nem.* 10.4; Herodotus 2.91.6; Euripides *Ion* 989–98; Apollodorus *Bibl.* 2.3.2, 2.4.2–3; Ovid *Met.* 4.790–803.

32. Homer (*Il.* 5.741, 8.349, 11.36, *Od.* 11.634) refers to the terror of the disembodied Gorgon's head but does not connect it to the mortal Medusa.

33. For the sweet voice of Medusa, see Hesiod *Th.* 275 (*liguphōnoi*) with West 1966 *ad loc.*

34. Cf. Euripides *Ion* 989–91 (Athena is Medusa's destroyer, wears her skin as the aegis), Apollodorus *Bibl.* 2.4.3 (Athena destroys her beautiful rival), Pindar *Pyth.* 12.11–24 (Athena invents flute to imitate Gorgon cry). Athena's birth from the head of Zeus parallels the birth of Pegasus from the head of Medusa. The shared connection to the Libyan Lake Triton of Medusa (Herodotus 2.91.6; Pausanias 2.21.5, 3.17.3) and Athena "Tritogenia" (Hesiod *Th.* 895 with West 1966 *ad loc.;* Apollodorus *Bibl.* 1.3.6, 3.12.3), together with Medusa's place on Athena's breast, suggests that Medusa is, in fact, a doublet of Athena.

35. On Clytemnestra and the Furies, see Zeitlin 1978:158–59.

36. See Jameson (1990:216 and n.12; cf. Burkert 1992:85) on the decapitation of the Gorgon as emblematic of a Greek initiation test. The feminine threat signified by hair may explain the frequent portrayal of Gorgons as bearded (noted by Jameson 1990:217).

37. On the equation of maiden = filly = ephebic Gorgon, see Gershenson 1989, Jameson 1990:216, Vernant 1991:111–38.

38. Pausanias 2.21.7; on Gorgophone, cf. Apollodorus *Bibl.* 1.9.5, 2.4.5, 3.10.3. Feldman (1965) locates the origins of the Gorgon in the guttural growl of animals, etymologically connecting *Gorgo, gorgos,* and *gorgoumai* to the Sanskrit root *garg.* On connections of Gorgons to Argos, see Jameson 1990.

39. The Homerid's portrait of the virgin daughters of Celeus whose hair "streamed about their shoulders" (*Hymn. Hom.* 2.176–78) is typical for the ancient Greeks. On freely flowing hair for unmarried girls in ancient Judaism, see Rashi ad Talmud *Ketubot* 15B, "*Verosha Parua*" (with her hair down, in disarray): "With her hair [flowing down] on her shoulders, thus they were accustomed to take out virgins from their father's house to the marriage house." Later Rabbinic sources such as the fifteenth-century *Beit Hadash* (*Tur, Even HaEzer* 21 "*lo yelchu*") continue to ex-

empt virgins from head covering. For discussion see Epstein 1948:48–52. For contemporary Rabbinic dissent on virgins' hair, see discussion in Joseph 1985:13.b–e,
pp. 41–44.

40. Cf. Swidler 1976:215 and n. 52.

41. So Carson 1990:160. This fragment is from a third-century C.E. papyrus with
some corruptions restored in the translation: Schibli 1990:50–51. Although the
precise purpose of the cloth is unclear in the fragment, most scholars understand
the *pharos* (cloth or robe) as the unveiling gift (also called *anakaluptēria*) rather than
the veil or headcovering itself: Fraenkel 1973:244, Kirk and Raven 1963:61, Schibli
1990:64–66.

42. See Hesiod *Op.* 72–82 and Vernant 1989:69.

43. Quote and paraphrased summary from Carson 1990:163, with extensive
bibliography of ancient and modern sources on p. 163, n. 55; on the *anakaluptēria*
and the vexed question of its precise timing, cf. Toutain 1940, Oakley 1982, Redfield
1982:192, Sissa 1990:94–98, Schibli 1990:64–69, Oakley and Sinos 1993:25–26.
For general summary of Greek wedding ceremonies with illustrations, see Daremberg-Saglio, s.v. *matrimonium,* especially 1649–53, Oakley and Sinos 1993; cf. Redfield 1982.

44. Bergren 1989:22. Bergren's trenchant observations on the significance of
the veil as homologous with the *zōnē* or belt, both symbolizing female sexuality as
something that must be uncovered by men at their own peril, appear in her discussion of *Homeric Hymn* 5, where she argues that the veiled Aphrodite is the paradigm of how all mortal virgins present themselves to men.

45. *Andrasin orathēnai:* Suda; Harpocration s.v. *anakaluptēria;* Schol. ad Euripides
Orestes, 284, cited in Toutain 1940:350 n.1. Ancient lexicographers offer words with
roots in the semantic sphere of seeing as synonyms for the *anakaluptēria,* e.g., the
optēria (Pollux 2.59, 3.36; Moeris Atticus s.v. *optēria;* Hesychius s.v. *optēria*) and the
theōrētra (Harpocration s.v. *anakaluptēria*); references cited in Oakley 1982:113 n.1.
Carson 1990:163–64 treats the ritual from the woman's point of view.

46. Festus s.v. *nuptias,* Lindsay 1913:174. On the saffron-colored veil of Roman
brides see, e.g., Lucan 2.361, Martial 12.42.3, Pliny *HN* 21.46, Jerome *Ep.*12. See
also *The Aldobrandini Wedding* (Rome, Vatican Museum), a painting in which the
bride is shown seated and heavily veiled in preparation for the wedding (reproduction in Maiuri 1953:30). The decorous veil held up before the bride's face, called
the *pudicitia* gesture in Roman portraiture, signifies chastity in the plastic arts, including coinage: Neumann 1965:85–89, North 1966:308. On Roman marriage ceremonies in general, see Daremberg-Saglio, s.v. *matrimonium,* 1654–58, Balsdon
1962:181–85.

47. Festus s.v. *Senis crinibus,* Lindsay 1913:454. For the braiding into *sex crines*
bound by *vittae* see also Plautus *Most.* 224, *Mil. glor.* 791; Tertullian *De virg. vel.* 12;
Servius *Ad Aen.* 7.403; Propertius 5.3.15; Tibullus 1.6.67; Valerius Flaccus 8.6; Ovid
Ars Am. 1.31, *Tr.* 2.522, *Pont.* 3.3.51. Marquardt (1886:46 n.3) concludes from Propertius 5.11.23 and Valerius Maximus 5.2.1 that the bride's fillets differed from the
virgin's in that they were double.

The braiding custom is nicely illustrated in the great frieze in the Villa of the
Mysteries at Pompeii, where a young woman sits with a female attendant at her side

and with Eros holding a mirror as she arranges her hair in distinct locks; for illustration and discussion see Brendel 1980, fig. 18 and p. 119 and n. 60; cf. Maiuri 1953:61. The importance of hairdressing in Roman wedding ritual can also be seen in a painting from the Archaeological Museum in Naples (reproduced in Veyne 1987:70).

48. Festus s.v. *caelibari hasta*, Lindsay 1913:55. According to Festus the act was performed with a spear taken from the slain and discarded body of a gladiator, so that the bride would be joined to her husband in the same way as the spear had been joined to the body of the gladiator; or because matrons were under the protection of Juno Curitis, who got her name from the spear she bore, called *curis* in the Sabine language; or because the spear portended the birth of strong men; or because by marriage law, the bride is subject to her husband's *imperium*, and the spear represents the substance of arms and imperial power. On the etiology of the Roman custom see also Plutarch *Vit. Rom.* 15.26E, cf. *Mor.* 285 *Quaest. Rom.* 87; Ovid *Fast.* 2.559–60 with note of Frazer (1929, vol. 2, 441–45). For a possible Brahmin parallel see Leach 1958:155.

49. Bloch 1980:32–33, Chill 1979:286. The word *huppah* is associated with a cloud cover in Is. 4.5, recalling the Roman etymology of Latin *obnubit* discussed above.

50. Ben-Yehuda 1959 s.v. *kalah* 2,2379 n.2.

51. Cf. Deut. 23:1, 27:20; Lev. 18:7–8, 20:11; metaphoric in Ezek. 16:8.

52. Epstein 1948:50 and n. 122 citing Talmud *Sanhedrin* 58B. Epstein (38–39, cf. Epstein 1942:44) argues on the basis of the Assyrian Code that the veiling ceremonial establishes the status of legitimacy for the Jewish wife.

53. *Mechilta, Mishpatim* ad Exod. 21:8, *Targum Onkelos* and *Targum Jonathan ad loc.*, Talmud *Kidushin* 18B, as cited by Epstein 1948:38 n. 61.

54. Jewish brides in antiquity wore diadems and crowns, which were outlawed only after the destruction of the Temple; Talmud *Sotah* 49A and B.

55. E.g., Lev. 1:4; 3:2, 8, 13; 4:4, 15, 24, 29, 33; 9:4. For the Greek parallel see Foley 1982:163.

56. On the *badeken*, see Chill 1979:280–81, who notes the custom of blindfolding the bride in some contemporary oriental and Hassidic communities and in the old community of Jerusalem.

57. Bloch 1980:31, Sperling 1982:405, #950 with *Contras Aharon*.

58. Epstein 1948:49 and n. 117 citing Midrash *Exodus Rabba* 41.6; *Tanhuma Ki Tissa*, p. 112; *Yalkut Shimeoni*, Song 4:9; *Derech Eretz* 6.2 (ed. Higger, p. 122); cf. Mildola, *Huppat Hatanim*, p. 45. In certain modern Jewish communities, supportive surrogates such as the rabbi and communal dignitaries performed the *badeken* on behalf of the groom: Sperling 1982:406, footnote; *Kitzur Shulhan Aruch* 470.3.

59. Sperling 1982:405, #950 with *Contras Aharon;* cf. *Tur, Even HaEzer* 61 with *Beit Hadash ad loc.;* Ashkenazi 1968:175 ad *Ketubot* 17A.

60. Nagler 1974:44–63; cf. Nagler 1967, Redfield 1982:195. On the vexed question of what the headdress of Homeric women actually looked like, see discussions of the archaeological evidence in Lorimer 1950:385–89; Marinatos 1967:B20–22; Heubeck and Hoekstra 1989:187 ad *Od.* 13.388.

61. Euripides *Hipp.* 198–202, 244–46; cf. 131–34, 218–21 and Rabinowitz 1986:132. On evidence for womens' headdress in classical Greece, see Krause

1858:72–135; Bekker 1889:459–60; Baumeister 1889, s.v. *Haartracht,* 617–19; Bremer 1912:2128–35.

62. Varro *Ling.* 7.44; cf. Festus s.v. *tutulum,* Lindsay 1913:484–85. Lucan (2.358) describes the matron's headdress as a *corona turrita,* a towered crown. For illustration of this arrangement in a bridal coiffure see Daremberg-Saglio s.v. *matrimonium,* 1655 fig. 4871. On evidence for covered hair as the norm for matrons in the early Republic, see Marquardt 1886:582–83.

63. For an exhaustive survey see Krause 1858:229–37. See also Marquardt 1886:602–6; Steininger 1912; Daremberg-Saglio s.v. *coma,* 1367–71.

64. Ovid *Ars Am.* 1.31; cf. *Tr.* 2.247, 252, *Fast.* 4.133, *Pont.* 3.3.51; Propertius 4.11.34. *Meretrices* (harlots) were precluded from wearing the fillets. For illustration see Wilson 1938:140–41 and figs. 92a and b (vestal's fillets). Another traditional headcovering for women, a kerchief called the *rica,* was used for sacrifice and may have persisted into the Empire as a sign of matronly modesty; Aulus Gellius 7.10.4 and Marquardt 1886:583; cf. Varro *Ling.* 5.130.

65. Cf. Bonfante and Jaunzems 1988:1405.

66. When women sacrifice they veil their heads with a *rica* (Varro *Ling.* 5.130; cf. Plutarch *Mor.* 266C *Quaest. Rom.* 10), a pose illustrated in a scene of the Emperor Septimius Severus and his wife Julia Domna at sacrifice, both with covered heads, from a relief on the arch of the Argentarii in Rome (reproduced in Dudley 1967, fig. 76). In mourning, according to Plutarch, Roman women wear white headdresses (Plutarch *Mor.* 270 D *Quaest. Rom.* 26), although at the funeral of a parent daughters, in contrast to sons, go with uncovered heads and unbound hair in an act that inverts customary gender roles (Plutarch *Mor.* 267 A–B *Quaest. Rom.* 14).

67. Brides and vestals share a common hairdo; Festus, s.v. *senis crinibus,* Lindsay 1913:454; cf. Beard 1980:15–16; Daremberg-Saglio, 1655 and figures 4056, 4057. Vestals at sacrifice wore the *suffibulum,* an oblong cloth with a colored border fastened under the chin, as did the state priest for certain rituals; Festus, s.v. *suffibulum,* Lindsay 1913:474–75; Varro *Ling.* 6.21.

68. According to Festus, the *flaminica* wears the *tutulus* (s.v. *tutulum,* Lindsay 1913:484–85) and the *rica* fastened to the *tutulus* (s.v. *ricae,* Lindsay 1913:342; cf. Paulus s.v. *rica,* Lindsay 1913:369; Festus s.v. *rica,* Lindsay 1913:368). The *rica* of the *flaminica* includes a twig from an *arbor felix;* Aulus Gellius 10.15.28. The *flaminica* also wears the *flammeum,* the flame-colored veil of the bride; Festus, s.v. *flammeo,* Lindsay 1913:79. For other hair taboos on the *flaminica* see Ovid *Fast.* 3.397–98, 6.229 with Frazer 1929 *ad loc.,* Vanggaard 1988:40–44, 88–104, passim.

69. Valerius Maximus 6.3.10; Plutarch *Mor.* 267C *Quaest. Rom.* 14, writing after Valerius Maximus, clearly has confused the story; cf. MacMullen 1980:208 n.3.

70. MacMullen 1980 with additional sources in n. 4. Polybius 15.27.2 reports the case of an incident in third-century B.C.E. Ptolemaic Egypt in which political rivalries were played out by taking the mother-in-law of one of the rivals and dragging her through the streets without her veil; Pomeroy 1984:51 with n. 54. Jewish sources provide a parallel in the Mishnaic case of a man fined 400 zuzim by Rabbi Akiva for uncovering the head of a woman in public; Mishnah *Baba Kama* 8.6; *Avot de R. Natan* A 3.10–14.

71. Mishnah *Ketubot* 7.6 and Talmud *Ketubot* 72A and B. Cf. *Tosephta Sotah* 5.9;

Talmud *Gittin* 90A; Jerusalem Talmud *Sotah* 16B; Midrash *Numbers Rabba* 9.12. For discussion of the law, see most fully Frimer 1980:46–137; cf. Epstein 1927:212–13, Epstein 1948:41, Swidler 1976:121–23. On the antiquity and the universality of headcovering as the norm for married Jewish women, see most fully Krauss 1945:274–97 and Epstein 1948:36–60.

72. On clothing, Mishnah *Sotah* 1.5 (= Talmud *Sotah* 7A); Talmud *Sotah* 8A links dishevelment of clothing to Num. 5:18. On the hair symbolism see Talmud *Sotah* 8B–9A; Midrash *Numbers Rabba* 9.16; cf. Susanna 32 (Apocrypha). The ceremony itself, in which the woman was taken before the high priest and given "bitter waters" to drink, was abolished by Rabbi Yohanan ben Zakai soon after the destruction of the Second Temple in 70 c.e., "when adulterers increased in number"; Mishnah *Sotah* 9.9. According to Rabbi Akiva (late first, early second century c.e.) the test would be ineffective unless the jealous husband, too, were free of guilt; Talmud *Sotah* 28A, 47B. For discussion, see Epstein 1948:216–34, Swidler 1976:151–54, Frymer-Kensky 1984.

73. Talmud *Ketubot* 72A deduces the requirement for "nondisheveled hair" as the norm for married Jewish women from the *sotah* ceremony; cf. Midrash *Numbers Rabba* 9.33. See Rashi ad Talmud *Sotah* 7A (*"Vesoter et śe'arah mikliato"*), who deduces the norm to have been some type of braiding. Elsewhere, however, Rashi (ad Talmud *Sotah* 8A) states re *"uparah"* that the language refers to uncovering rather than "disheveling" or "undoing," i.e., that headcovering and not simple braiding was the norm for married women; for discussion and sources on this question see Epstein 1948:39–40 n. 66, Krauss 1945:274–77.

74. For the parallel value placed on female silence in Greco-Roman culture, see Plutarch *Mor.* 142 *Coniug. Praecept.* 32: "Phidias made the Aphrodite for the Eleans with one foot on a tortoise to typify womankind keeping at home and keeping silence," with discussion in Heckscher 1953.

75. On the industrious, virtuous "bee woman" type of the seventh-century B.C.E. Greek poet Semonides (Diehl, frag. 7.85–91; cf. Phocylides of Miletus, frag. 3) as the instantiation of *"sophrosyne"* for women in classical Greece, see North 1977. The necessity even for *female* fertility in marriage is eliminated through hair symbolism in the variant on the Hesiodic succession myth which has Athena born, not from the head of Zeus, but from his beard; Onians 1951:233 n. 2 citing *Myth. Vat.* 1.176, 2.37.

A strain of Jewish opposition to this tendency is preserved in a Mishnah which permits a husband to abrogate the assumption of nazirite vows by his wife precisely because, at the end of the nazirite period, she would have to cut off all her hair and would appear repulsive to him; Mishnah *Nazir* 4.5; cf. Talmud *Nazir* 28A–B; discussion in Epstein 1948:55–60.

76. Talmud *Yoma* 47A; Jerusalem Talmud *Megillah* 72A; Midrash *Leviticus Rabba* 20.11, *Numbers Rabba* 2.26. Kimhit's date is circa 17 B.C.E. (early Rabbinic period); cf. Swidler 1976:122.

77. Cf. Hallpike (1987:155), who notes that in the case of the early Frankish kings, who were essentially warriors, long hair was celebrated as a distinctive mark of royal status to the extent that "cutting the hair disqualified a member of the royal family from succession to the throne."

78. Plutarch (*Mor.* 267 *Quaest. Rom.* 14) suggests that a son covers his head at the funeral of a parent to indicate that sons honor fathers as gods.

79. The gesture is illustrated on the Altar of Peace, erected by Augustus (*Res Gestae,* 12) and dedicated in 9 B.C.E. The altar is enclosed by sculptures showing the mythical Aeneas with his head covered at sacrifice (Simon 1967, pl. 30); in another panel Agrippa, pictured in the entourage of Augustus in procession to the dedication ceremonies, wears his toga drawn over his head in the identical gesture (Simon 1967, plates 13 and 14), as does Augustus himself (Simon 1967, plates 10, no. 2 and 11). Unlike the Greeks, Roman men covered their heads at sacrifice. Plutarch (*Mor.* 266C *Quaest. Rom.* 10) explains that the practice was to prevent distraction by an ill-omened sound, adducing as parallel Aeneas, who while at sacrifice covered his head to avoid distraction. See also Vergil *Aen.* 3.405–9 with Servius ad 407; Dionysius of Halicarnassus *Ant. Rom.* 12.16; Festus, s.v. *Saturnia,* Lindsay 1913; cf. Lucretius 5.1198; Ovid *Fast.* 3.363; Suetonius *Vitell.* 2. Exceptions where the Romans follow the Greek practice of sacrificing bare-headed are noted in Macrobius *Saturn.* 3.6.17; Plutarch *Mor.* 266E *Quaest. Rom.* 11; Dion. Hal. *Ant. Rom.* 1.34.4, 6.1.4; Festus s.v. *Saturnia, Saturno,* Lindsay 1913; Macrobius *Saturn.* 1.8.2; Servius ad Vergil *Aen.* 3.407; cf. Frazer 1929 vol. 4, 133 ad Ovid *Fast.* 6.31.

The difference in practice may reflect contrasting Greek and Roman conceptions of the nature of transactions with divinity. Intent on "up there," the Greeks seem to feel that nothing should come between the person and the divinity during the sacrificial transaction; to sacrifice with an uncovered head ensures that communication will be direct and unblocked. The Romans, ever focused on the here and now, worry about ill-omened interruptions which they seek to block out by the barrier of a headcovering. The Greek custom of sacrificing with uncovered head may also be explained as part of a general Greek aversion to submissive postures in relation to the gods, as characterized by Jameson (1988:963): "The Greek in his addresses to the supernatural stood upon his dignity." Cf. the medieval Rabbinic legal code *Tur* (*Orach Hayim, Hilchot Brachot* 7 with *Beit Hadash ad loc. "umechase rosho"*), whose author remarks of the Jewish gesture—similar to the Roman sacrificial practice—of covering the head with the *talit* (prayer shawl) at moments of high sanctity in the prayer service: "[It] subjugates the human heart and brings men to fear of Heaven."

80. That the perpetually covered head is the most striking sign of the *flamen* can be seen from efforts to derive the word from a Latin root related to the cap. Varro (*Ling.* 5.84; cf. Festus s.v. *flamen dialis,* Lindsay 1913) erroneously derives the title *flamen* from *filum* (strand) because priests in Latium always kept their heads covered (*capite velato erant semper*) and bound with a fillet. Plutarch, too, derives the word *flamen* from the priest's peculiar headdress, called here the *pileus,* which he is prohibited from removing; Plutarch *Vit.* 64C *Num.* 7, *Mor.* 274C *Quaest. Rom.* 40; cf. Dionysius of Halicarnassus *Ant. Rom.* 2.64.2. Since the *flamen dialis* is forbidden "to be in the open air without his cap [*apex*]," for the *flamen* to go bareheaded in his house is interpreted as a recent concession; Aulus Gellius *NA* 10.15.17–18. A certain Sulpicius was deprived of his priesthood because the *apex* fell from his head at sacrifice; Valerius Maximus 1.1.4; Plutarch *Vit.* 300C *Marc.* 5. Suetonius (frag. 168 p. 268 [Re], quoted in Servius *ad Aen.* 2.683) lists and describes three types of

priestly headgear: *apex, tutulus, galerus.* The *galerus* (leather cap) with the peaked *apex* can be seen on the right long wall of the Ara Pacis frieze with its four *flamines* in procession after Augustus; Simon 1967:17 and plates 10 (no. 2), 12, 13. The *flamen*'s hair itself is hedged with taboos regarding its cutting and disposal; Aulus Gellius *NA* 10.15.12,15–16. For discussion see Vanggaard 1988:40–44, 92–93.

81. On the vexed question of the antiquity of today's mandatory headcovering for Jewish males, see Krauss 1945:266–73, Epstein 1948:32, Idit 1972, Bloch 1980:104–6. These all conclude that headcovering, which in antiquity was optional and a matter of custom for important men, gradually came to be endorsed as a universal requirement. On the evolution of the modern *yarmulke* (skullcap), see Plaut 1955.

82. Slaves and common people in ancient Greece wore a cap called the *kunē;* workers wore the narrow-brimmed felt or leather hat (*pilos*); travelers of every social rank wore the wide-brimmed Thessalian hat (*petasos*). Otherwise, men mostly were bareheaded; Plato (942d *Leg.* 12) may be expressing the aristocratic sensibility when he cautions against corrupting the native strength of the hair by covering the head. Roman men in the archaic period were also in the habit of going out bareheaded, using the toga drawn up over their head or the *cucullus* (hood) attached to their cloak as need be. The conical felt cap (*pileus*) was used chiefly by freedmen. At the Roman Saturnalia, where everyone would wear the *pileus* (Mart. 11.6.4, 14.1.2), it was regarded as a sign of the inversion of social roles. For a recent discussion of Greek and Roman headcoverings, see Bonfante and Jaunzems 1988, passim. For a survey of headcoverings for Jewish men in antiquity, see Krauss 1945:251–65.

83. Talmud *Eruvin* 100B describes the bride as "one who is veiled like a mourner and banished from people"; cf. *Pirkei de Rabbi Eliezer* 14.

84. Midrash *Genesis Rabba* 17.8 passim; cf. Sperling 1982:406, 952, citing *Yalkut Reuveni,* chapter on Genesis.

85. Cf. O'Brian 1983. The nuptial coronet or *stephanē* remains a central symbol of Greek weddings from Minoan-Mycenean times through the present day; Mylonas 1945:563, cf. Oakley and Sinos 1993:16 and figs. 28–30 et passim.

86. Hom. *Od.* 2.120, of Mycene; Hom. *Il.* 21.511, of Artemis; Hom. *Od.* 8.267, Hesiod *Th.* 196, *Hymn. Hom.* 5.6, 175, of Aphrodite; *Hymn. Hom.* 2.224, 384, 470, Hesiod *Op.* 300, of Demeter.

87. For discussion see Onians 1951:130, 135 n.9, 165–67, 231 et passim, and my note 15 above.

88. Nagler (1974:58 n. 44) draws a parallel between Hera's *krēdemnon* and Zeus's gleaming mist (*Il.* 14.351), which conceals the couple making love even while pointing to the fertility of their *hieros gamos* (sacred wedding). Cf. Hom. *Od.* 5.232 (= *Od.* 10.545, of Circe), where Calypso completes her toilet by donning a *kaluptrēn.*

89. Liddell and Scott 1968, s.v. *liparos.*

90. Contra Heubeck and Hoekstra 1989:188 ad Hom. *Od.* 13.388, who explain the Homeric formula *lipara krēdemna* as deriving from an original meaning of *krēdemnon* not as a textile but as a metallic head binder, like a crown, which might aptly be described as "shining." On this view Homer, who understood the *krēdemnon* as the veil or shawl with sides hanging down worn by his contemporaries, retains the original descriptor although it is no longer apt. If this argument is correct, the *lipara*

krēdemna would be simply a synonym for a bright (golden) crown, such as that of Aphrodite described above.

91. On the association of virile fertility and the life force itself with wetness, see Giacomelli 1980. This notion surely informs Callimachus's description of Apollo's hair (*Ap.* 38–41) as locks that distill fragrant healing oils upon the ground. The same idea informs the Roman use of the Latin adjective *nitidus* (gleaming) applied to the head (*caput*), e.g., Horace *Carm.* 1.4.9, Tibullus 1.8.16, or to the hair (*caesaries, capillus, coma*), e.g., Vergil *Georgics* 4.337, Tibullus 1.7.51, 2.5.7–8, Ovid *Her.* 20.166. The adjective *nitidus* associates hair with glossy moisture and heavenly radiance, a connection perhaps originating in the Indo-European identification of Zeus with sky and weather; see *Oxford Latin Dictionary* s.v. *niteo* 1.4, *niditus* 1.4.5. Another instance of the association of the head and moisture with specific fertility implications is the Hebrew custom of anointing the king's hair with oil, e.g. 1 Sam. 10:1 (Saul), 16:13 (David).

92. Nagler notes that *lipara* is the most common epithet of *krēdemna;* 1974:58 n. 44. The veil (*kaluptrēn*) of Hecuba, the "super-mother" of Priam's many sons and daughters, is also *liparēn* in *Il.* 22.406.

93. Nagler cites an interesting inversion of the formula in the parodist Matron's description of the entrance of a *hetaira* who holds in front of her face a filthy, greasy *krēdemnon;* 1974, 67 n.5.

94. Translation adapted from Jones and Ormerod 1977, vol. 2, 131–33.

95. Festus, s.v. *nuptias,* Lindsay 1913:174: "Aelius and Cincius [on the derivation of *nuptias*]: since the head of the bride is veiled [*obvolvatur*] with a flame colored veil, [an act] that the ancients termed '*obnubere.*' For this reason [they say] that the law also bids veil [*obnubere*] the head of him who has slain a parent, that is to say, '*obvolvere.*' "

96. For an explicit exposition of the hierarchy of female–male–God in Judaism, see Abudraham 1963:25. In his discussion of women's exemption from "time-bound" commandments, Abudraham resolves any potential conflict between a woman's obligations to God and her obligations to her husband in favor of the latter—or as Milton said of Eve, "He for God only, she for God in him."

REFERENCES

Abudraham, David ben Joseph
    1963 [1541] *Abudraham HaShalem.* Jerusalem: T'hiya.
Allen, Thomas W., ed.
    1965 *Homeri Opera,* vol. 5. Oxford: Clarendon.
Ashkenazi, Betzalel
    1968 *Shitah Mekuvetzet (Asefat Z'kenim).* Jerusalem: Ma'oz Meir.
Austin, R. G., ed.
    1960 *M. Tulli Ciceronis Pro M. Caelio Oratio.* 3rd ed. Oxford: Clarendon.
Bal, Mieke
    1987 *Lethal Love: Feminist Literary Readings of Biblical Love Stories.* Bloomington: Indiana University Press.
Balsdon, J. P. V. D.
    1962 *Roman Women: Their History and Habits.* New York: J. Day.

Barnes, Hazel E.
1974 "The Look of the Gorgon." In *The Meddling Gods: Four Essays on Classical Themes*, 1–51. Lincoln: University of Nebraska Press.

Baumeister, A.
1889 *Denkmäler des klassischen Altertums*. Munich and Leipzig: R. Oldenbourg.

Beard, Mary
1980 "The Sexual Status of Vestal Virgins." *Journal of Roman Studies* 70:12–27.

Beit Hadash
Commentary on *Tur* code by Yoel Sirkes (ca. 1570–1641), printed in standard editions of *Tur.*

Bekker, I.
1889 *Charicles or Illustrations of the Private Life of the Ancient Greeks*. Trans. F. Metcalfe. 8th ed. London: Longmans, Green, and Co.

Ben-Yehuda, Eliezer
1959 *Thesaurus Totius Hebraitatis et Veteris et Recentioris*. New York and London: Thomas Yoseloff.

Berg, Charles
1951 *The Unconscious Significance of Hair.* London: George Allen and Unwin.

Bergren, Ann L. T.
1989 "The Homeric Hymn to Aphrodite: Tradition and Rhetoric, Praise and Blame." *Classical Antiquity* 8(1): 1–41.

Bloch, Abraham P.
1980 *The Biblical and Historical Background of Jewish Customs and Ceremonies*. New York: Ktav.

Bömer, Franz, comm.
1969 *P. Ovidius Naso Metamorphosen*. Buch I–III. Heidelberg: Carl Winter.

Bonfante, Larissa, and Eva Jaunzems
1988 "Clothing and Ornament." In *Civilization of the Ancient Mediterranean: Greece and Rome*, ed. by Michael Grant and Rachel Kitzinger, 3:1385–1413. New York: Scribner's.

Boswell, John
1980 *Christianity, Social Tolerance, and Homosexuality: Gay People in Western Europe from the Beginning of the Christian Era to the Fourteenth Century*. Chicago: University of Chicago Press.

Bremer, Walther
1911 *Die Haartracht des Mannes in archaisch-griechischer Zeit*. Dissertation. Giessen.
1912 "Haartracht und Haarschmuck. Griechenland." In *Paulys Real-Encyclopädie der Classischen Altertumswissenschaft*, 7:2109–35. Stuttgart: Metzler.

Brendel, Otto J.
1980 *The Visible Idea: Interpretations of Classical Art*. Washington, D.C.: Decatur House Press.

Burkert, Walter
1975 "Apellai und Apollon." *Rheinisches Museum* 118:1–21.
1985 *Greek Religion*. Trans. John Raffan. Cambridge: Harvard University Press.

1992   *The Orientalizing Revolution: Near Eastern Influence on Greek Culture in the Early Archaic Age.* Trans. Margaret Pinder and Walter Burkert. Cambridge: Harvard University Press.

Burn, A. R.
1966   *The Pelican History of Greece.* Baltimore and Harmondsworth, England: Penguin.

Carson, Anne
1990   "Putting Her in Her Place: Woman, Dirt, and Desire." In *Before Sexuality: The Construction of Erotic Experience in the Ancient Greek World,* ed. by David M. Halperin, John J. Winkler, and Froma I. Zeitlin, 135–69. Princeton: Princeton University Press.

Chill, Abraham
1979   *The Minhagim: The Customs and Ceremonies of Judaism, Their Origins and Rationale.* New York: Sepher-Hermon.

Cooper, Wendy
1971   *Hair: Sex, Society, Symbolism.* New York: Stein and Day.

Corson, Richard
1980   *Fashions in Hair: The First Five Thousand Years.* Chester Springs, Penn.: Dufour.

Daremberg, Charles, and Edmund Saglio
1877–1919   *Dictionnaire des antiquités grecques et romaines.* Paris: Hachette. [Daremberg-Saglio]

David, Ephraim
1992   "Sparta's Social Hair." *Eranos* 90:11–21.

Detienne, Marcel
1977   *The Gardens of Adonis: Spices in Greek Mythology.* Trans. Janet Lloyd, with an introduction by J.-P. Vernant. Sussex: Harvester Press.

Diehl, E.
1949–1952   *Anthologia Lyrica Graeca.* 3rd ed. Leipzig: Teubner.

Diels, H., and W. Kranz
1951   *Die Fragmente der Vorsokratiker.* 6th ed. Berlin: Weidmann.

Dover, Kenneth J.
1978   *Greek Homosexuality.* Cambridge: Harvard University Press.

Dudley, Donald
1967   *Urbs Roma.* London: Phaidon Press.

Ehrhardt, Christopher
1971   "Hair in Ancient Greece." *Echos du Monde Classique* 15:14–19.

Eisenstein, Judah David, ed.
1915   *Otzar Midrashim* ("Treasury of Midrashim"). New York.

Eliade, Mircea
1959   *Cosmos and History: The Myth of the Eternal Return.* Trans. Willard R. Trask. New York: Harper.
1960   *Myths, Dreams, and Mysteries.* Trans. Philip Mairet. London: Harvill.

Englert, John, and Timothy Long
1973   "Functions of Hair in Apuleius' *Metamorphoses*." *Classical Journal* 68: 236–39.

Epstein, Louis M.

1927   *The Jewish Marriage Contract: A Study of the Status of Women in Jewish Law.*
New York: Jewish Theological Seminary. (Reprinted: Arno, 1973.)

1942   *Marriage Laws in the Bible and the Talmud.* Cambridge: Harvard University
Press.

1948   *Sex Laws and Customs in Judaism.* New York: Bloch.

Evelyn-White, Hugh G., trans.

1914   *Hesiod: The Homeric Hymns and Homerica.* Loeb Classical Library 57. Cambridge, Mass., and London: Harvard University Press and Heinemann.

Feldman, Thalia

1965   "Gorgo and the Origin of Fear." *Arion* 4:484–94.

Ferenczi, Sándor

1952 [1923] "On the Symbolism of the Head of Medusa." In *Selected Papers,*
2:360. New York: Basic Books.

Firth, Raymond

1973   "Hair as Private Asset and Public Symbol." In *Symbols Public and Private,*
262–98. Ithaca: Cornell University Press.

Foley, Helene P.

1982   "Marriage and Sacrifice in Euripides' *Iphigenia in Aulis.''Arethusa* 15:
181–201.

Fraenkel, Hermann

1973   *Early Greek Poetry and Philosophy.* Trans. M. Hadas and J. Willis. New York
and London: Harcourt Brace Jovanovich.

Frazer, James G., trans.

1921   *Apollodorus: The Library.* 2 vols. Loeb Classical Library 121–122. Cambridge, Mass., and London: Harvard University Press and Heinemann.

Frazer, James G., ed., trans., and comm.

1929   *Publii Ovidii Nasonis Fastorum Libri Sex. The Fasti of Ovid.* With translation
and commentary. 5 vols. London: Macmillan.

Freud, Sigmund

1950 [1922] "Medusa's Head." In *Collected Papers,* ed. by James Strachey, 5:105–
6. London: Hogarth Press.

Frimer, Dov I.

1980   "Grounds for Divorce Due to Immoral Behavior (Other than Adultery)
According to Jewish Law" (in Hebrew). Ph.D. dissertation, Hebrew University of Jerusalem.

Frymer-Kensky, Tikva

1984   "The Strange Case of the Suspected Sotah (Numbers V 11–31)." *Vetus
Testamentum* 34(1):11–26.

Gershenson, Daniel

1989   "The Beautiful Gorgon and Indo-European Parallels." *The Mankind
Quarterly* 29(4): 373–90.

Giacomelli, Anne

1980   "Aphrodite and After." *Phoenix* 34:1–19.

Gleason, Maud W.

1990   "The Semiotics of Gender: Physiognomy and Self-Fashioning in the

Second Century C.E." In *Before Sexuality: The Construction of Erotic Experience in the Ancient Greek World*, ed. by David M. Halperin, John J. Winkler, and Froma I. Zeitlin, 389–415. Princeton: Princeton University Press.

Hallpike, Christopher R.
1969   "Social Hair." *Man* n.s. 4(2):256–64.
1987   "Hair." In *The Encyclopedia of Religion*, ed. by Mircea Eliade, 6:154–57. New York and London: Macmillan.

Heckscher, W. S.
1953   "Aphrodite as a Nun." *Phoenix* 7:105–17.

Heubeck, A., and A. Hoekstra
1989   *A Commentary on Homer's Odyssey. Vol. II: Books IX–XVI.* Oxford: Clarendon.

Heubeck, A., S. West, and J. B. Hainsworth
1988   *A Commentary on Homer's Odyssey. Vol. I: Introduction and Books I–VIII.* Oxford: Clarendon.

Huppat Hatanim
        See Mildola, Rafael H.

Idit, Meir
1972   "Head, Covering of the." *Encyclopedia Judaica*, 8:1–6. Jerusalem: Keter.

Jakobson, Roman
1990   *On Language.* Ed. by Linda R. Waugh and Monique Monville-Burston. Cambridge: Harvard University Press.

Jameson, Michael H.
1988   "Sacrifice and Ritual: Greece." In *Civilization of the Ancient Mediterranean: Greece and Rome*, ed. by Michael Grant and Rachel Kitzinger, 2:959–79. New York: Scribner's.
1990   "Perseus, the Hero of Mykenai." In *Celebrations of Death and Divinity in the Bronze Age Argolid* (Proceedings of the Sixth International Symposium at the Swedish Institute at Athens, 11–13 June, 1988), ed. by Robin Hägg and Gullög C. Nordquist, 213–23. Stockholm: Paul Astroms.

Jones, W. H. S., H. A. Ormerod, and R. E. Wycherley, trans.
1977   *Pausanias: Description of Greece.* 5 vols. Loeb Classical Library. Cambridge, Mass., and London: Harvard University Press and Heinemann. [different translators for different volumes]

Joseph, Ovadia
1985   *Yabia Omer: She'elot VeTshuvot.* 2nd ed. Vol. 6. Jerusalem: Published by author.

Kerenyi, C., and C. G. Jung
1969   *Essays on a Science of Mythology: The Myth of the Divine Child and the Mysteries of Eleusis.* Bollingen Series XXII. Princeton: Princeton University Press.

Kirk, G. S.
1986   *The Iliad: A Commentary. Vol. 1: Books 1–4.* Cambridge: Cambridge University Press.

Kirk, G. S., and J. E. Raven
  1963   *The Presocratic Philosophers*. Cambridge: Cambridge University Press.
Kötting, Bernhard
  1986   "Haar." In *Reallexikon für Antike und Christentum*, ed. by T. Klauser,
          13:177–203. Stuttgart: Hiersemann.
Kovacs, Maureen Gallery, trans.
  1985   *The Epic of Gilgamesh*. Stanford: Stanford University Press.
Krause, Johann Heinrich
  1858   *Plotina oder die Kostüme des Haupthaares bei den Völkern der alten Welt*. Leip-
          zig: Dyk'sche Buchhandlung.
Krauss, Samuel
  1945   *Kadmoniot HaTalmud* (Hebrew translation of *Talmudische Archäologie*,
          1910). Tel Aviv: D'vir.
Leach, Edmund
  1958   "Magical Hair." *Man: Journal of the Royal Anthropological Institute* 88:147–
          68.
Levy, Amnon
  1989   *HaHaredim* ("The Ultraorthodox"). Jerusalem: Keter.
Liddell, H. G., and R. Scott
  1968   *A Greek-English Lexicon*. Oxford: Clarendon.
Lindsay, Wallace M.
  1913   *Sexti Pompei Festi de verborum significatu quae supersunt cum Pauli epitome*.
          Leipzig: Teubner.
Lissarrague, François
  1990   "The Sexual Life of Satyrs." In *Before Sexuality: The Construction of Erotic
          Experience in the Ancient Greek World*, ed. by David M. Halperin, John J.
          Winkler, and Froma I. Zeitlin, 53–81. Princeton: Princeton University
          Press.
Lobel, E., and D. Page, eds.
  1935   *Poetarum Lesbiorum Fragmenta*. Oxford: Clarendon.
Loraux, Nicole
  1990   "Herakles: The Super-Male and the Feminine." In *Before Sexuality: The
          Construction of Erotic Experience in the Ancient Greek World*, ed. by David M.
          Halperin, John J. Winkler, and Froma I. Zeitlin, 21–52. Princeton:
          Princeton University Press.
Lorimer, Hilda L.
  1950   *Homer and the Monuments*. London: Macmillan.
MacMullen, Ramsay
  1980   "Women in Public in the Roman Empire." *Historia* 29:208–18.
Maiuri, A.
  1953   *Roman Painting*. Lausanne: Skira.
Marinatos, Spyridon
  1967   *Kleidung, Haar- und Barttracht*. Archaeologia Homerica, vol. 1. Göttingen:
          Vandenhoeck & Ruprecht.
Marquardt, Joachim
  1886   *Das Privatleben der Römer*. 2nd ed. with A. Mau. Leipzig: S. Hirzel.

Mayor, J. E. B.
1901   *Thirteen Satires of Juvenal with a Commentary.* 2 vols. 2nd ed. London: Macmillan.
Melville, A. D., trans.
1986   *Ovid: Metamorphoses.* New York: Oxford University Press.
Merkelbach, R., and M. L. West, eds.
1967   *Fragmenta Hesiodea.* Oxford: Clarendon.
Mildola, Rafael H.
1796   *Huppat Hatanim.* Livorno. (Reprinted Jerusalem, 1983.)
Mylonas, George E.
1945   "A Signet-Ring in the City Art Museum of St. Louis." *American Journal of Archaeology* 49:557–69.
Nagler, Michael N.
1967   "Toward a Generative View of the Oral Formula." *Transactions of the American Philological Association* 98:269–311.
1974   *Spontaneity and Tradition: A Study in the Oral Art of Homer.* Berkeley and Los Angeles: University of California Press.
Nelson, Jill
1987   "Enough to Curl Your Hair: When Hair Style and Political Self Image Are Intertwined, Coif Confusion Ensues." *The Washington Post Magazine,* 6 December, pp. 44–45.
Neumann, G.
1965   *Gesten und Gebärden in der griechischen Kunst.* Berlin: De Gruyter.
Nisbet, R. G. M., and M. Hubbard
1975   *A Commentary on Horace: Odes Book 1.* Oxford: Clarendon.
North, Helen
1966   *Sophrosyne: Self-Knowledge and Self-Restraint in Greek Literature.* Ithaca: Cornell University Press.
1977   "The Mare, the Vixen, and the Bee: *Sophrosyne* as the Virtue of Women in Antiquity." *Illinois Classical Studies* 11:35–48.
Oakley, John H.
1982   "The Anakalypteria." *Archäologischer Anzeiger* 97:113–18.
Oakley, John H., and Rebecca H. Sinos
1993   *The Wedding in Ancient Athens.* Madison: University of Wisconsin Press.
Obeyesekere, Gananath
1981   *Medusa's Hair: An Essay on Personal Symbols and Religious Experience.* Chicago: University of Chicago Press.
O'Brian, Joan
1983   "Nammu, Ami, Eve and Pandora: What's in a Name?" *Classical Journal* 79:35–45.
Onians, Richard Broxton
1951   *The Origins of European Thought about the Body, the Mind, the Soul, the World, Time, and Fate.* Cambridge: Cambridge University Press.
Oxford Latin Dictionary
1982   Oxford: Clarendon.
Patai, Raphael
1978   *The Hebrew Goddess.* New York: Avon.

Perrin, Bernadotte
  1914   *Plutarch's Lives.* 10 vols. Loeb Classical Library. London and New York: Heinemann and Macmillan.
Plaut, W. Gunther
  1955   "The Origin of the Word 'Yarmulke.'" *Hebrew Union College Annual* 26:567–70.
Pomeroy, Sarah B.
  1984   *Women in Hellenistic Egypt from Alexander to Cleopatra.* New York: Shocken.
Rabinowitz, Nancy S.
  1986   "Female Speech and Female Sexuality: Euripides' *Hippolytos* as Model." In *Rescuing Creusa: New Methodological Approaches to Women in Antiquity,* ed. by Marylin Skinner. *Helios Special Issue* 13(2):127–40.
Rashi (Solomon Yitzhaki, 1040–1105 C.E.)
            Torah Commentary. Printed in standard edition of Hebrew Bible.
            Talmud Commentary. Printed in standard edition of Talmud.
Redfield, James
  1975   *Nature and Culture in the Iliad: The Tragedy of Hector.* Chicago: University of Chicago Press.
  1982   "Notes on the Greek Wedding." *Arethusa* 15:169–99.
Richardson, N. J., ed.
  1974   *The Homeric Hymn to Demeter.* Oxford: Clarendon.
Rose, H. J.
  1959   *A Handbook of Greek Mythology.* New York: Dutton.
Rouse, W. H. D.
  1902   *Greek Votive Offerings.* Cambridge: The University Press.
Schibli, Hermann S.
  1990   *Pherekydes of Syros.* Oxford: Clarendon Press.
Scholem, Gershom
  1972   "Lilith." *Encyclopaedia Judaica,* 11:245–49. Jerusalem: Keter.
Schredelseker, Paul
  1913   *De superstitionibus Graecorum quae ad crines pertinent.* Dissertation. Heidelberg.
Segal, Charles
  1982   *Dionysiac Poetics and Euripides' Bacchae.* Princeton: Princeton University Press.
Shulchan Aruch by Rabbi Joseph Karo (1488–1575)
  1927   Berlin: Chorev.
Simon, Erika.
  1967   *Ara Pacis Augustae.* Greenwich, Conn.: New York Graphic Society (also Tübingen: Verlag Ernst Wasmuth).
Sissa, Giulia
  1990   *Greek Virginity.* Trans. Arthur Goldhammer. Cambridge: Harvard University Press.
Slater, Philip E.
  1968   *The Glory of Hera: Greek Mythology and the Greek Family.* Boston: Beacon.

Sommer, Ludwig

    1912A   "Haaropfer." In *Paulys Real-Encyclopädie der Classischen Altertumswissenschaft*, 7:2105–9. Stuttgart: Metzler.

    1912B   *Das Haar in Religion und Aberglauben der Griechen.* Inaugural-Dissertation. Münster.

Sperling, Abraham Isaac

    1982 [1890]   *Sefer Ta`ame HaMinhagim Umekore HaDinim* ("The Book of the Reasons for the Customs and Sources for the Laws"). Jerusalem: Eshkol.

Steininger, R.

    1912   "Haartracht und Haarschmuck. Rom." In *Paulys Real-Encyclopädie der Classischen Altertumswissenschaft*, 7:2135–50. Stuttgart: Metzler.

Swidler, Leonard

    1976   *Women in Judaism: The Status of Women in Formative Judaism.* Metuchen, N. J.: Scarecrow Press.

Toutain, J.

    1940   "Le rite nuptial de l'anakalypterion." *Revue des Etudes Anciennes* 42:345–53.

Tur

    Legal code, by Jacob b. Asher (Baal HaTurim, ca. 1270–1343). 1st edition, Pieve de Sachi, 1475; Warsaw, 1863.

Van der Valk, M., ed.

    1971   *Eustathii Archiepiscopi Thessalonicensis Commentarii ad Homeri Iliadem pertinentes.* Vol. 1. Leiden: Brill.

Vanggaard, Jens H.

    1988   *The Flamen: A Study in the History and Sociology of Roman Religion.* Copenhagen: Museum Tusculanum Press.

Vernant, Jean-Pierre

    1989   "At Man's Table: Hesiod's Foundation Myth of Sacrifice." In *The Cuisine of Sacrifice among the Greeks*, ed. by Marcel Detienne and Jean-Pierre Vernant, trans. by Paula Wissing, 21–86. Chicago: University of Chicago Press.

    1991   *Mortals and Immortals: Collected Essays.* ed. by Froma I. Zeitlin. Princeton: Princeton University Press.

Veyne, Paul

    1987   "The Roman Empire." In *A History of Private Life. I: From Pagan Rome to Byzantium*, ed. by Paul Veyne, trans. by A. H. Goldhammer, 5–233. Cambridge, Mass., and London: Belknap Press of Harvard University Press.

Weinrich, Otto

    1924/1925   "Eine delphische Mirakel-Inschrift und die antiken Haarwunder." *Sitzungsberichte der Heidelberger Akademie der Wissenschaften, Philosophisch-Historische Klasse* 7:1–11.

West, M. L., ed.

    1966   *Hesiod Theogony.* Oxford: Clarendon.

Wilken, G. A.

    1886   "Über das Haaropfer und einige andere Trauergebräuche bei den Völkern Indonesiens." *Revue Coloniale Internationale* 2:225–69.

Wilson, Lillian M.
    1938   *The Clothing of the Ancient Romans.* Baltimore: Johns Hopkins University
            Press.
Zeitlin, Froma I.
    1978   "The Dynamics of Misogyny: Myth and Mythmaking in the Oresteia."
            Arethusa 11:149–84. (Reprinted in *Women in the Ancient World: The Are-
            thusa Papers,* ed. by John Peradotto and J. P. Sullivan, 159–94 [Albany:
            State University of New York Press, 1984].)

FIVE

⸺⸺

Veils, Virgins, and the Tongues
of Men and Angels

Women's Heads in Early Christianity

Mary Rose D'Angelo

*It appears very trifling for men, commissioned to do so great a work on earth,
to give so much thought to the toilets of women.*
ELIZABETH CADY STANTON, *THE WOMAN'S BIBLE* (1899)

Elizabeth Cady Stanton's wonderment at the preoccupation of early Christian male writers with women's clothing—and, in particular, headdress—
directs our attention to the real foreground of early Christian writings on
women's heads: the minds of men. For early Christian men, as, it seems,
for men of antiquity in general, women's heads were indeed sexual members, and at least two of these men, Paul and Tertullian, expended much
thought and no little ink in efforts to enforce the sexual character of
women's heads. Their association of women's heads and genitals seems to
be entirely conscious; in the case of Tertullian, it is startlingly explicit. It
is far from clear, on the other hand, that early Christian women experienced their heads as sexual organs. While it is possible to discern traces
of the women's religious clothing and hairdressing practices in the works
of these men, we have no direct access to the meanings the women themselves gave them. Antiquity provides some clues suggesting that these meanings may have differed widely from male interpretations of women's bodies
and dress. But for the most part, the women of early Christianity are visible
to later generations only through the eroticizing veil of the male gaze.

Two early Christian texts exercise the powers of theology and exegesis
in the interests of the demand that women veil their heads. In 1 Corinthians
11:2–16 (usually dated between 52 and 60 C.E.), Paul attempts to ration-
alize his prescription that women who pray and prophesy in the assembly
must be veiled. *De virginibus velandis* (That virgins must be veiled) is a tract
written by the North African ecclesiastical rhetor Tertullian around the
year 211, as he moved deeper into the rigors and ecstasies of the New

131

Prophecy, a proto-charismatic movement of early Christianity, also known as Montanism.[1] The two texts have much in common. Both base themselves in the supposed demands of nature, both extrapolate their prescriptions from the creation accounts of Genesis, both decapitate the women of the community in the interests of the superior status of men. All of this is hardly surprising: the interpretation of 1 Cor. 11:2–16 is an issue of debate in Tertullian's Carthage, and Tertullian seeks to use this passage, as well as the writings of some of Paul's early interpreters, as justification for his own demands.

But there are significant commonalities in the situations of the two writers as well. First, Paul and Tertullian are both attempting to change the current practice; in both cases, it is the unveiled women who can claim to have tradition on their side. Second, both write in the context of communities which are in the process of establishing themselves, and both must deal with the issue of religious innovation in a culture in which antiquity is the test of truth. Third, in both communities, prophecy is a central form of discourse, and women share in the prophetic gifts. Fourth, angels attend upon the assembly in both contexts and play a role not only in the visions and revelations but also in the conduct of the community.

1 COR. 11:2–16:
A WOMAN MUST HAVE AN AUTHORITY UPON HER HEAD

Amid attempts to moderate the Corinthian church's enthusiasms for the wisdom he taught them and the charismatic power they experienced at his preaching, Paul launches into a tortured exposition of the right tradition with regard to women's heads:

11:2 I praise you because you remember me in everything, and as I handed over to you, you hold fast my traditions.

3 But I want you to know that the head of every man is Christ, the man head of woman, and God the head of Christ.

4 Every man praying or prophesying with his head covered shames his head,

5 But every women praying or prophesying with her head uncovered shames her head; for it is one and the same thing with a shaven woman.

6 For if a women does not cover herself, let her also be shorn. But if it is shameful for a women to be shorn or shaven, let her be covered.

7 For a man ought not to cover his head, being the image and glory of God, but the woman is a man's glory.

8 For man is not from woman, but woman from man,

9 And man was not created on account of the woman, but woman on account of the man.

10 Therefore, the woman ought to have an *exousia* upon her head on account of the angels.

11 But neither woman without man nor man without woman in the Lord,

12 For as the woman from the man, so also the man through the woman, but all things are from God.

13 Judge for yourselves: is it proper for a woman to pray to God with her head uncovered?

14 Does not nature itself teach you that if a man has long hair, it is a dishonor to him?

15 But if a woman has long hair, it is a glory to her, because her hair is given to her in place of a garment.

16 But if someone thinks to be contentious, we do not hold such a custom, nor do the churches of God.

The translation above attempts to preserve the ambiguities of 1 Cor. 11:2–16, a cryptic and convoluted passage whose every line, indeed, every word, seems to have inspired disputes in the scholarly literature. To this interpreter, at least, Paul's goal is clear: he wants the women of the Corinthian community to cover their heads when they pray or prophesy in the assembly.[2] This goal emerges in the commands he gives: "Let her be shorn [or] . . . let her be covered. . . . Judge for yourselves: is it proper for a woman to pray to God with her head uncovered?" (5–6, 13).[3] 1 Corinthians 14 shows that praying and prophesying imply addressing the community and leading it in prayer; at least in 1 Cor. 11:3–16 Paul assumes that this sort of leadership is open to women, and makes no attempt to control it.[4]

The arguments with which Paul supports his demand for the veil are much less clear. Considering that women generally did wear headcoverings in the Greek-speaking imperial world, the difficulty with which Paul makes his case is striking.[5] He first puts forward a set of arguments from theology and scripture (3–10) which are themselves difficult to elucidate, but whose general trend is clear enough. They begin from the claim that the man is head of the woman, as God is of Christ, and Christ of the man (3). The woman, then, is head of no one. Indeed, she is virtually decapitated; the commands to be veiled or shorn are introduced with a sort of pun in which the women's own head and her man/husband seem to be conflated: a woman who prays without covering her head shames her head/husband.[6]

Some scholars have suggested that the word "head" is to be seen here as meaning "source" rather than "ruler."[7] It is probable that the use of "head" here does imply "source." In 1 Cor. 11:7–9 Paul draws upon Genesis 1–2 (1:27, 2:18, and 2:21–23) to claim that the woman's creation is derivative, that she is from and for the man. Thus her relation to God as source is second to the man's; she is (only) the glory of a man, who is the image and glory of God (11:7). In such a context, "head" as "source" does not exclude "head" as "ruler" but justifies it.[8]

The conclusion to 11:7–9 ought to be: a woman must be married, and must be submissive to her husband. But Paul does not draw this conclusion, either here or anywhere in the undisputed letters. The conclusion that he does draw (11:10) is difficult in the extreme: therefore a woman ought to have an *exousia* (authority) upon her head, because of the angels. The Greek word *exousia* does not refer to authority only as an abstraction; rather, it can also designate a spiritual being, or a class of spiritual beings. It is possible that here too Paul attempts a pun: a woman ought to have an *exousia*, that is, an authority or husband, upon her head. Thus the verse would claim that women must be married.[9] But among both contemporary and ancient interpreters the word *exousia* is almost universally understood to refer to a covering or veil, and interpreted to mean the veil as a sign of authority.[10] Its exact import is disputed; it can be seen as a sign of a husband's authority over the woman, or of her own authority over her own head.[11] But the difference is less than is sometimes supposed; whether the veil confesses her submission or supplies her deficiency, the woman's own unveiled head remains deficient.

Equally problematic is the final phrase: "on account of the angels." Nothing has prepared the twentieth-century reader for the introduction of angels at this point. A wide variety of theories have been advanced to identify "the angels" and to explain why they require women's heads to be veiled. Commentators from Tertullian on have taken the view that Paul requires women's heads to be veiled lest the angels be sexually tempted, as were the sons of God in Gen. 6:1–4 who figure so prominently in *1 Enoch*.[12] Since verse 10 draws a conclusion to the arguments from Genesis 1–2, the angels in question may be the angels who were present at the creation of the first human beings and who presided over their sojourn in paradise (like the angels of the *Apocalypse of Moses*) or who objected to their creation (like the angels of *Genesis Rabbah*).[13] It has also been suggested that the angels are the guardians of the liturgical order in the Corinthian assembly, as they are in the community reflected in the Qumran texts.[14] Angels play a significant role in the cosmological lives of Paul and the Corinthians. It is apparently the tongues of angels that the Corinthians believe they speak in glossolalia (13:1), and the Corinthian preference for celibacy may reflect their claim to "live like the angels."[15] With human beings, angels are the spectators at cosmic contests in which Paul is put on display (4:9–13), and the Corinthians can expect that they themselves will judge the angels (6:2–3). Thus the angels appear to be ambiguous and mysterious figures in Corinth, who might either enforce the order of the assembly or avail themselves of its sexual disorder.

Paul's use of the Genesis texts not only removes the woman's ability to act as head, but also robs her of her role as source of life, explicitly denying that the man is from the woman (11:8). He does not explicitly require submission to a husband; but this text and 1 Cor. 12:12–31 will provide the materials for a new use of Genesis in Ephesians 5:25–31. There the husband is head of the wife who is his flesh (Gen. 2:23–24), and the woman has become fully decapitated: she neither is a head nor has one.

Paul himself seems not to be entirely satisfied with his case thus far. In 1 Cor. 11:11–12, he backs off from the argument from the creation accounts of Genesis, relativizing his claim of the derivative character of the woman's creation and conceding her a role in procreation and perhaps also "in the Lord."[16] But he in no way modifies his demand. Verses 13–16 supply three more or less new arguments, from propriety, nature, and custom. In 3–10 Paul attempts to shame the unveiled women, insisting on the veil because of the low and secondary character of the woman. Having evoked that shame, he can afford to shift tactics; in 13–15 he appeals to the women's *amour propre*, without in any way qualifying his demand that they cover their heads in the assembly.

The twentieth-century reader tends to find Paul's argument from nature less than convincing, and indeed nearly risible. To the query "Does not *nature* itself teach you that if a man has long hair, it is a dishonor [*atimia*] to him?" we are inclined to answer, "no." His further postulate, "but if a woman has long hair, it is a glory [*doxa*] to her, because her hair is given to her in place of a garment," is likely to inspire the rejoinder, "then she ought not to need a veil." But for most of Paul's contemporaries, "nature" would have been little distinguished from the propriety invoked in 11:13, and the assumption that long hair is a dishonor to men but a glory to women would have been widely shared in the Romanized milieu of Corinth.[17]

But why does Paul believe that by putting long hair on a woman's head, nature indicates that she ought to wear a veil? This statement makes some sense if Paul sees an analogy between the woman's head, on which hair grows profusely, and the genitals of both men and women, where hair also grows more abundantly, and which (at least in Paul's view) must be covered in public.[18] Men's heads are different, in that they can be shaven or go bald without causing shame (1 Cor. 11:4–6).

Paul's concern with women's heads in 1 Cor. 11:3–16 finds an echo in the discussion of spiritual things in 1 Corinthians 12–14 that usually goes unnoted. In 1 Corinthians 12–14 he seeks to relativize the Corinthians' preference for speaking in tongues as a sign of the possession of the spirit. The body image of 1 Cor. 12:12–31 is a plea for diversity and harmony in the exercise of communal function, which insists that body parts (charismatic functions) must differ in order to make up a body, i.e., not everyone needs to speak in tongues. Throughout 1 Cor. 12:12–31 Paul develops the body image in the service of his argument that any gift or service manifests the spirit in the community, though prophecy (like apostleship) is superior to speaking in tongues.[19] In the course of this expanded analogy, Paul makes a special point with regard to the private parts:

> What we consider to be the more dishonorable parts [*ta atimotera*] of the body we dress with greater honor [*timēn*], and our shameful parts [*ta askhēmona hēmōn*] have greater seemliness [*euskhēmosunēn*], whereas our seemly parts [*ta euskhēmona*] have no need [of it]. But God has so composed the body, giving greater honor [*timēn*] to the one who is lacking. (12:23–24)

The elaboration of the image in 12:23–24 probably intimates that the gift of speaking in tongues, as the equivalent of the flashier clothing, is not a sign of the greater honor accorded to those who practice it, but rather a cover-up of their "shame."

Paul does not forget other issues when he focuses on one. When he observes in 12:22 that the members of the body that seem to be weaker are more necessary, he probably thinks of his apostolic defense, especially 4:8–13, but also of his counsel of concern for the weak in conscience in 8:7–13. It may be that 12:23–24 functions not only to undercut the prestige of tongues but also to reinforce the commands of 11:4–6 and the argument of 11:14–15. Women's heads are like, or are, the shameful (that is, sexual) members, which require a covering—thus as nature clothed them with hair and it is a glory to them, "we" must dress them in greater honor, for they have need of seemliness.[20] Thus glorious hair, like the spectacular aspects of tongues, becomes an indicator of what is shameful.[21]

This combination of sexual innuendo (11:4–6, 13–15) with the claims of creation and of nature (11:3–10, 14–15) is heavy rhetorical artillery. What is the situation that raises Paul's concern to such a level? It seems that, in requiring women to cover their heads when they pray and prophesy, Paul is trying to change established practice in the Corinthian community, perhaps even practice he himself taught them. He begins his argument by conceding the Corinthians' fidelity to his traditions (11:2), and closes it by insisting that neither he nor the other churches hold "this custom" (11:16), that is, women praying and prophesying with uncovered heads. The use of "pray" and "prophesy" in 1 Corinthians 14 makes clear that these words indicate a type of community leadership within a charismatic setting; the women of Corinth share in the leadership of the assembly, which seems to proceed by the spontaneous experience and sharing of gifts of word and wisdom (cf. 1:5–7). To do this they remove the veils which were a normal part of the dress of mature respectable women in public settings.[22]

While we have no direct access to the rationale behind the "custom" in Corinth, the letters of Paul give us grounds for speculation about the "tradition" upon which it is based. It has long been recognized that Gal. 3:26–28 preserves a tradition associated with the baptismal practice of the early Christian mission.[23] This tradition might well be the source of conflict over gender roles: it proclaims, "All you who have been baptized into Christ have put on Christ. There is among you neither Jew nor Greek, neither slave nor free, no 'male and female.'" The context in 1 Corinthians gives some clues that this tradition may indeed be at issue in Corinth. In 1 Cor. 12:13, Paul cites a similar baptismal tradition, but does not include the problematic pair "male and female." In 1 Cor. 7:20–24, he asserts that slavery and freedom, circumcision and uncircumcision, are nothing in Christ, in order to dissuade the Corinthians from seeking either divorce or marriage. He may have attempted to avoid the more problematic consequence of the declaration "no 'male and female'" by interpreting it as "no [advantage for] married and unmarried."

Reconstructions of the position of the Corinthian women beginning from Gal. 3:28 have tended to focus upon theological, exegetical, and even philosophical rationales for the Corinthian women's practice. It is equally important to reflect upon its relation to baptismal practice. No direct evidence about baptismal ceremonies survives from this very early period, but it is tempting to use later baptismal practice to imagine a liturgical function for Gal. 3:27–28 in the light of later rituals. In later years, candidates were baptized in the nude, then ceremonially reclothed and led into the congregation.[24] In light of this pattern, Gal. 3:27–28 might be seen as preserving a greeting to the newly baptized. After the bath they were all clothed in a single full-length garment (the *chiton* or *enduma*), without the outer garments, headgear, and ornaments that would normally reflect sexual and social distinctions.[25] As they were presented to the assembled community, the presider commented upon their new and uniform clothing: "All you who have been baptized into Christ have put on [*enedusasthe*] Christ. There is among you neither Jew nor Greek, neither slave nor free, no 'male and female.'"[26] Not all marks of distinction could be obliterated by the *enduma*. Slave collars or brands might not be hidden by it.[27] But in the context of baptism the common reclothing would be a powerful sign against such marks of servitude. It may be that, for the women of the community, the baptismal reclothing did not include the veil, and their uncovered heads were thus a sign of their new status. In the antique Jewish novel *Aseneth,* the eponymous heroine, Aseneth, is told that she need not wear a veil on the day of her wedding/entry into Judaism; on that day, her head is like the head of a young man.[28]

The women in the Corinthian community (and, despite 11:16, perhaps of other communities as well) may have rejected the wearing of veils on the basis of their experience of "putting on Christ" in baptism. They would thus have sought to continue the baptismal practice within the assembly, asserting that the gendered, sexual meaning given to their heads was abrogated "in Christ"—through their baptism and within the community.[29] They ritually affirm their equality to men when they speak in the assembly, as a sign of the authority of their prophetic voices.

I might then theorize that Paul sexualizes, or rather resexualizes, the heads of the women prophets in the community for the same reasons that Howard Eilberg-Schwartz suggests that the rabbis sexualized women's heads—in order to silence women's voices.[30] But in fact Paul does not silence the women's voices, but takes their prophetic role for granted.[31] Women prophets, and indeed women who function in the mission as ministers, apostles, and laborers, are a given in Paul's reality. He must take them into account, not merely tolerating them, but relying upon their support and patronage, as he does in his appeal to the Romans.[32] It is specifically when the women pray and prophesy in the assembly that Paul requires a headcovering. 1 Cor. 14:34–35 does indeed command women to be silent in the assembly. But the provenance of this passage is uncertain, and while the textual evidence of interpolation is not strong, the conflict with 1 Cor. 11:4–6 is nearly insuperable.[33] Thus it seems most likely that 1 Cor. 14:34–35 voices the views of a zealous disciple of the "Paul" of the Pastorals.[34]

Thus Paul does not silence the women prophets of the Corinthian community but rather seeks to control the circumstances under which they prophesy. Ross Kraemer has analyzed the Corinthian situation in the light of Mary Douglas's anthropological theories and has suggested that the significance of Paul's need to control the heads of prophesying women is directly connected with his interest in a higher degree of social definition in the other aspects of the Corinthian assembly's ecstatic experiences. In the face of Corinthian "antiritual" attitudes and practice, Paul struggles to reassert social constraints, and in particular the distinction of women from men.[35] On the basis of their participation in the ecstatic and charismatic gifts of the community, Kraemer concludes, the women of the Corinthian assembly have attained "a status, authority and prestige which Paul found extraordinarily offensive and problematic."[36]

Paul, and perhaps others of the Corinthian community, would almost certainly have defined the area of that offense as the area of sexual morality. The Corinthian community is a new community; even if Paul does not fully distinguish early Christianity from Judaism, Christianity is certainly new within cities like Corinth. It celebrates its newness in a cultural context in which innovation in religion is highly suspect, is associated with immorality, especially sexual immorality, and is excusable only on the basis of some claim to ancient authority. Precisely in sexual mores, the early Christian community in general and the community in Corinth in particular stretch the boundaries of what is acceptable. In 1 Corinthians 7 Paul seeks to protect the community against "immoralities" that might follow from the preference for celibacy which Paul himself shares (7:1–2) and which he endorses also for women (7:39–40). He thus affirms the prior claims of marriage, at least preexisting marriage. For Paul and the Corinthians, refusing sexual activity brings freedom. But marriage keeps the spouse within the bonds of sex (7:4). A woman may not divorce and remarry; neither may a man. A wife may not refuse sex, nor may a husband. The woman does not have authority (*exousiazei*) over her own body; her husband does. Likewise, a man's body is subject to his wife's sexual authority. But the reciprocity that goes for the "body" does not go for the head; a woman must have an "authority" upon her head which is not necessary for the man. If Paul's commands on behalf of marriage and sex are not easy to reconcile with his counsels of virginity and restraint (*enkrateia*), both are preceded and, it seems, introduced by the very clear sanctions against "immorality" in 6:12–20. 1 Corinthians 5 also demonstrates that in Paul's mind things in Corinth have gotten beyond what is morally acceptable.

Paul's anxiety about female sexual morality as a threat to communal mores appears also in Rom. 1:18–32, where female sexual perversion, with female homoeroticism as its prime example, heads the list of vices that demonstrate the God-forsakenness of those who refused to recognize God's eternal and invisible nature. As male homoeroticism involves the feminization of at least one partner in the eyes of Paul and his contemporaries, so female homoeroticism reveals itself as perverse autonomy. Any assertive woman, but especially a sexually assertive woman, is an unnatural and perverted woman.[37] In 1 Cor. 11:3–10 it is specifically female derivativeness, the secondary creation of woman inscribed by means of the texts of Genesis, her "natural" lack of autonomy, that must be signaled by the veil. Paul sees the choice of bareheadedness as an assertion of autonomy with sexual overtones.

Thus for Paul the veil, like the support of marriage, is necessary to protect the practices he has approved—or accepted—in other areas: first and foremost, that a woman may pray and prophesy in the assembly, but also that a woman may remain single. There is even an acknowledgment (though hardly an approval) that a woman may separate from her husband, in Paul's insistence that a woman who does so must not remarry.[38] Of course this does not mean that in requiring the veil, Paul merely concedes to external mores what he hopes will satisfy outsiders. On the contrary, the reference to the angels shows that he experiences the threat to communal mores as real and internal.

THE HEADS OF WOMEN AND THE EYES OF MEN

What, then, makes the woman's head sexual? I would like to suggest that the answer is implicit in 1 Cor. 11:2–16: what sexualizes the female head is the sexual authority, the dominance of the male gaze. That it is specifically (though not only) the woman's head which is sexualized might be explained in terms of a new anthropological principle which we may call the "ankle principle." At the beginning of the twentieth century, women's ankles were highly eroticized because they could sometimes, but not always, be seen, because they had to be observed partially and in stolen glances. More generally, that part of a woman's body which is sometimes but not always, or partly but not wholly, vulnerable to a man's gaze is particularly erotic. Thus a woman's head stands for her genitals by a kind of erotic metonymy. In the *anakaluptēria* (unveiling) of Greek wedding rituals, the bridegroom removed the veil that covered the bride's face as a sign of his right to also "unloosen her girdle."[39]

A wide variety of texts from the first centuries of the common era illustrate the relation between the male gaze and the sexualization of the woman's head. Among the most entertaining of these is that of the North African novelist, philosopher, and sometime magician, Apuleius, the second-century magic realist. In *Metamorphoses* (*The Golden Ass*), Apuleius's Lucius (in his pre-Ass state) gives a stunning description of the erotic attractions of women's hair (2.8). He prefaces it with the assurance that he makes it his prime concern (*cura*) first, in public, to *see* the head and hair of women and afterward, at home, to *enjoy* them. He identifies hair and head as the *praecipua*—foremost, conspicuous, most important—parts of the body, the ones that leap first to the eye. Like Paul, he makes an analogy between clothing and hair—though for Apuleius the function of both is to make the body more alluring, with colorful, luxuriant brilliance. Of course, discarding clothing only improves its function in Apuleius's (or at least Lucius's) eyes. The same cannot be said of hair; again like Paul, he finds a bald woman a horrifying idea (2.8–9).

It is clear that Lucius's twin goals of publicly seeing and privately enjoying women's hair involve some effort. But his effort does not go unrewarded. The panegyric on women's hair introduces the interview in which Lucius makes an assignation with the young serving girl Fotis (2.10). After a tantalizing postponement of this pleasure, Lucius describes the rich abandon of its fulfillment (2.16–17). Fotis transforms herself into a vision of Venus, stripping off her clothes, then, in response to Lucius's pleas, letting down her luxuriant hair, and "with her rosy palm rather overshadowing her smooth [hairless, probably depilated] femininity out of industry rather than covering it with modesty" (2.17).[40] In the preliminary interview Lucius achieves the sight of her hair; later he achieves the enjoyment of it, as a prelude to the vision and enjoyment of her "smooth femininity."

It should not be assumed, of course, that Lucius's precoital rhapsodies represent normal Roman mores. On the contrary, propriety and good taste would be deeply disappointing to the reader who has been promised a Greek, and indeed a Milesian, tale. Our passage is clearly intended to be one of the "good parts" of the novel. When Lucius, having at last cast himself upon the mercy of the moon Goddess, draws near to the rose wreath that will bring him salvation from his en-Assment, he describes the initiates in the Isis-procession by the shining shaven heads of the men and the women's pomaded hair swathed in a light covering (11.10).

This solemn picture of the initiates conforms better to the perspective of Roman moral sobriety that is voiced by Valerius Maximus in the early part of the first century:

> There was also the harsh marital severity of Gaius Sulpicius Gallus. He divorced his wife because he had caught her outdoors with her head uncovered: a stiff penalty, but not without a certain logic. "The law," he said, "prescribes you for my eyes alone to which you may prove your beauty. For these eyes you should provide the ornaments of beauty, for these be lovely: entrust yourself to their more certain knowledge. If you, with needless provocation, invite the look of anyone else, you must be suspected of wrongdoing."[41]

Thus the head of a woman should be covered in order to reserve her person for the gaze of the husband alone; and the woman who does otherwise is guilty of "provocation," of "inviting" the gaze of another. Valerius's inclusion of the vignette marks it as "memorable," i.e., an extreme case; it represents normal mores no more than does *The Golden Ass*. But neither is G. Sulpicius Gallus presented as a bad example. Valerius includes the anecdote with two other examples of severity toward women and concludes: "And so, long ago, when the misdeeds of women were thus forestalled, their minds stayed far from wrongdoing."[42]

Texts from Judaism of the period also reveal the conviction that the exposing of women's heads to the gaze of men is a sexual violation. For a man to remove a woman's veil in public is both insult and injury. A story in *Avot de Rabbi Natan A* 3 provides a particularly good example about a man who "transgressed the words of Rabbi Akiba" and uncovered a woman's head in the marketplace.[43] When Akiba fined him 400 zuz (a very substantial sum of money), he tried to avoid the fine by luring the woman to uncover her own head publicly in order to use up oil worth a very small amount. Akiba decides against him, asserting: "The one who injures himself, albeit he is not permitted to do so, is not culpable; but if others injure him, they are culpable. She who abused herself is not culpable, but thou who didst abuse her, go and give her 400 zuz."[44]

Thus the woman's self-respect is involved; the veil is a sign of her dignity and to remove it is an insult as well as an assault and marks her as a "common" woman.[45] But for Rabbinic writers, as for Valerius's Roman audience, the veil is also a sign of submission, and particularly of sexual submission. *Avot de Rabbi Natan A* 1 makes this clear. The passage is a comment upon Gen. 3:16:

> "[Your desire will be for your husband,] And he shall rule over thee:" for a man demands gratification openly, but a women demands it in her heart, her head covered like a mourner and as though she were bound in prison and banned from all men.[46]

"Gratification" here refers to sexual gratification. The woman's sexual desire must be cloaked and hooded. The headcovering is the guardian of those arrangements of sexual politics according to which a man has the sexual initiative and a woman does not.[47]

Lucius, Sulpicius Gallus, and the man who "transgressed the words of R. Akiba" (or rather Apuleius, Valerius Maximus, and the compiler of *Avot de R. Natan A*) all express the other side of these comments from *Avot de R. Natan A*. If a woman must cover herself and so dissimulate her desire, then the woman who uncovers herself announces her own sexual availability. In so doing she usurps the male initiative. A woman who bares her head before the assembly both invites and affronts the male gaze. She "asks for it," and has no right to give her gesture a different meaning—as the woman in the story about Akiba did, and as the wife of Sulpicius Gallus (or the women she represents) might well have done also. In Corinth, the women who uncover their heads when they prophesy seem to be rejecting sexual meaning for their heads or voices. They assert their status as visionaries, as seers and the subjects of vision, rather than as the objects of the male gaze. But in the eyes of Paul they put on a spectacle for men and angels, affronting the cosmic arrangements of Genesis.[48] Whether the angels are offended or eager observers of women's heads, their gaze is male.

AFTER PAUL

Did Paul win in his own time? We have no direct evidence of how Paul's strictures in 1 Cor. 11:3–16 were received among the women of Corinth. It is probable that Paul not only had supporters in Corinth but actually wrote in support of some members of that congregation.[49] It is noteworthy that he never speaks directly to the women; rather, he uses third-person imperatives (5–6) until he addresses himself to the congregation as a whole (13–16). He saw no need to return to this issue; but this may signal either his satisfaction at the Corinthians' response, or his discretion in response to their rejection of his strictures.[50] The later interpreters of Paul, who speak in his person, prescribe submission to a husband (Col. 3:18–19, Eph. 5:22–23), forbid women to have rich clothing, braided hair, teaching, authority over men, and early celibacy (1 Tim. 2:8–15, 5:3–16), and require silence in the assembly (1 Cor. 14:34–35). They no longer see the headcovering as an issue—whether because Paul had succeeded in making it the rule, or because their intent to put an end to the liberties it once symbolized makes the veil irrelevant.

In the succeeding centuries, there remained contexts in which women were able to resist and to reject the strictures attached to the categories "male" and "female" and to dispense with the veil. Among these is the choice of virginity and the highly ambiguous status attained by virgins.[51]

The second-century *Acts of Paul and Thecla* presents Thecla as proposing to cut off her hair in order to follow Paul (25). It seems that this interpreter of Paul has taken 1 Cor. 11:6 very seriously indeed; Thecla, offered the choice between being veiled and being shorn (1 Cor. 11:6), appears to have chosen a haircut. Later, after the deliverance from martyrdom in which she bestows on herself the baptism Paul has refused her, she makes over her *chiton* into a man's cloak (40) and, with Paul's blessing, emulates him in preaching the gospel (41). Her choice of male apparel and short hair is clearly intended to expedite her journeys and mission. It is increasingly thought that the stories about Thecla were legends which derived from groups of ascetic women.[52] The first four centuries of Christianity present enough reports about, and prohibitions against, ascetic women who disguised themselves as men to make clear that the choice was made by at least some extraordinary women.[53] Thecla's story may give us some insight into the meaning these women attached to it.[54]

Tertullian's writings give a glimpse of a less drastic option undertaken by a broader range of Christian women. In the Carthage of the early third century, custom still accorded to virgins the right not to be veiled. Though both Tertullian and his opponents see this practice as a manifestation of local custom, it was not limited to North Africa; Tertullian claims that Greece and certain unnamed barbarian communities "hide" their virgins, but not that all other communities do so (*De virginibus velandis* 2.1). The practice had ritual significance: the virgin removed the veil that she normally wore outdoors (*De orat.* 22.9, *De virg. vel.* 13.1),[55] "that she might enter distinct and distinguished [*notabilis et insignis*] into the assembly, that she might show forth the honor of sanctity in the freedom of her head" (*De virg. vel.* 9.1).[56] The practice clearly had the approval and support of the local ecclesiastical authorities, who saw it as both a glory to the church and an incentive to girls to choose virginity (and probably as a kind of compensation to their families).[57] But as the practice of the unveiled women prophets of Corinth is known only from Paul's arguments against them, so the unveiled virgins of Carthage are known only from Tertullian's attempt to eliminate them.

TERTULLIAN: "THAT VIRGINS MUST BE VEILED"
(*DE VIRGINIBUS VELANDIS*)

Tertullian's most extensive and direct treatment of the need to veil women's heads is the treatise *De virginibus velandis*. The title is usually translated "On the Veiling of Virgins," but the intensely polemical character of the work suggests that the gerund would be better translated on the model of Cato's famous slogan *Carthago delenda est*. The treatise played a role in the increasing tensions between the New Prophecy (or at least Tertullian) and the

Catholics in Carthage. Montanist claims both to prophetic experience and to a stricter moral discipline were central in proselytizing, as well as in controversy; Tertullian seems to have been attracted by both.

Tertullian's concern with this issue, or with other aspects of the behavior of women, cannot be blamed on his association with the New Prophecy; he had insisted on the propriety of veiling virgins at prayer already in *De oratione,* well within his earlier "Catholic period."[58] He also claims to have addressed the question in Greek (*De virg. vel.* 1.1). He appears to have put his objections to one bishop, perhaps the bishop of Carthage, who responded in terms of his reluctance to change the dispositions of his predecessor (*De oratione* 22.10, *De virginibus velandis* 1–3). The basic outlines of the argument he would later put forward in *De virginibus velandis* are already apparent in the few chapters of *De oratione* he devotes to the question. In *De oratione* he begins by bewailing the diversity of practice that prevails among the churches in this regard (20.1, 21.1). He makes a linguistic case that Paul clearly included virgins among women when he required women to cover their heads (22.1–4). It is shameful for virgins, he claims, as well as for women to be "shorn." He further theorizes that the diction of Gen. 6:2 is such that the women in question must not have been wives, but virgins or widows (22.7). It is age, he asserts, that determines when a virgin becomes a woman and should wear a veil. Indeed, she is no longer a virgin, but is married to time (22.8). He suggests that a virgin who wears a veil does not perpetrate a lie, but rather shows herself to be a bride of Christ (22.9). To those with scruples about changing tradition, he opposes good judgment and consistency (22.10). He concedes briefly that perhaps one need not force virgins to be veiled, but only in order to insist that likewise one ought not to force them not to be covered. Finally he "pronounces and attests" that virgins who have been betrothed, whose "flesh has once shuddered at the kiss and touch of a man," must be veiled (22.10).

By the time Tertullian wrote *De virginibus velandis,* he was deeply involved with the concerns of the New Prophecy. A number of details in the text make this clear. If he does not yet castigate the Catholics as "psychics" (unspiritual), he does refer to the "multinubists" (3.4; i.e., Christians who remarry after the death of a spouse). He answers the charge that the veiling of virgins constitutes *novitas* in discipline not by claiming its antiquity, but by insisting that those who hear the Paraclete prophesying *now* (i.e., the faithful who respond to the New Prophecy) cover their virgins (1.5–7). Further he invokes an angelic revelation to one of "our" women to determine the extent of the veil.

Although all the arguments of *De oratione* reappear in this text, Tertullian's approach to them has changed. The relatively measured tone of *De oratione* has been replaced by anxious virulence and an acrid and prurient sarcasm. Many factors contribute to the shifts in Tertullian's arguments, not least the fact that devoting a whole treatise to the subject allows the scope to let himself go rhetorically. Among such factors are certainly his need to defend the New Prophecy and his increasing despair of convincing the Catholic authorities of its rightness. In *De virginibus velandis* Tertullian's audience is not primarily the unveiled virgins, but their male supporters; he turns to the virgins only at the close of the treatise (16.3), but in fact addresses his remarks there to all women alike (16.3–17.5). The text is conceived as a discourse among the men who (at least in his view) make the decisions.[59] More explicit attention is given to the arguments of the defenders of unveiled virgins, arguments which by now doubtless have also become more explicit under Tertullian's constant rhetorical battering. This is especially the case with what Tertullian probably sees as the ultimate goal of the treatise: the demolition of the distinction between woman and virgin, which the Catholics base on 1 Corinthians 7.[60] This distinction, which has the effect of exempting virgins from the rulings of 1 Cor. 11:3–16, is also what is celebrated in the practice of the North African church.[61] More enlightening than the specific shifts in Tertullian's argument are the two new and interrelated motifs with which it is imbued: the danger of the gaze, and the danger of honor and glory.

De virginibus velandis returns constantly to these twin dangers. In Tertullian's view, for a virgin to be seen or to be distinguished by any sort of honor nullifies her virginity. What others acclaim as a sign of holy liberty is for him an index of license (*libido* 2.4, *licentiam* 3.2). "Every publication of the good of a virgin is an experience [*passio*] of *stuprum*" (3.4).[62]

Especially it is the gaze, the eyes, of men that violate virginity, and the eyes and aspect of virgins (as of other women) also endanger men. A virgin, like any other woman, should strive not to be seen at all, and if she must limit her own vision, so much the better for her; let her take the example of Arab women (17.2). The covering Tertullian demands (whether for woman or for virgin) must cover her head and neck well down her back, and should be such as to make it impossible for another to look into her face, and for her to look at others (17.1–3). Tertullian alike impugns the motives of the virgins who dispense with the veil and of their male defenders:

> Such eyes wish a virgin to be seen as has a virgin who wishes to be seen. The same sorts of eyes mutually desire each other. It is of the same lust [*libido*] to be seen and to see. To blush if he sees a virgin, marks a holy man, as it does a holy virgin if she is seen by a man. (2.4)

The women who wish to be unveiled are virgins of men, and not of God.[63] Even virgins who begin with no bad motive are endangered by the practice:

> while they are penetrated by many unstable eyes, while they are aroused by the fingers of those who point, while they are too much loved, while they grow hot amid continual embraces and kisses.[64]

The connection between sight and sexuality, between eye and genitals, between gaze and fornication is hardly unique to Tertullian; the same equations are made in ancient anatomy and psychology, and in the poetry of love, as well as in Christian moral and ascetic writings.[65] Popular culture also linked the penetrating character of the phallus and of the eye.[66] Greek and Roman representations of the phallus often included an eye in its head. This motif, as well as other representations of the phallus, seems to have been widely used as an apotropaic device against the evil eye. One particularly striking representation is a first-century B.C.E. terracotta which depicts two anthropomorphized phalluses sawing an eye in two.[67]

If Tertullian makes so explicit an identification between the male sexual organ and the male gaze, he also makes a most explicit conjunction between the virgin's genitals and her head: "Impose a veil extrinsically on her who has a covering internally. Let her whose lower parts are not bare have her upper parts likewise covered" (12.1).[68] When Tertullian demands a covering for the virgin "whose lower parts are not bare," he probably refers to the pubic hair that grows when "her shame is everywhere clothed," at puberty (11.4).[69] The *tegumen intrinsecus* that warrants the veil is more probably the hymen, unknown to most Greek anatomical science, but apparently a part of anatomy in the Latin world.[70] In the startling revelation which warrants the length of the veil, an angel appears in a dream to a woman seer of Carthage, beating her "elegant" neck, sarcastically inviting her to bare herself to her loins (*lumbos;* it seems to mean the lowest part of her back), since she has not yet gotten anywhere. Presumably this angel was an offended guardian of the communal order rather than an eager suitor.

While Tertullian's focus on the gaze is by no means new, it is integrated into his special understanding of the Christian discipline as progressively revealed.[71] He claims Rebecca as a truly Christian woman because she covered her face at Isaac's approach. Thus she showed her recognition of the new disciplinary revelation of Christ that marriage and *stuprum* alike are accomplished by the gaze and the mind (*de aspectu et anima*), not merely in the body (11.3). Behind this strange encomium lies Tertullian's exegesis of Matt. 5:28, one his favorite texts.[72] He generally uses the verse to show that Christ extends the law to sins of the will; but at some points the will is understood as active in the gaze: "He defines not only the man who had already invaded another's wedlock to be an adulterer, but likewise him who had contaminated [a woman] by the concupiscence of his gaze."[73] Tertullian explains his strictures on women's dress as protection for men, who are susceptible to this sin of concupiscence in response to women's beauty. But they are also a protection for women, who may not be allowed impunity when they have been the cause of another's perdition.[74]

If unveiled virgins are a danger to themselves, how much more to men and angels! Now Tertullian is quite certain that the women the angels lusted after must have been virgins, for "who can presume that such angels would desire tainted bodies and the leavings of human lust" (7.2).[75] Such a dangerous face ought to be hidden not only from the angels but also from human eyes (7.3). So dangerous is the sight of women to men that mother should veil herself for the sake of son, sister for the sake of brother, daughter for the sake of father: "All ages are endangered in you. Put on the armor of modesty, surround yourself with a rampart of chastity, cover your sex with a wall which neither allows your eyes beyond it nor admits others' in" (16.3–4).

If men are endangered by women's gaze, this is only because their own eyes and desire might be engaged by it. The woman's gaze does not and cannot sexualize the man. Partly this is because of his innate dignity; he need not be covered, because "he does not naturally have an abundance of hair, because it is not shameful for him to be shaven or shorn, because it was not on his account that the angels transgressed, because he is the glory and image of God, because his head is Christ" (8.1). But it also seems that Tertullian, like others of his time, believes that women will not be aroused by the sight of a man (17.3).[76] A woman is also sexually endangered by her own gaze, but its dangers come not from seeing men but from too great an idea of her own importance, from spiritual and sexual autonomy.

Tertullian is as deeply offended by the idea that virgins should be honored by the church as he is convinced of the danger of their exposed heads. Honors for virgins, as for other women, offend against the "natural inferiority" prescribed for women (*De cor. mil.* 14.1). No other exceptions are made for virgins in the discipline of the church, he asserts; like other women, virgins are forbidden to speak in the church, teach, baptize, offer, or claim any "manly gift" (*virilis muneris*) or priestly function (*sacerdotalis officii; De virg. vel.* 9.1). Not only does a virgin not deserve to be honored as is a man, she ought not to be accorded the privileges of widows (as has been done by a certain unnamed bishop), or the respect due to experienced and proven wives (of one husband only, of course; 2–3). It is worse still, indeed "inhuman," for female virgins, who ought as women to be subject in every regard, to proffer any honorific sign of their virginity, when *male* virgins are accorded no such sign (10.1–2). Indeed, the males ought to get more credit, since men are "greedier and hotter for women" and therefore have to work harder at continence (10.3).[77] The continent who have been married and experienced sex (e.g., Tertullian) deserve the most of all, but get no special honor (10.3–4).

"The least mention of virginity seems to elicit cruelly sarcastic winks," Giulia Sissa remarks in her study of Greek virginity.[78] In Tertullian's *De virginibus velandis,* winks have given way to a constant rhetorical sneer. He speaks of virgins who do not wish to be covered as "virgins of men," as "virgins who can ask something of men," as "marketable heads."[79] Tertullian's particular ire is raised by the claim that the unveiled heads of virgins are a kind of recruiting device, the means by which others are invited to a life of virginity—in his term, soliciting (14.1). Virgins attracted in this way are really responding to a kind of coercion, he claims, and the public celebration they receive is likely to lead them to betray their virginity. Once they have done so they will boldly continue to go uncovered to hide their sin and, he insinuates, will ultimately resort to abortion. God, he hints, has frequently helped the children of such virgins to birth, while their mothers made war against them (14.2–3).

So dangerous is ecclesiastical adulation of virgins, Tertullian claims, that even the eyes of women are to be avoided. The veil should be invoked as a defense not only against temptation, scandal, envy, but even against what the gentiles call "*fascinum* . . . the unhappy result of too great praise and glory," which may come from envy of the devil but also may be God's judgment on the proud (15.1–2). Sometimes translated "fascination," *fascinum* means the spell or enchantment, the work of the evil eye or cursing mouth; *fascinum* also names the antidote, the phallus, widely used as a charm to avert it.[80] *Fascinum* could produce a wasting that was parallel to the pangs of love.[81] Children and victorious generals especially needed protection; but young marriageable girls were particularly vulnerable to erotic enchantment.[82] Thus Tertullian manages to insinuate a warning that the virgin's supposed sign of the honor of sanctity, her free and unveiled head, actually puts her in danger of sexual slavery and degradation.

Tertullian goes beyond disparagement of the unveiled virgins, to question virginity itself; indeed, he requires it to disappear. Virginity that is known is not virginity; a virgin can only be a virgin if she is not acknowledged (14.5). "She denies the woman who hides the virgin," he counsels with approval (15.3)—perhaps because she disappears entirely. At one point he esteems virginity as less meritorious than continence because the virgin has not experienced or struggled with sexual desire (10.1–4), while elsewhere he hints that she undergoes sexual experiences (11.4, 12.1). Already in *De oratione* the convolutions of his attempts to include "virgin" in the use of "woman" in 1 Cor. 11:2–16 led him to argue that a girl who has come of age is a nonvirgin (22.8),[83] and in *De virginibus velandis* this claim is given a longer, more complex justification (11.1–12.2). Tertullian does not seem to carry this strange claim into other works.[84] What, then, is the concern that drives him to these rhetorical extremes?

What Tertullian seeks to undermine is the ecclesiastical meaning of virginity, the honor that it receives from the church. When he asks, "Do virgins adorn and commend the church before God, or the church virgins?" his question is clearly rhetorical (14.1). But it is less clear whether the expected answer is "the latter" or merely "no." Less clear still is whether

Tertullian could really expect his audience to give either of these answers. There can be little doubt that the Christians of third-century Carthage believed that virgins *do* adorn the church, as well as that the church adorns virgins. So too Tertullian probably intended a *reductio ad absurdum* when he argued that man is head of a virgin as of a woman, "unless a virgin is some monstrous third sex with her own head" (7.6). But what he disparages is the long and widely held conviction that virginity does indeed bestow transcendence of sex, indeed of gender. The virgin, if she is not a third sex, has "left behind the things of woman," so as to become male, or more often "manly," or even to live the life of the angels.[85] The Catholics of Carthage undoubtedly believe that a virgin does indeed have a head of her own, and the Carthaginian practice that displayed "the honor of sanctity in the freedom of her head" (9.1) probably proclaimed the message that a virgin is not subject to a husband, but only to Christ.[86]

Tertullian himself does not completely reject these views; in *De cultu feminarum* he uses the promise of an angelic nature to motivate women not to avail themselves of the inventions of the fallen angels (cosmetics and jewelry) whom they will judge.[87] He will even allow a virgin the status of not-woman—but only if she "hides the virgin," and submits in every way to a womanly role (*De virg. vel.* 15.3). He acknowledges that women have a role in the clergy (*ordines*) through continence.[88] Although he insists that discipline denies women the right to speak in the assembly, teach, baptize, and offer, he knows also that there are grounds on which the right to baptize has been claimed for women, and he may well know of women who claim other "manly gifts, priestly functions."[89] If the New Prophecy in Carthage did not actually allow women to speak or teach in the assembly, its members did hear the word of God through women.[90]

Tertullian acknowledges the role of women prophets in the New Prophecy. Of its founding prophets, he cites Prisca less frequently than Montanus, and Maximilla not at all.[91] But among the prophets of Carthage, he cites women, though without their names. They experience revelations during the assembly (*De anima* 9.4) and encounter angels in dreams (*De virg. vel.* 17.3). The long and extremely reverent description in *De anima* of the processes by which one women prophet received her revelations leaves little room for doubting Tertullian's esteem for the women prophets of Carthage. While it is far from certain that Tertullian was the editor of the *Passion of Perpetua*, he can hardly have been unaware of her visions and fate.[92]

De virginibus velandis appears to have been written at a crucial point for Tertullian's own development; it is usually seen as one of the very last treatises composed before his break with the Catholics of Carthage. As I mentioned above, Tertullian's concern with the practice of veiling does not originate with his Montanism, nor does his anxiety about women as a source of sexual temptation, nor his insistence on female inferiority. He must have known that Christianity was seen by outsiders as appealing primarily to women, children, and slaves, and allowing them the upper hand.[93] He saw the ordinary duties of the Christian woman as likely to offend against the dignity, if not the morals, of a pagan husband (*Ad uxorem* 2.4). The prominence of women prophets in the New Prophecy formed part of the evidence that the Catholics used against the movement.[94] The Catholics could not deny that women can be prophets.[95] But prophets are always suspect and subject to testing, and being women does them no good.

While Tertullian's concern is not the veiling of women prophets, the presence of women prophets in the community may have inspired his concern. His increasing commitment to the New Prophecy may well have increased his anxiety about honors bestowed on women. *De corona militis,* generally thought to have been written in the same year as *De virg. vel.,* also insists that any sign of honor is inappropriate to women (14.1). His outrage at honors for virgins may well reflect his anxiety about the dangerous proximity of women to angels and spiritual power in the holy reality to which he increasingly gave his allegiance. The best defense is a good offense: the New Prophecy, in his view, does not allow women an inappropriately honorific role; on the contrary, it is the Catholics who do so, in allowing virgins to go unveiled. The paraclete is now revealing a stricter and more all-encompassing discipline which the New Prophecy puts into practice. Virgins are not to be exempt from the veil, but to recognize that they can escape from the disabilities of being women only by submitting fully to them (15.3). If some women are to be heard, then all women, including and especially virgins, are not to be seen.

All this raises the question of whether the innovation Tertullian sponsors is already the practice of the New Prophecy (as is usually assumed), or whether its members too must be convinced of Tertullian's view of what "our" virgins ought to do (1.1).[96] Tertullian seems to imply that there are virgins in Carthage eager to hide beneath the veil, when he depicts them as dragged into the public eye with their veils ripped from their heads by a sacrilegious hand (e.g. that of the bishop of Carthage; 3.4–5). One might reconstruct a little drama, a competition in humility and chastity between Montanists and Catholics, in which the Montanists bring their virgins to church ostentatiously veiled, the unveiled Catholic virgins complain that they are scandalized, and the bishop rules that all virgins must unveil in the assembly. But it is clear that what Tertullian really seeks is not permission for but requirement of veiling. How *many* Montanist virgins are "blushing that they be publicly known, trembling that they be uncovered, summoned as if for violation [*stuprum*]" (3.4)? Is Tertullian the defender of virgins who wish to veil, or must virgins veil to vindicate his views? Do we really hear the voices of the unveiled virgins in the Catholic complaint of scandal? Or is the "scandal" really the concern of others—the bishop of Carthage, or male leaders of the New Prophecy other than Tertullian—who fear that the veil will prove a stumbling block both to recruiting virgins and to retaining them? Or are the complaining virgins no more than Tertullian's straw women?

The revelation Tertullian cites as testimony for the required length of the veil may give us a chilling glimpse into the experience of one of the women of Carthage. The dream, in which an angel lashes the woman seer and invites her to strip, evokes a scene from a wall painting in the Villa of the Mysteries at Pompeii, in which a winged figure raises a rod at a woman whose back is exposed to below her waist.[97] Burkert's interpretation of the painting suggests that the scene may be an allegory that draws on the tradition in which frenzy is expressed by flogging; the young woman is about to feel the stroke of divine, Dionysiac madness.[98] The dream of the visionary at Carthage may reflect the way this conflict over women's persons and heads has invaded her experience; the angelic voice that mediates her divine madness speaks in the sarcastic tones of Tertullian, accusing her of inviting the gaze in which she is sexualized and condemned.[99] As visionary, she sees herself as exhibitionist, and her angelic medium as offended voyeur.[100]

This too is speculation; the women of Carthage remain veiled from our interrogation. Nor do we know how well Tertullian succeeded; he never returns to the topic, and in fact seems to become less concerned with the behavior of women in every regard. It may be that he won in both camps, Catholic and Montanist; or that he lost, but was satisfied with the stricter discipline of the New Prophecy in other areas; or that he was less anxious once the final break was made (although *De pudicitia* hardly suggests that he had lost interest in Catholic discipline). Perhaps he simply felt that he had said it all so well as to have no need to repeat himself. Then again, he may have given a public reading of his works on women every year.

As for the Catholics of Carthage, we have no idea how they took Tertullian's treatise. Some forty years later the Carthaginian bishop Cyprian wrote a treatise on the dress of virgins, but the veil seems not to have been an issue. Cyprian's target is wealthy virgins, and he shows no small talent for misogynist sarcasm and innuendo. But unlike Tertullian, he is quite certain that virgins adorn the church: "This is the flower of the ecclesiastical seed; the beauty and ornament of spiritual grace . . . the image of God responding to the sanctity of the Lord."[101] By the fourth century, the veil seems to have become the sign of a virgin; the veiling of a virgin signaled her commitment to lifelong virginity. But in this context the veil became a mark of distinction and an honor, assumed in splendid communal ceremonies that reflected both marriage rituals and baptism.[102]

On many levels, the rhetorical excesses, the overwrought moral rigor, and the ultimate schismatic bitterness of Tertullian make him an easy mark. But it should not be forgotten that in the long run, both Tertullian and Paul won. They won not only in terms of the literal imposition of veils and headcovering on women and virgins for many centuries, but also in the larger battle they saw themselves fighting over the unveiled heads of women, the battle to shelter the divine and revelatory, the words of the spirit and the eyes of the angels, from the sexualized presence of women. They won not insofar as they differed from Cyprian and his predecessors in Carthage, from the later and earlier clerical sponsors of virginity, from the male charismatics of Corinth, but insofar as they were at one with them. The arguments from Genesis and nature that now sound so strange and unconvincing invoked the mythic foundations of their shared world in order to sustain its structure. And they won too, in that the women whose heads were at issue remain veiled against our inquiry, cloaked in the male discourse that at once discloses and hides their presence. We cannot know the meaning they gave their gestures, or the hopes and expectations that accompanied them. These women are visible only through the eyes of the male controversialists, who do not see them either, for they are locked into the *fascinum* of their own eroticizing gaze.

NOTES

This essay draws upon research funded by a National Endowment for the Humanities Summer Stipend (1980) and an American Council of Learned Societies Fellowship (1986–87).

1. The movement originated in Phrygia; the name Montanism refers to the male among the three prophets (Montanus, Maximilla, and Prisca) who are credited with founding it. It was characterized by strong apocalyptic expectation in its earlier stages and by concerns with sexual and ascetic discipline, especially in its later stages. It was eventually regarded as heretical. Braun 1977:712 dates *De virginibus velandis* to 211 C.E. All dates for the treatise are based on internal evidence. It appears to be one of the last before Tertullian's rupture with the Catholics and is usually considered to be close in time to *De corona militis* and *De exhortatione castitatis*. The treatise has received relatively little scholarly attention. For discussion of the questions see Stücklin 1974:92–93.

2. Even this is disputed; some scholars claim that a hairstyle is at issue rather than a headcovering; Schüssler Fiorenza 1983:226–30. For the opposing view (which I share), see MacDonald 1988:276–82 and the literature there, also Brooten 1988. Pagett 1984 contends that the Corinthians insist upon the veil for women, and that Paul argues that women do not need a veil. Others urge, on the basis of 11:14–15, that the behavior of the Corinthian men is equally at issue; see especially Murphy-O'Connor 1980, Brooten 1985. Walker 1975 argues that 11:3–16 is not to be attributed to Paul at all but is to be seen as the product of three *different* interpolators.

3. Thus the suggestion that men's hair practices are at issue in Corinth is unlikely; no imperatives are directed to men in the passage. See also Wire 1990, esp. 117–18.

4. For a discussion of 1 Cor. 14:34–35 see below.

5. Levine, this volume.

6. See also Wire 1990:117–18.

7. See on this Bedale 1954; also Wire 1990:279, n. 2. Fitzmyer 1989:504–6 discusses other literature.

8. See also Fitzmyer 1989:506–11.

9. See also Wire 1990:117.

10. See Fitzmyer 1974.

11. See especially Hooker 1964.

12. Tertullian, *De virginibus velandis* 7.2–4; also *De oratione* 22.5–6, *De cultu feminarum* 1.2.1–3.3, 2.10.3, *De corona militis* 14.2. For early versions of the legend of the sons of God/watchers/angels see *1 Enoch* 6–12, 15, *Testament of Reuben* 5.1–6. Tertullian knows the legend from *1 Enoch; De cult. fem.* 3.1–3. On the watchers and views of women in antique Christianity, see Prusak 1974, Küchler 1986, Yarbro Collins 1988.

13. *Apoc. Mos.* 7.2, 17.1–5, 22.1–3, 27.1–2, 29.1–6, 32.2, 33.5, 35.2, etc.; *Genesis Rabbah* 8.4–6, 8. On the basis of *Gen. R.* 8.10, Wire theorizes that the angels, like the men of the community, must be protected from distraction from the glory of God (1990:120–22).

14. So Fitzmyer 1974.

15. Mark 12:25 // Matt. 22:30, Luke 20:36; Balch 1972.

16. On the complexities of the use of Genesis here, see D'Angelo 1988.

17. John Winkler claims that Greek-speaking antiquity bears out anthropologists' suggestion that "what 'natural' means in many . . . contexts is precisely 'conventional and proper' "; 1990:17.

18. An analogy between women's heads and the private parts was first suggested to me by Rowan A. Greer in 1973. Giulia Sissa suggests that Galen sees beards, eyelashes, foreskin, pubic hair, and buttocks as natural sources of modesty and dignity; Sissa 1990:112. The passage in question (Galen, *De usu partium* 11:14) describes the last three as providing covering and ornament (*skepēn de kai kosmon*). Galen does not then conclude that they ought to be further covered. He explains women's need for long hair on their heads in the same way (*skepēs heneka kai kosmou*), but believes that they have this in common with men.

19. The Corinthians seem to use tongues as the mark by which they distinguish the spiritual from the unspiritual. See Hurd 1965:193.

20. The idea that 1 Cor. 11:2–16 and 12:23–24 were connected in Paul's mind was also Greer's suggestion.

21. On the idea that adornment and cosmetics conceal what is shameful and repulsive, see Richlin, this volume.

22. See the lengthy discussion of the practice and its etiologies in Levine, this volume; also Wire 1990:122–23. On the headcovering as a norm for women in antiquity, see MacDonald 1988:276–82 and the literature there; Kraemer 1992:146. Thompson 1988 concludes that women were free to make a choice in this area and that 1 Cor. 11:10 acknowledges that right (*exousia;* 1988:113).

23. See on this Wire 1990:122–26.

24. This is a generalized picture, based on a wide variety of liturgies, narratives, and homilies from the third through the fifth centuries. It is clear that from a very

early period the candidates were baptized nude. The *Apostolic Tradition* attributed to Hippolytus specifies that the baptizands be stripped, reclothed after baptism, and then brought into the assembly (21.3–20) (note that this document is a reconstruction; see Dix 1937:lii–lxxxi). A number of legendary accounts of baptism mention the unclothing and reclothing; see e.g. *The Acts of Thomas* 121, 133. In *Acts of Paul and Thecla* 38, the heroine puts on her garments after her deliverance/baptism, interpreting the action in terms of the resurrection. In the fourth century, Egeria relates that in Jerusalem the candidates are baptized nude, then clothed, and as "infants" led into the Anastasis with the bishop and from there to the Basilica of the Cross, where the congregation is assembled (*Itinerary* 38.1–2). Theodore of Mopsuestia speaks of reclothing in a "garment that is wholly radiant," "a white garment that shines" (*On Baptism* 4; trans. A. Mingana, 1933:68). See also the description of the rite in Tonneau and Devreesse 1949:xxxi. Theodore also explains a practice of placing a linen stole over the head immediately before the actual bath to proclaim the freeing of the candidate by analogy with freedmen's practice of wearing a linen headcovering both at home and in the marketplace; Theodore of Mopsuestia, *On Baptism* 3 (trans. Mingana, 1933:47). Gregory of Nazianzus shows that by the late fourth century the baptismal garment was important enough to be the occasion of ostentation (*Homily* 40, *On Baptism* 25). See also Margaret Miles 1989, who has argued that in the fourth century the experience of public (or semi-public) nudity was central to the baptismal experience, and experienced differently by women than by men; 1989:24–52.

25. The basic article of clothing for men and women, both slave and free, was the indoor garment (*enduma* or *indutus*), the *chiton* or *tunica*. Women wore a floor-length garment of this type, while men's were usually shorter. But men of certain occupations (priests for instance, and some musicians) and in certain settings, especially ritual settings, wore full-length versions also. Distinctions in dress for men and women and for ranks of society (including slaves) were made with the fabrics, outdoor garments, and ornaments; see Bonfante and Jaunzems 1988:1390, 1398, 1403–4, Wright and Lawler 1970, Pomeroy 1975:181–82, Boulanger 1919:766–69, Amelung 1899, col. 2309, 4b, 2332–33. The toga, of course, was the badge of citizenship in the empire, at least officially. Theoretically all "barbarians" would have had their native dress (see e.g. Tacitus, *Germania* 17) but, for the most part, Jews in the Greek-speaking world seem to have dressed as Greeks. From the Oppian Law to the "Women's Senate" of Elagabalus, attempts were continually made to restrict certain fabrics and ornaments to the upper ranks of society, and especially to keep women from displaying wealth in clothing; Pomeroy 1975:179–82.

26. See also Meeks 1974:183–84 and note 82; 1983:151, 155, 237 nn. 49, 68.

27. On slave collars, see Hopkins 1978:121; also the illustration in Veyne 1987:59. Seneca's highly rhetorical claim that the senate rejected distinctions in dress for slaves lest the latter realize how few free persons enslaved them only indicates that no distinction in dress was stipulated by law (Seneca, *De clementia* 1.24). We know that some visible distinctions existed; the "liberty cap" (*pilleus*), for instance, for freedpersons, and the toga for citizens. See also Theodore of Mopsuestia, *On Baptism* 3 (trans. Mingana, 1933:47), on freedmen's use of a linen headcovering. Branding was used as a punishment for such offenses as running away and stealing.

During the imperial period branding was extended to free citizens, thereby essentially marking them with the shame of slavery. See Betz 1971, esp. A 2, 658–59.

28. *Aseneth* 15.1 (see Philonenko 1968:180–81); also *Acts of Thomas* 13–14, 121.

29. More complex theological rationales for the women's practice of uncovering their heads have been offered by a number of scholars. MacDonald explains the theology behind the practice as an assumption of androgyny on the basis of baptism and suggests a philosophical theology like Philo's as its source or context; 1987:66–102, 1988, Brooten 1988; so also Jervis 1993:235–38, Boyarin 1993:8–12. Wire deduces that the women of Corinth based their practice in the claim that they fully participate in the image of God (1990:127), but elsewhere suggests that the women may have seen no impropriety in what they were doing because of the housechurch setting—they had their heads uncovered in the house, where women were not required to cover their heads (1990:183).

30. Eilberg-Schwartz, this volume.

31. So also Kraemer 1992:149.

32. D'Angelo 1990B:72–82, Brooten 1977.

33. Attempts to reconcile 1 Cor. 11:4–6 and 1 Cor. 14:34–35 are futile. There is nothing in the vocabulary or contexts to distinguish the women of 1 Cor. 14:34–35 or to indicate that this is some special group within the larger group of the women of the congregation; rather, 1 Corinthians 14 suggests that any of the community might offer prayer or prophesy in the assembly. Wire 1990:149–58 gives an excellent review of the textual evidence. But her conclusions are by no means certain. She reveals the difficulty of including 14:34–35 in 1 Corinthians 12–14 when she points out that the passage, if it is integral to 1 Corinthians 12–14, must be seen as its climax. She attempts to demonstrate that this is the case; but if indeed this passage is the climax of 1 Cor. 12:1–14:1, Paul can hardly be as good a rhetorician as she claims.

34. Kraemer 1992:149 suggests that the interpolation is anti-Montanist; however, it does not seem to have been used against the New Prophecy by its opponents.

35. Kraemer 1992:146–50; see also Wire 1990:188–93, Neyrey 1986:151–56. Boyarin 1993 and Jervis 1993 argue from different perspectives that Paul seeks here to reassert gender distinctions.

36. Kraemer 1992:146.

37. Brooten 1985:67–69; see also Winkler, who contends that sex is "unnatural" for Artemidorus and for antiquity in general when it does not involve men, penetration, and an appropriate display of dominance relationships (1990:39–40).

38. On asceticism and the problems raised by divorce and remarriage for Christian women, see D'Angelo 1990a:94–95.

39. So Sissa 1990:94–99; also on the *anakaluptēria,* see Levine, this volume.

40. "Smooth" or "hairless" emphasizes her youth and may imply that she is prepubescent, but is more likely to be a tribute to Roman cosmetic art, which included depilation of body hair, including the pubis, for women; see Martial 3.74, and the funerary inscription of Allia Potestas (*CIL* 6.37965; translation in Lefkowitz and Fant 1982:137, #143), also Ovid, *Ars amatoria* 3.194 (cited by Richlin, this volume). Pliny's recipes for depilatories seem intended primarily for women and slave boys; *Natural History* 28.249, 255, 30.132–34, 32.136. Men who depilated themselves were considered at best finicky (Suetonius, *Caesar* 45) but more usually

effeminate; see Martial 2.62, 3.74, 10.65, Dio Chrysostom *Discourse* 33.48ff., and the literature collected by Maud Gleason 1990:397–406. Tertullian lists depilation as a vanity men should avoid (*De cult. fem.* 2.8.2); strangely, I can find no such stricture on women in his work.

41. Valerius Maximus, *De dictis et factis memorabilibus* 6.9 (translation in Lefkowitz and Fant 1982:176, #190). Valerius was a contemporary of Tiberius; G. Sulpicius Gallus was consul in 166 B.C.E. Sulpicius Gallus's real motives are not relevant to my purposes; in fact, Plutarch believes that he divorced his wife for covering her head rather than uncovering it (*Quaestiones Romanae* 267C). The point is that in the first century, Valerius Maximus finds this motivation credible enough to ascribe it to Gallus.

42. Translation in Lefkowitz and Fant 1982:176, #190.

43. *Avot de R. Natan A* 3. See also *Baba Qamma* 8.6, Babylonian Talmud *Baba Qamma* 90b. The words he transgressed seem to be those in *Babba Qamma* 8.6: "R. Akiba said: Even the poorest in Israel are looked upon as freemen who have lost their possessions, for they are sons of Abraham, Isaac and Jacob" (tr. Danby 1933:343).

44. Tr. Goldin 1955:27.

45. The word used is *bĕzûyāh;* Goldin translates "slut."

46. *Avot de R. Natan A* 1, tr. Goldin, 10. Cf. *Avot de R. Natan B* 9 and *Gen. R.* 17.8; in both of these the reference to Gen. 3:16 is less than clear. Cf. Bab. Talmud *Erubin* 100b.

47. Bab. Talmud *Erubin* 100b includes a discussion about whether it is meritorious for a wife to invite her husband to have sex; the conclusion is that it is meritorious to make sex attractive to him but that she ought not to make an explicit demand upon him.

48. On the status of female visionaries as both subject and object of visions see Castelli forthcoming, Matter forthcoming.

49. See Dahl 1977; also Wire 1990:189–93.

50. Galatia appears not to have participated in the collection; the community is not mentioned in Rom. 15:26. Perhaps Paul's intransigent letter to them lost him their support.

51. Castelli 1986.

52. MacDonald 1983:34–53.

53. See the "Life of St. Pelagia the Harlot" in Kraemer 1988:316–35, #125; also Castelli 1986:75–76.

54. Bynum concludes that women's cross-dressing in the Middle Ages was inspired by practical rather than symbolic motives; 1987:291.

55. While Tertullian insists that the virgins and all respectable women veiled their heads outdoors, other texts raise some questions about this; Tertullian himself points out that Jewish women cover their heads so consistently that they can be distinguished by the practice (*De cor.* 4).

56. Brown suggests that virgins might have sat together in a prominent place, 1988:80–81; he appears to make this suggestion on the basis of *De virg. vel.* 9.2–3 (see p. 80, n. 85), where Tertullian complains of a virgin who was accorded a seat among the widows.

57. On the question of virgins and family politics, see Brown 1988:190–94, 260–62.

58. Other works of Tertullian's Catholic period include *Ad uxorem* 1 and 2, *De cultu feminarum* 1 and 2.

59. Some scholars have suggested that Tertullian's ultimate quarrel is with the bishop of Rome; Stücklin 1974:106–8.

60. The central verse seems to be 7:34 (*De virg. vel.* 4.2–5).

61. Stücklin 1974:141 claims that Tertullian uses the word *virgo* in four different senses, without making any clear distinction of unmarried woman (*Ledige*) from child (*Kind*), girl (*Mädchen*), and technical virgin (*Unberührte*). This is true, and entirely deliberate on Tertullian's part; he wishes to make clear that the *only* valid distinction is between fully grown woman and underage girl child. Stücklin also discusses the degree to which virginity was institutionalized in Carthage in the early third century (150–58). It would seem from *De virg. vel.* 9.2–3 that widows belong to the clergy (*ordines*) while virgins do not. See Gryson 1976:20–22.

62. *Stuprum* is the legal charge made under the *Lex iulia de adulteriis* in cases involving illicit sex with an unmarried girl of the citizen class. Tertullian probably uses *passio* to encompass both the male viewer's (active) lust and the virgin's passive reception of it.

63. Actually "virgins of human beings" (*hominum*); but it seems probable that Tertullian wants to give the phrase sexual overtones.

64. *Dum percutitur oculis incertis et multis, dum digitis demonstrantium titillatur, dum nimium amatur, dum inter amplexus et oscula assidua concalescit* (14.5).

65. Leyerle 1993 gives an excellent summary not only of St. John Chrysostom's thought on this topic, but also a wide sampling of the theme in Greek moral thought from the Presocratics on. See also the entirely approving pronouncement of Propertius: *Si nescis, oculi sunt in amore duces* (If you don't know it, eyes are leaders in love) (*Elegiarum* 2.15.12).

66. Johns 1982:60–75.

67. Ibid. 68, fig. 51. Johns points to the likeness of form between schematic representations of the eye and the vulva, and suggests that the vulva also functioned apotropaically, but also points out that the vulva may represent the evil eye itself.

68. *Impone velamen extrinsecus habenti tegumen intrinsecus. Tegantur etiam superiora cuius inferiora nuda non sunt* (12.1).

69. Here he makes no reference to the practice of depilation for women; see n. 40 above.

70. Soranus alone seems to have heard of its existence, which he denies; see Sissa 1990:108–17, 165–77 (Soranus cited 113–14). Note, however, that Tertullian's treatment of Mary's virginity in *De carne Christi* 23 does not require belief in the hymen; it could reflect the understanding of virginity described by Sissa. Note that Tertullian's three kinds of virginity also assume that virginity is a renewable state: *De exhortatione castitatis* 1.

71. See Cardman 1985.

72. Tertullian identifies adultery and *stuprum*, making them synonymous; *De pud.* 64.

73. *De poen.* 3. See also *De idolatria* 2, 23, *De resurrectione carnis* 15, *De anima* 15, 40, 48, *De pudicitia* 6.

74. *De cultu feminarum* 2.2.4–6.

75. See above, p. 134, and note 12.

76. He believes men to be "hotter"; see 10.3. See also Miles's discussion of the order of baptisms; she suggests that women were baptized last because they were farthest from the state of innocence. But the simplest explanation is that it was not expected that they would be aroused by seeing the men baptized (1989:48). Cf. Babylonian Talmud *Berachot* 61a and Bab. Talmud *Erubin* 18a, where a woman is required to walk behind a man if they go on a journey, not to acknowledge his superiority, but lest he see her legs when she lifts her skirts and be aroused.

77. *Avidior et calidior in feminas.* This idea seems connected to antique biology's view of the male as more hot and dry and the female as more cold and wet; see Brown 1988:18–21. Tertullian seems to have preferred works to grace.

78. Sissa 1990:91.

79. Cf. Plutarch, *Apothegmata Laconica* 232C: "When someone inquired why they [the Spartans] took their girls into public places unveiled but their married women veiled, he [Charillus] said, 'Because the girls have to find husbands, and the married women have to keep those who have them!'" (tr. Babbitt 1968:393). The point is the witty explanation, not that this is a custom unique to the ancient Spartans.

80. Tertullian's ideas about the word *fascinum* are likely to have come from Pliny the Elder; see *Historia naturalis* 28.7.35, 39, also Kuhnert 1909.

81. Virgil, *Eclogue* 3.103.

82. See Winkler's study of erotic spells, primarily from the Greek magical papyri; 1990:71–72, 85–98.

83. *Nulla virgo est ex quo potest nubere* (She is no virgin from the time she is able to marry) (22.8).

84. See, e.g., *De ex. cast.* 1, where Tertullian classifies virginity from birth as the first type of virginity.

85. Cf. Gen. 18:11; Philo *De posteritate Caini* 134; *Quaestiones in Genesin* 4.15, 66; *De mutatione nominum* 130–47, esp. 137; *Gospel of Thomas,* Logion 114; for analyses of Christian texts see Castelli 1986:73–77, Miles 1989:53–77.

86. See Tertullian's description of the veiled virgins as *tanto magis liberae quanto Christi solius ancillae:* "the more free insofar as they are servants to Christ alone" (3.2); he has probably appropriated this boast from the unveiled virgins, whom he sees as serving and pleasing men.

87. *De cultu feminarum* 1.2.; the references are to the "sons of God" in Gen. 6:1–4 and *1 Enoch,* also to 1 Cor. 6:2–3.

88. *De exhortatione castitatis* 13.7; on the widows as an *ordo* see also Gryson 1976:20–22.

89. *De virginibus velandis* 9.1; *De baptismo* 17.4; see also Kraemer 1988:221–45, #93–109, Rossi 1991.

90. Tertullian certainly upholds the proscriptions of 1 Cor. 14.34–35 and 1 Tim. 2:8–15, but insists on the right of women to prophesy (*De virg. vel.* 9.1, *Adv. Marc.* 5.8.11). It seems that the North African Montanists got around prohibitions against women speaking in the assembly by hearing and testing the women prophets after the assembly; *De anima* 9.4.

91. Prisca in *De ex. cast.* 10, *De res. car.* 11; Montanus in *De fuga* 9 (bis), *Adv. Prax.* 8, *De pud.* 21.

92. On the dialectic of visionary experience and voyeuristic objectification of the female martyr in this text, see Castelli forthcoming.

93. See Origen, *Contra Celsum* 3.44; see also Kraemer 1992:128–31.

94. Eusebius, *Hist. eccl.* 5.14, 18; see also pejorative references to "Montanus and the women" throughout the materials in 5.14–19. Origen calls female ecstatic prophecy into question, but in the context of the Delphic oracle. Fox 1987:407 claims that Origen represents "the assumptions that Montanus could not overthrow." This seems overstated, especially since Fox himself tries to argue that the woman prophet of *De anima* was not a member of the New Prophecy, but represents a common feature of early Christian life (410–11).

95. Perhaps because of the scriptural precedents; see Eusebius, *Hist. eccl.* 5.17.

96. It seems that most interpreters have taken the "our" in 1.1 ("our virgins") to refer to the North African church, while referring the *nobis* and *nostrae* in 17.3 to the Montanists.

97. Johns 1982, color plate 24.

98. Burkert 1987:104.

99. For a description of the way that communal disputes can influence the experience of prophecy, see Tertullian, *De anima* 9.

100. See in contrast Castelli's (1993) analysis of Perpetua's vision of herself as a male youth.

101. Cyprian, *De habitu virginum* 3: *flos est ille ecclesiastici germinis, decus et ornamentum gratiae spiritalis . . . Dei imago respondens ad sanctimoniam Domini*, in G. Hartel, ed., 1873:189.

102. So Brown 1988, who cites decisions of the councils of Saragossa and Carthage determining the age at which a virgin is allowed to assume the veil (261 n. 8), and recreates a description of the ceremony from Ambrose (355).

REFERENCES

Amelung, W.
  1899   "Chitōn." *Paulys Real-Encyclopädie der Classischen Altertumswissenschaft*, 3(2):2309–35.
Aseneth
     See Philonenko.
Avot de Rabbi Natan
     See Goldin.
Babbitt, Frank Cole
  1968   *Plutarch's Moralia*. Loeb Classical Library 3. Cambridge: Harvard University Press.
Balch, David L.
  1972   "Backgrounds of I Cor. VII: Sayings of the Lord in Q; Moses as an Ascetic *Theios anér* in II Cor. III." *New Testament Studies* 18:351–64.
Bedale, S.
  1954   "The Meaning of *kephalē* in the Pauline Epistles." *Journal of Theological Studies* n.s. 5:211–15.

Betz, Otto

1971   "Stigma." *Theological Dictionary of the New Testament,* ed. by Gerhard Friedrich, trans. and ed. Geoffrey W. Bromiley, 7:657–64. Grand Rapids: Wm. B. Eerdmans.

Bonfante, Larissa, and Eva Jaunzems

1988   "Clothing and Ornament." In *Civilization of the Ancient Mediterranean: Greece and Rome,* ed. by Michael Grant and Rachel Kitzinger, 3:1385–1413. New York: Charles Scribner's Sons.

Boulanger, Andre

1919   "Vestis." *Dictionnaire des antiquités grecques et romaines,* ed. by Charles Daremberg and Edmond Saglio, 5:764–71. Paris: Librairie Hachette.

Boyarin, Daniel

1993   "Paul and the Genealogy of Gender." *Representations* 41:1–33.

Braun, René

1977   *Deus Christianorum: Recherches sur le vocabulaire doctrinal de Tertullien.* 2nd ed. Paris: Etudes Augustiniennes.

Brooten, Bernadette J.

1977   " 'Junia . . . Outstanding among the Apostles' (Romans 16.7)." In *Women Priests: A Catholic Commentary on the Vatican Declaration,* ed. by L. Swidler and A. Swidler, 141–44. New York: Paulist.

1985   "Paul's Views on the Nature of Women and Female Homoeroticism." In *Immaculate & Powerful: The Female in Sacred Image and Social Reality,* ed. by Clarissa W. Atkinson, Constance H. Buchanan, and Margaret R. Miles, 61–87. Boston: Beacon.

1988   "Response to Dennis Ronald MacDonald, 'Corinthian Veils and Gnostic Androgynes.' " In *Images of the Feminine in Gnosticism,* ed. by Karen King, 293–96. Philadelphia: Fortress.

Brown, Peter

1988   *The Body and Society: Men, Women and Sexual Renunciation in Early Christianity.* New York: Columbia University Press.

Burkert, Walter

1987   *Ancient Mystery Cults.* Cambridge: Harvard University Press.

Bynum, Caroline Walker

1987   *Holy Feast and Holy Fast: The Religious Significance of Food to Medieval Women.* Berkeley and Los Angeles: University of California Press.

Cardman, Francine

1985   "Tertullian on Doctrine and the Development of Discipline." *Studia Patristica* 16, ed. by Elizabeth A. Livingstone (Papers Presented to the Seventh International Conference on Patristic Studies, 1975), 136–42. Berlin: Akademie-Verlag.

Castelli, Elizabeth

1986   "Virginity and Its Meaning for Women's Sexuality in Early Christianity." *Journal of Feminist Studies in Religion* 2:62–85.

Forth-   "Visions and Voyeurism: Holy Women and the Politics of Sight in Early
coming   Christianity." Protocols of the Center for Hermeneutical Studies. Berkeley, Calif.

Cyprian   *See* Hartel.

Dahl, Nils Alstrup

1977   "Paul and the Church at Corinth according to 1 Cor 1:10–4:21." *Studies in Paul: Theology for the Early Christian Mission,* 40–61. Minneapolis: Augsburg.

Danby, Herbert

1933   *The Mishnah.* Oxford: Oxford University Press.

D'Angelo, Mary R.

1988   "The Garden Once and Not Again: 1 Cor 11:11–12 as an Interpretation of Gen 1:26–27." In *Genesis 1–3 in the History of Exegesis: Intrigue in the Garden,* ed. by Gregory Robbins, 1–42. New York and Toronto: Edwin Mellen.

1990a   "Remarriage and the Divorce Sayings Attributed to Jesus." In *Divorce and Remarriage: Religious and Psychological Perspectives,* ed. by William P. Roberts, 78–106. Kansas City: Sheed and Ward.

1990b   "Women Partners in the New Testament." *Journal of Feminist Studies in Religion* 6:65–86.

Dix, Gregory

1937   *The Apostolic Tradition of Saint Hippolytus.* Vol. 1. London: Society for Promoting Christian Knowledge.

Fitzmyer, Joseph A.

1974   "A Feature of Qumran Angelology and the Angels of 1 Cor 11:10." In *Essays on the Semitic Background of the New Testament,* 187–204. Missoula, Mont.: Scholars Press. (First published *New Testament Studies* 4 [1957–1958]:48–58; reprinted with new postscript in *Paul and Qumran,* ed. by Jerome Murphy-O'Connor, 31–47 [London: Chapman, 1968].)

1989   "Another Look at KEPHALE in 1 Corinthians 11:3." *New Testament Studies* 35:503–11.

Fox, Robin Lane

1987   *Pagans and Christians.* New York: Alfred A. Knopf.

Galen   *See* May.

Gleason, Maud

1990   "The Semiotics of Gender: Physiognomy and Self-Fashioning in the Second Century C.E." In *Before Sexuality: The Construction of Erotic Experience in the Ancient Greek World,* ed. by David M. Halperin, John J. Winkler, and Froma I. Zeitlin, 389–415. Princeton: Princeton University Press.

Goldin, Judah S.

1955   *The Fathers According to R. Nathan* [Avot de Rabbi Natan]. New Haven: Yale University Press.

Gryson, Roger

1976   *The Ministry of Women in the Early Church.* Trans. Jean Laporte and Mary Louise Hall. Collegeville, Minn.: Liturgical Press.

Hartel, G. (ed.)

1873   *C. Thasci Caecilii Cypriani Opera Omnia. Corpus Scriptorum Ecclesiasticorum Latinorum* 3.1. Vienna.

Hooker, Morna D.
  1964   "Authority on Her Head: An Examination of 1 Cor. xi.10." *New Testament Studies* 10:410–16.
Hopkins, Keith
  1978   *Conquerors and Slaves.* Sociological Studies in Roman History 1. Cambridge: Cambridge University Press.
Hurd, John C.
  1965   *The Origin of 1 Corinthians.* London: SCM.
Jervis, L. Ann
  1993   "But I Want You to Know . . .": Paul's Midrashic Intertextual Response to the Corinthian Worshipers (1 Cor 11:2–16)." *Journal of Biblical Literature* 112:231–46.
Johns, Catherine
  1982   *Sex or Symbol? Erotic Images of Greece and Rome.* London: British Museum Publications.
Kraemer, Ross S.
  1988   *Maenads, Martyrs, Matrons, Monastics: A Sourcebook on Women's Religions in the Greco-Roman World.* Philadelphia: Fortress.
  1992   *Her Share of the Blessings: Women's Religions in Paganism, Judaism and Christianity in the Greco-Roman World.* Oxford: Oxford University Press.
Küchler, Max
  1986   *Schweigen, Schmuck und Schleier: Drei neutestamentliche Vorschriften zur Verdrängung der Frauen auf dem Hintergrund einer frauenfeindlichen Exegese des Alten Testaments im antiken Judentum.* Novum Testamentum et Orbis Antiquus 1. Freiburg (Schweiz): Universitätsverlag; Göttingen: Vandenhoeck & Ruprecht.
Kuhnert, E.
  1909   "Fascinum." *Paulys Real-Encyclopädie der Classischen Altertumswissenschaft* 6(2):2009–14.
Lefkowitz, Mary R., and Maureen B. Fant
  1982   *Women's Life in Greece and Rome.* Baltimore: Johns Hopkins University Press.
Leyerle, Blake
  1993   "John Chrysostom on the Gaze." *Journal of Early Christian Studies* 1:159–74.
MacDonald, Dennis Ronald
  1983   *The Legend and The Apostle: The Battle for Paul in Story and Canon.* Philadelphia: Westminster.
  1988   "Corinthian Veils and Gnostic Androgynes." In *Images of the Feminine in Gnosticism,* ed. by Karen King, 276–92. Philadelphia: Fortress.
  1987   *"There Is No 'Male and Female' ": The Fate of a Dominical Saying in Paul and Gnosticism.* Harvard Dissertations in Religion. Philadelphia: Fortress.
Matter, E. Ann
  Forth-   "Monastic Women and Spiritual Autobiography: Exhibitionism, Voy-
  coming   eurism and Visionary Experience. A Response to Elizabeth Castelli."
           Protocols of the Center for Hermeneutical Studies. Berkeley, Calif.

May, Margaret Tallmage, trans.
  1968   *Galen: On the Usefulness of the Parts of the Body.* Ithaca: Cornell University Press.
Meeks, Wayne A.
  1974   "The Image of the Androgyne: Some Uses of a Symbol." *History of Religions* 13:165–208.
  1983   *The First Urban Christians.* New Haven: Yale University Press.
Miles, Margaret
  1989   *Carnal Knowing: Female Nakedness and Religious Meaning in the Christian West.* Boston: Beacon.
Mingana, A.
  1933   *Commentary of Theodore of Mopsuestia on the Lord's Prayer and on the Sacraments of Baptism and the Eucharist.* Woodbrooke Studies: Christian Documents 6, edited and translated with a critical apparatus. Cambridge, England: W. Heffer & Sons.
Murphy-O'Connor, Jerome
  1980   "Sex and Logic in 1 Corinthians 11:2–16." *Catholic Biblical Quarterly* 42:482–500.
Neyrey, Jerome
  1986   "Body Language in 1 Corinthians: The Use of Anthropological Models for Understanding Paul and His Opponents." In *Semeia 35: Social Scientific Criticism of the New Testament and Its Social World,* ed. by John H. Elliott, 129–70. Society of Biblical Literature. Decatur, Ga.: Scholars Press.
Pagett, A.
  1984   "Paul on Women in the Church: The Contradictions of Coiffure in 1 Corinthians 11:2–16." *Journal for the Study of the New Testament* 20:69–86.
Philonenko, Marc
  1968   *Joseph et Aséneth: Introduction, texte critique, traduction et notes.* Studia Post-Biblica 13. Leiden: Brill.
Pomeroy, Sarah
  1975   *Goddesses, Whores, Wives, and Slaves: Women in Classical Antiquity.* New York: Schocken.
Prusak, Bernard
  1974   "Woman Seductive Siren and Source of Sin? Pseudepigraphical Myths and Christian Origins." In *Religion and Sexism,* ed. by Rosemary Radford Ruether, 89–116. New York: Simon and Schuster.
Rossi, Mary Ann
  1991   "Priesthood, Precedent and Prejudice: On Recovering the Women Priests of Early Christianity, Containing a Translation from the Italian of 'Notes on the Female Priesthood in Antiquity' by Giorgio Otranto." *Journal of Feminist Studies in Religion* 7:73–94.
Schüssler Fiorenza, Elisabeth
  1983   *In Memory of Her: A Feminist Theological Reconstruction of Christian Origins.* New York: Crossroad.

Sissa, Giulia

    1990   *Greek Virginity.* Trans. Arthur Goldhammer. Revealing Antiquity 3. Cambridge: Harvard University Press.

Stücklin, Christoph

    1974   *Tertullian, De Virginibus Velandis: Übersetzung, Einleitung und Kommentar. Ein Beitrag zur altkirchlichen Frauenfrage.* Europäische Hochschuleschriften Series 23, vol. 26. Bern: Herbert Lang; Frankfurt: Peter Lang.

Tertullian

    1954   Quinti Septimi Flori Tertulliani *Opera, Pars I Opera Catholica, Pars II Opera Montanistica. Corpus Christianorum, Series Latina* 2. Turnhout: Brepols.

Thompson, Cynthia

    1988   "Hairstyles, Headcoverings and St. Paul: Portraits from Roman Corinth." *Biblical Archaeologist* 51:99–115.

Tonneau, Raymond, and Robert Devreesse

    1949   *Les homélies catéchétiques de Théodore de Mopsueste.* Vatican City: Biblioteca Apostolica Vaticana.

Veyne, Paul

    1987   "The Roman Empire." In *A History of Private Life. I: From Pagan Rome to Byzantium,* ed. by Paul Veyne, trans. Arthur Goldhammer, 5–233. Cambridge, Mass., and London: Belknap Press of Harvard University Press.

Walker, William O.

    1975   "1 Corinthians 11:2–16 and Paul's Views Concerning Woman." *Journal of Biblical Literature* 94:94–110.

Whitaker, E. C.

    1970   *Documents of the Baptismal Liturgy.* London: SPCK.

Winkler, John J.

    1990   *The Constraints of Desire: The Anthropology of Sex and Gender in Ancient Greece.* New York and London: Routledge.

Wire, Antoinette Clark

    1990   *The Corinthian Women Prophets.* Philadelphia: Fortress.

Wright, Frederick Adam, and Lillian B. Lawler

    1970   "Dress." *Oxford Classical Dictionary,* 2nd ed., 364–65. Oxford: Clarendon Press.

Yarbro Collins, Adela

    1988   *The Gospel and Women.* Orange, Calif.: Chapman College.

SIX

The Nakedness of a Woman's Voice,
the Pleasure in a Man's Mouth

An Oral History of Ancient Judaism

Howard Eilberg-Schwartz

A woman's voice is nakedness.
BABYLONIAN TALMUD, BERACHOT 24A

There is an interesting parallel between the statement from the Babylonian Talmud in the above epigraph and some of Freud's comments in one of his early case studies of hysteria. Both assume that a woman's voice and mouth are associated with her genitalia. Freud makes these comments in the context of discussing the case of Dora, a young woman who periodically developed symptoms affecting her mouth and voice. For stretches at a time, Dora lost the ability to speak and developed an irritating cough. Through Dora's analysis, Freud was drawn to the conclusion that Dora had erotic feelings for a family friend whom Freud calls Herr K. Freud speculates that on one occasion when she was embraced, Dora felt the pressure of his erect member against her groin. But because she could not acknowledge her feelings, they were displaced and expressed in her mouth. Her mouth had symbolically become her vagina.[1]

Perhaps Freud has made an important discovery here about the workings of the unconscious, about the indirect and hence disguised expression of sexual meanings through their diversion to other parts of the body. And yet to accept his interpretation is to ignore another important question: What is it that led him to associate Dora's mouth with her vagina? Stated this way, the burden of the question shifts away from the workings of Dora's unconscious, and toward Freud's activity as an interpreter. As an interpreter, Freud is in fact repeating a cultural process that transcends psychoanalytic discourse, for Freud is by no means the first man to make an association between a woman's mouth and the vagina. Indeed, the displacement from the lower to the upper body of a woman is a phenomenon that has appeared in a diversity of cultural settings. The question thus arises as to whether Freud is unknowingly participating in a process that he is simultaneously trying to describe. My purpose here is not to challenge

Freud's analysis of Dora, a task that has already been adequately performed by others,[2] but rather to pursue an alternative understanding of this symbolic slippage from the mouth to the vagina. While unconscious processes may very well be at work in this sort of symbolism, I want to show that it is also part of a much broader symbolic process which involves ideas about gender and cultural reproduction and which is rooted in specific kinds of social relations.

The specific focus of this essay is the eroticization of the female mouth in ancient Judaism. My initial focus is on Rabbinic Judaism (200–600 C.E.), although I will show that the erotic symbolism of the female mouth is rooted in cultural processes already at work in ancient Israelite religion as well. My strategy is to begin with sources that most explicitly treat a woman's mouth as erotic and then work backward as a way of tracking the symbolic processes involved in this linking of the female mouth, voice, and sexuality.

The eroticization of the female mouth, I argue, takes its place in a larger cultural process that treats the mouth as a male organ of reproduction and dissemination.[3] In raising the issue of the male mouth, I am seeking to complicate the overly simplistic constructions that conflate masculinity and the phallus. As this essay shows, masculinity is a construction that also claims other parts of the body, in particular the mouth. And it is the fecundity of the male mouth that both requires and generates an eroticization of the female mouth. In many ways, then, the male mouth serves as a replacement for the phallus, for it absorbs the symbolic concerns that often are invested in the male sexual organ. The linking of the mouth and the phallus that is discussed here might be taken as an instance of what has recently come to be called "phallogocentrism," those cultural or theoretical systems in which there is a conflation of the phallus and the logos (speech, thought).

And yet this association of the mouth and masculinity is rendered problematic, indeed put at risk, by the association of the mouth with the vagina. In considering this possibility, I am aware of how masculinity as a gender construction is always precarious and in danger of being undermined by the very constructions that sustain it. My larger purpose, then, is to show how the transference between the vagina and mouth is, at least in one religious tradition, part of a broad and complex cultural dialectic. This analysis in turn renders questionable the nature of Freud's insight, for it raises the possibility that psychoanalytic discourse may itself embody and reproduce the very symbolic process it seeks to disclose.

THE NAKEDNESS OF THE FEMALE VOICE

It would be wrong to assume that ancient Judaism everywhere and always makes an association between a woman's mouth, voice, and sexuality. To make such a generalization would be a reification of cultural systems with complex and conflicting impulses. And yet there are several sources in which the female mouth and voice are laden with sexual meanings.

Consider first the Rabbinic statement that "a woman's voice is nakedness." This assertion appears in the Babylonian Talmud (Berachot 24a) at the end of a discussion of what constitutes indecent exposure in a woman:

Rabbi Isaac said: "[An exposed] handbreath in a woman is nakedness." To what does this refer? Shall I say if one gazes at her? But has Rabbi Sheshet not already said, "Why does Scripture list the ornaments worn outside the clothes with the ornaments inside [when the Israelites took ornaments from the women of Midian, Num. 31:50]? To tell you that whoever gazes on the little finger of a woman, it is as if he gazes at her foul place." [Since Sheshet's earlier statement already prohibits looking even at a woman's little finger, Isaac's comment must refer to something else; otherwise it would be redundant.]

Rather, [Isaac's statement] refers to one's own wife and pertains to the matter of reciting the Shema prayer. [That is, a man cannot recite the Shema if he can gaze on an exposed handbreath in his wife.]

R. Hisda said, "[Exposure of] a woman's leg is nakedness, as it says [Isa. 47:2, referring to the fair maiden Babylon] 'Grasp the handmill and grind meal. Remove your veil, strip off your train, bare your leg, wade through the rivers' and it is written immediately following 'your nakedness shall be uncovered, and your shame shall be exposed.' "

Said Samuel, "A woman's voice is nakedness, as it says 'For your voice is sweet and your face is comely' " [Song 2:14].

Said Rabbi Sheshet, "The hair of a woman is nakedness, as it says, '[Behind your veil] your hair is like a flock of goats' " [Song 4:1].

As this passage begins, it seems that the concern with a woman's indecent exposure is global, pertaining to any and all contexts. But as the discussion unfolds the focus narrows; the concern with indecent exposure is relevant in particular to the context in which a man is reciting the Shema, one of the most important prayers that a man must recite to God. In reciting the Shema, a man is required to separate himself from any indecency, including his own nakedness, which must not be visible, as well as other offensive things such as urine or feces. After considering various situations in which a man might inappropriately recite the Shema—for example, when sleeping in a bed with another naked man or with naked members of his family—the discussion shifts to a woman's body. What kinds of exposure are indecent in a woman? The text lists the exposure of a handbreath of a woman's skin, her little finger, her leg, her hair, and her voice. According to Samuel, "a woman's voice is nakedness, as it says, 'For your voice is sweet and your face is comely' " (Song of Songs 2:14).[4] This statement does not directly link a woman's mouth with the vagina. But by eroticizing the voice, and by linking it to the exposure of other body parts including the vagina, the sound of a woman's voice is defined as indecent exposure, at least in the presence of a man who is reciting the Shema and perhaps in other contexts as well.[5]

Erotic associations of the female voice are also evident in a second excerpt from the Babylonian Talmud (Nedarim [Vows] 20a–b). As this text unfolds, the female voice and mouth are increasingly linked to sexual intercourse until, by the end, the idea of speaking to a woman is itself a way of euphemistically representing sexual intercourse.

> It was taught [on the authority of the early sages], "Never become accustomed to making vows since in the end you will violate oaths. Do not make a practice of visiting a non-observant Jew [*am haaretz*], because in the end he will feed you untithed food. And do not make a practice of visiting a non-observant priest, for in the end he will feed you heave-offering [which is only to be consumed by priests]. And do not engage overly much in conversation with the woman, for in the end you will come to illicit intercourse [or adultery] [*nî'ûf*]."

The discussion begins with a list of activities from which one should desist in order to avoid being led to various serious trespasses involving the mouth, such as violating oaths or eating untithed food. And finally, "Do not engage too much in conversation with a woman, for this will lead you to illicit intercourse [or adultery] [*nî'ûf*]." Thus what begins as a list about how to avoid actions that will lead to trespasses involving the mouth ends with a cautionary statement about how one's mouth can lead to sexual impropriety. The opening of a woman's mouth will be just the first of other, more serious openings.

This trail of associations next generates worries about the danger of gazing at various parts of a woman's body. It is as if the text is itself exhibiting the dangers of the female voice, shifting the reader's attention from her voice to the exposure of her body.

> Rabbi Aha in the name of Rabbi Yoshayiah says, "Whoever gazes at a woman will stumble in sin, and whoever looks at a woman's heel will have children [or sons] who are abnormal." Said Rab Yosef, "[This applies] even to his own wife with menstrual impurity."[6] Said Simeon ben Lakish, "The word 'heel' which is mentioned refers to the place of decay [the vagina], which is opposite the heel."[7]

At this point the text abruptly breaks into a discussion of the virtues of being "shamefaced" and fearing of God. It is as if the thought of seeing the woman's "place of decay" is too much to bear. The gaze is shifted from where it does not belong to the thought of God. Males are reminded that according to Scripture it is the fear of God that is to be before their faces, not unseemly sights, such as the lower parts of a woman's body. Those who are not shamefaced, the text concludes, must not have had their forefathers present at the revelation of God at Sinai.

> It was taught, [in Scripture it says, "And Moses said to the people, be not afraid, for God has come only in order to test you and so that] the fear of Him may be before your faces [and that you do not sin]" [Exod. 20:17]. "Fear of him" means modesty [*bôšet*], and "do not sin" teaches that modesty leads to fear of sin. On the basis of this they said: It is a good sign in a man if he is modest. Others say: Any man who does not become embarrassed easily is a sinner. And one who does not have a modest countenance, it is certain that his forefathers did not stand on Mount Sinai.

With this delicate reminder, the text returns to its logical and apparently inevitable progression of thought. Having begun with a woman's voice, and then gazed upon her body, the text turns to the matter of intercourse itself. One sage, R. Yohanan b. Dahabai, reportedly learned from the ministering angels how various forms of sexual misconduct create deformities in the offspring. "Overturning the table," that is, performing intercourse doggie style,[8] leads to the offspring's lameness; looking at "that place" causes blindness, kissing it causes muteness. Conversation during intercourse in turn causes deafness in the child. The point is difficult to miss: misuse of an organ during intercourse will cause deformity in future offspring in that very same organ. Whereas originally the sages were worried that conversation with a woman would lead to sex with her, they are now concerned about the impropriety of talking to a woman with whom one may appropriately have sex. Talking to a woman during intercourse is thus grouped with other inappropriate forms of sexual expression. Moreover, its placement in the list is significant. Sandwiched between kissing and looking at the vagina, conversation during intercourse is regarded as analogous to cunnilingus, and the woman's mouth as a vagina.

Not all sages share this restrictive view. As proof of an opposing viewpoint, a story is next recounted of Imma Shalom, who is asked by sages why her children are so exceedingly beautiful. She replies:

> [My husband] does not "converse" [i.e., have intercourse] with me either at the beginning of the night or the end of the night but only at midnight, and when he "converses" he exposes a spot and covers a spot and he is like one who is moved by a demon. And I asked him, "What is the reason?" And he answered, "So I will not set my eyes on another woman and have his [that is, my] sons become illegitimate."

Since this story simultaneously undercuts and confirms earlier suspicions, it serves as a fascinating conclusion to the discussion of the female voice. The discussion began with worries about speaking to a woman and now ends with unnamed sages asking a woman a question. It seems that the fears about a woman's voice have disappeared. And yet the question they ask and the answer they receive confirm the worries that were previously voiced. After all, they should have anticipated that she would tell them about how her husband has intercourse with her, in response to their interest in the beauty of her children. Beautiful children, as the previous discussion suggests, are the product of modest sexual behavior. Thus the case of Imma Shalom both contradicts and confirms the sages' worst fears. Talking to her does lead to a discussion of intercourse and to a graphic portrayal of the bedroom scene. And still more ironically, the woman herself uses "conversation" as a metaphor for sexual intercourse itself, a metaphor which appears elsewhere (B. Talmud, Berachot 3a). It is as if once asked, Imma Shalom confirms the association of eroticism and the female voice. There are multiple ironies here. A woman speaks to men and refers to sexual intercourse with her husband as "conversation." In doing so, she is simultaneously being modest by using euphemistic language and at the same time confirming the erotic associations of the female voice. For the present purposes, it is this imaginative linking of intercourse and conversation with a woman that is of concern. Thus we need not follow this discussion as it continues to unfold, for it leaves behind the question of the female voice, moving on to more permissive judgments about what kinds of pleasures are permitted during intercourse.

What sorts of symbolic and social processes led the sages to eroticize the female voice in this way? Is this simply the expression of Rabbinic worries about male desire, a desire which always carries the danger of leading to illicit sexual relations? Or is there something else that makes the female voice so tantalizing to the Rabbinic imagination? As I shall now suggest, the eroticization of the female voice is the logical consequence of a developing symbolic system which is itself rooted in the specific nature of the Rabbinic community. Furthermore, the meaning of these associations becomes evident only when we ask about the male mouth. The failure of secondary theoretical literature to attend to the male mouth is indicative of the way that that literature reproduces the structures of the discourse it is analyzing. Discussion of the female mouth as vagina, without attention to the male mouth, is to speak only from the gaze of the male. The male mouth is behind the voice but not an object of the voice. For this reason, it is not at all evident what role the eroticization of the female mouth serves. What is called for is an oral history of Judaism, a history that says what the mouth in general represents and what kind of cultural symbolism it speaks.

AN ORAL HISTORY OF JUDAISM

The eroticization of the female voice is closely linked to the emergence of the male mouth as an important organ for the reproduction and dissemination of Torah. Elsewhere, I have shown how the themes of procreation and genealogy, which are of utmost importance in Israelite religion, are extended by the early rabbis to Torah study and Torah knowledge.[9] That is not to deny that the sages continued to share earlier Israelite concerns about procreation and genealogy. But as the learning of Torah emerged as the paradigmatic religious act in the Rabbinic community, it absorbed the symbolic capital which had earlier been invested in procreation. That is, concerns about reproduction and transmission are symbolically extended from the human body to Torah knowledge itself. For the rabbis, the reproduction of Torah knowledge and clear lines of Torah dissemination are of paramount concern. This symbolism is already evident in the earliest Rabbinic sources: to some extent in the Mishnah (ca. 200 C.E.), the earliest Rabbinic document, and even more clearly in Avot (ca. early third century), the first Rabbinic text to reflect in a sustained way on the meaning of Torah study.

The Mishnah, for example, already develops an analogy between teacher-disciple and father-son relationships. As the Mishnah puts it, one's father brings one into this world, while one's teacher brings one into the world to come (Mishnah Baba Meṣia 2:11; Mishnah Keritot 6:9). By ignoring the role of the mother, a symmetry is established between being a father and being a sage. In addition to the analogy between birth and rebirth, which is explicit here, there is an implied comparison between procreation and Torah study. This analogy between the father-son and the rabbi-disciple relationships goes deeper than most interpreters have realized. A disciple's responsibilities are analogous to those of a son. Just as a son must perpetuate his father's lineage and protect its purity, a disciple must preserve his rabbi's teaching and transmit it without contamination to posterity. The genealogy of Torah knowledge is thus reminiscent and imitative of priestly genealogies. "Moses received the Torah from Sinai and transmitted it to Joshua, and Joshua to the elders, and the elders to the Prophets and the prophets transmitted it to the men of the Great Assembly" (Avot 1:1). This concern with Torah genealogy manifests itself in a Rabbinic concern with attributions: Rabbi So-and-so said in the name of Rabbi So-and-so. According to the Tosefta, a work which probably postdates the Mishnah, one who does not raise up disciples in effect loses his status as rabbi. "If a scholar has disciples and disciples of disciples, he is quoted as Rabbi; if his [immediate] disciples are forgotten, he is quoted as Rabban; if both are forgotten, he is quoted by his name" (Tosefta Eduyot 3:4). It is as if the title of rabbi is authorized by the production of a genealogy.

Not surprisingly, the explicit aspiration of the sages is to increase and disseminate Torah and raise many disciples. "One who does not increase [Torah knowledge] decreases it. One who does not learn is worthy of death" (Avot 1:13). The word "increase" (*marbeh*), which is used repeatedly in Avot, derives from the root *rbh*, the same root that is used in the formulation of the requirement that humans be fruitful and multiply (*rĕbû*) (Genesis 1:28, Mishnah Yebamot 6:6). Given their preoccupation with reproducing Torah knowledge, it is not surprising that the sages are obsessed with various ways in which Torah study might be interrupted or Torah knowledge diminished. One who forgets a single detail of what he has learned or one who interrupts his memorization of Torah to admire a blossoming tree is compared to a person who has committed a capital offense (Avot 3:7, 8). The sages' obsessive concern about the loss of Torah knowledge is reminiscent of their concerns about the waste of semen (Mishnah Niddah 2:1). One sage is even praised for never losing "a drop" (Avot 2:8). It is hard to miss the association between a "drop" of Torah and a "drop" of semen, which is referred to in the same document several passages later (Avot 3:1). Torah production, then, is a cultural equivalent of physical reproduction. A sage creates a genealogical line through the transmission of Torah. His link to perpetuity is dependent on the success and commitment of his intellectual heirs.

It is within this symbolic context that we can understand the first Rabbinic statement which explicitly denigrates conversation with women (Avot 1:5). Yose b. Yohanan of Jerusalem reportedly said, "Do not multiply conversation with the woman." It is this very statement that triggered the associations to a woman's body and sexual intercourse in the text previously considered (Babylonian Talmud, Nedarim 20a). But here, in its earliest appearance in Rabbinic literature, the denigration of the woman's voice occurs without its eroticization. The fear is not that conversation with a woman will lead to illicit sexual activity. Rather, the text simply comments that the sages "said this in reference to a man's wife, all the more so another man's wife. Hence the sages have said, 'He that talks much with women brings evil upon himself and neglects the study of the Torah and will eventually inherit Gehinnom [hell].' " In this case, multiplying conversation with a woman causes one to neglect the study of Torah, with the result that one will not be involved in "increasing Torah." In fact, this expression "neglecting words of Torah" (*bôṭēl mi-dibĕrê-tôrāh*) is reminiscent of the language the sages use to describe a man who neglects his obligation to be fruitful and multiply (*bôṭēl mi-pĕriah ûrĕbiah*) (Mishnah Yebamot 6:6).

Since the reproduction and transmission of Torah is homo-lineal, that is, from one male to another, talking to a woman is wasting words that could better be spent on Torah study. The denigration of the female voice thus explains why women, who otherwise have all the physical equipment necessary for reproducing Torah, are otherwise excluded from the genealogy of knowledge. Here, then, is the beginning of a symbolism that eventually, and perhaps even naturally, gives rise to the association between a woman's voice and sexuality. A woman's voice is disruptive to Torah learning, which is conceptualized as the male form of cultural reproduction. It is only male mouths that are the proper organs for the dissemination of Torah. Since women's voices are not seminal, their mouths are simply vaginas. Eroticizing the female voice, then, serves several purposes simultaneously. It defines speaking to a woman as an illicit form of reproductive activity, like masturbation, a waste of precious words that could better be directed elsewhere. At the same time, it compares speech with a woman to sexual intercourse, which is itself considered disruptive to the reproduction of Torah.[10]

As we shall now see, this symbolic construction is not exclusively a phenomenon of Rabbinic Judaism. A similar symbolism is already in the process of formation, although not fully developed, in Israelite religion. Rabbinic ideas represent more fully elaborated versions of these earlier conceptions.

THE OPEN MOUTH

The association between the female mouth and vagina is evident in several contexts in the Hebrew Bible. Consider first the prophecy of Hosea, a prophet who is well known for personifying Israel as an adulterous woman who whores after other nations.[11] According to Hosea, God demands that the Israelites rebuke their mother Israel "for she is not My wife and I am not her husband. And let her put away her harlotry from her face, and her adultery from between her breasts" (Hosea 2:4). The metaphor of adultery is used here to describe Israel's whoring after other gods. The sexual imagery is evoked both by the terms "harlotry" and "adultery" and by the reference to the breasts. Most interpreters construe this statement as referring to some sort of jewelry, clothing, or makeup that signifies Israel's status as harlot.[12] Israel will remove these from her face and breast to signify "her" renewed recommitment to God.

But there is another layer of meaning operating here that cannot be ignored. As Hosea emphasizes elsewhere, it is through the mouth and speech that Israel opens herself up to foreign gods. Israel's face, therefore, or more specifically her mouth, is equivalent to the vagina. This association becomes more explicit as the metaphor unfolds. According to Hosea (2:19), God envisions a day of reconciliation.

> Assuredly, I will speak coaxingly to her and lead her through the wilderness and speak to her tenderly. . . . And in that day, declares the Lord, you will call [Me] *Ishi* [My husband]. And no more will you call [Me] *Baali* [My husband/My Baal]. For I will remove the names of the Baals from her mouth and they shall nevermore be mentioned by name. (Hosea 2:16–19)

As this makes evident, the restoration of God's relationship involves removing the word "Baal," the name of another god, from Israel's mouth. It is the presence of that name in her mouth that constitutes the adultery. And it is the restoration of God's name to her mouth that makes God once more her proper husband.

A similar substitution of the mouth for the vagina occurs in Ezekiel's extended portrayal of God as the lover and protector of Israel, who is met-aphorically a woman (Ezekiel 16). Ezekiel employs the image of sexual intercourse to describe metaphorically the relationship of God and Israel. Israel goes whoring after other gods: "You spread your legs at all passersby" (Ezek. 16:25). But in the end God says, "I will establish My covenant with you and you shall know that I am the Lord. Thus you shall remember and feel shame and you shall be too abashed to open your mouth again, when I have forgiven you for all that you did, declares the Lord God" (Ezek. 16:62–63).[13] Here again we have the familiar contrast between whoring after other gods and fidelity to the Lord. Note, however, the shift from the imagery of the open legs to the closed mouth. Israel opens her legs to all passersby. But when she again knows God, her mouth will remain shut. The closing of the mouth may indicate that Israel can no longer assert herself, as Greenberg suggests (1983:292). To leave off the analysis here, however, entirely misses the way in which the focus shifts from the opening of Israel's vagina to the closing of her mouth. Israel, as a collectivity, opens her vagina to other nations. But at the individual level it is the mouth that gives of-fense.

There are other passages as well that may presuppose an association between the female mouth and vagina. "The mouth of forbidden women [*zārôt*] is a deep pit. He who is doomed by the Lord falls into it" (Prov. 22:14). "My son, listen to my wisdom; incline your ear to my insight . . . while your lips hold fast to knowledge. For the lips of a forbidden woman drip honey; her mouth [*ḥikkāh*] is smoother than oil" (Prov. 5:1–3). "Your lips, O my bride, drop honey, honey and milk are under your tongue" (Song 4:11). It would be a mistake, however, to overgeneralize these asso-ciations, since there are many contexts in which the female mouth is a positive image—for example, the woman of worth who opens her mouth with wisdom (Prov. 31:26), an image that is related to the feminine image of wisdom.[14]

As indicated above, discussion of the female mouth would be incomplete without attention to the male mouth and its role in the religious symbolism of ancient Israel. The male mouth is regarded as the organ for the dissem-ination and occasionally even the reception of God's word. This function of the mouth is thus responsible for worries about the purity of the mouth. For example, when Isaiah is first called by God, he cries out:

> Woe is me; I am lost! For I am a man of unclean lips and I live among a people
> of unclean lips. . . . Then one of the seraphs flew over to me with a live coal

which he had taken from the altar with a pair of tongs. He touched it to my lips and declared, "Now that it has touched your lips, your guilt shall depart and your sin be purged away." Then I heard the voice of my Lord saying "Whom shall I send?" (Isa. 6:5–8)

Isaiah cannot serve as God's mouthpiece until his mouth has been purified and becomes a pure conduit for the divine word.

This theme of the male mouth is also developed in various myths concerning the relationship of Moses and God, most of which are attributed to early Biblical sources (J and E). In response to God's initial call, Moses protests that he is heavy of mouth and heavy of tongue (Exod. 4:10), an idea that prefigures in obvious ways the passage from Isaiah discussed above. Elsewhere (in the Priestly narrative), Moses is described as uncircumcised of lips (Exod. 6:12), an expression about which I shall have more to say below.

Indeed, the unfolding relationship between Moses and God can be described as a dance of intimacy in which the mouth and face play key roles. Initially, God appears to Moses in the burning bush (Exod. 3:4).[15] While God only instructs Moses to remove his sandals, Moses averts his face as well. This foreshadows Moses' protests about the inadequacy of his mouth and tongue (Exod. 4:10). God rebukes Moses for his reluctance. "Who has made the human mouth? . . . Is it not I the Lord? Now therefore go and I will be with your mouth and will tell you what to say" (4:11–12). Once more Moses expresses his reluctance, whereupon God compromises: "There is your brother Aaron the Levite. He, I know, speaks readily. . . . You shall speak to him and put words in his mouth—I will be with your mouth and with his mouth as you speak and tell both of you what to do— and he shall speak for you to the people. Thus he shall be your spokesperson [lit. he will be a mouth for you] and you will be a god for him" (4:14– 16).[16] The relationship of Moses and Aaron is thus analogous to that of Moses and God. Aaron is Moses' mouth(piece) just as Moses is God's.

Some time later Moses and Aaron and other leaders go up the mountain and they see God (Exod. 24:9–11). The text, however, describes only what is under God's feet; the gaze is once again averted. According to another passage (Exod. 33:7–11), Moses would go into the cloud which had descended on the tent of meeting and the Lord would speak to Moses "face to face," as a man speaks to an intimate. This notion of unmediated communication ultimately becomes the defining characteristic of Moses' relationship to God (Num. 12:8, 34:10). Shortly thereafter (Exod. 33:13) Moses says to God, "If I have found favor in Your eyes, show me now Your ways." Here is not the place to analyze this passage in detail, but the use of the word *face* is exceedingly interesting: God responds by saying, "My face will go before you." God's face is obviously a synecdoche for God's whole being. Moses responds by saying, "If Your face does not lead us, do not move us from here" (33:14–15).

God eventually reassures Moses once more and promises to pass all the divine goodness before Moses' "face." But God cautions Moses that "you cannot see My face, for no one may see My face and live." To protect Moses, God indicates that the divine hand will be placed over Moses and when taken away Moses will see only the divine backside (33:19–23).

One last time Moses goes up the mountain. When he descends his face beams with light and the people are afraid to approach him (Exod. 34:29–30). But eventually they draw closer and Moses repeats what God has said. When he is finished speaking, Moses covers his face with a veil. He removes it only when he goes in to speak with God and he replaces it when he comes out (34:32–34). The removing of Moses' veil has obvious connections with the idea that God speaks to Moses "face to face." In one context, Moses is even said to speak to God "mouth to mouth" (Num. 12:8). This differentiates Moses from his siblings Aaron and Miriam, to whom God speaks in less direct fashion. The representation of God and Moses speaking "mouth to mouth" is a very intimate image: God does not speak into Moses' ear, but mouth to mouth the word is passed.

These passages suggest that the mouth is the organ of dissemination, and at times even reception, of the divine word. What is being represented here, accordingly, is a genealogy of knowledge that prefigures Rabbinic ideas about the reproduction and dissemination of Torah. Furthermore, we have in these passages an incipient idea of oral Torah, that is, a Torah that is passed from mouth to mouth. Divine knowledge is passed through men, from one mouth to the next. God puts words in Moses' mouth, who gives them to Aaron. And God speaks directly to Moses, who only uncovers his face to pass along received knowledge to Israel. This symbolism is given expression in later sources as well. "I am the Lord your God who brought you out of the land of Egypt, open wide your mouth and I will fill it" (Ps. 81:11).

This notion of the mouth as the organ for the dissemination and sometimes reception of the divine word, and hence as an organ whose control and purity are required, is fully developed in Biblical wisdom literature. Consider only two of the many examples. "He that guards his mouth preserves his life. He who opens wide his lips, it is his ruin" (Prov. 13:3). "The mouth of the righteous bears wisdom, but the treacherous tongue shall be cut off" (Prov. 10:31).

This notion of a cultural transmission that is intimately connected to the mouth flows alongside and draws upon another symbolism of transmission, which I have explored elsewhere.[17] I refer to the ideology of the seed. Within this cultural stream, the covenant between God and Abraham is passed genealogically through Abraham's seed, a notion of genealogy that is symbolized by the penis and circumcision. These two notions of transmission and continuity sometimes interpenetrate. According to Deutero-Isaiah, God says, "My spirit which is upon you and my words which I have placed in your mouth shall not be absent from your mouth, nor from the mouth of your seed, nor from the mouth of your seed's seed" (Isa. 59:21).

The male mouth, however, symbolizes more than just continuity. It also has potentially erotic associations, associations that are simultaneously powerful and problematic. As mentioned previously, the relationship between God and Israel is frequently conceptualized as that between husband and wife. In some cases, God is even said to metaphorically have intercourse with Israel (e.g., Ezekiel 16:8). We also know that idolatry is routinely represented as a feminized Israel whoring after other gods. Moreover, we have already seen how there is a slippage from the metaphor of Israel opening her legs in illicit sexual activity to the image of her opening her mouth to idolatry.

But this heterosexual metaphor, which works so well when speaking about Israel as a collectivity, is more problematic in contexts in which God speaks to individual male Israelites, such as Moses or other prophets. What at the level of the collectivity is conceptualized as God penetrating the female Israel is at the interpersonal level represented as God putting words in some male's mouth. Thus there is a series of structural homologies that are potentially available and sometimes exploited: not just the well-known relationship between revelation and intercourse, but also a homology between the metaphoric phallus of God and God's mouth, on the one hand, and the metaphoric vagina of Israel and the mouth of receptive Israelite males, on the other. The sliding between these two symbolic domains is evident, for example, in Ezekiel's description of God having intercourse with Israel: "Now when I passed by you and looked upon you and behold your time was the time of love, I spread my skirt over you and covered your nakedness and I took an oath to you and I entered into a covenant with you" (16:8). Interpreters have tended to think of this oath as a kind of marriage vow or pledge of fidelity, although there is no evidence of such a ceremony in ancient Israel.[18] Moreover, the word "oath" is never used as a description of a marriage pledge except in this context.[19] But it may be significant that an oath is sometimes associated with the penis. In two different early Biblical narratives, a patriarch instructs a servant or son to reach under the patriarch's thigh and take an oath. As many interpreters have noted, the thigh is here a euphemism for the penis, which is grasped while the oath is taken.[20]

To return to the love scene between God and Israel, the important point to note is how at the moment of intercourse the text abruptly breaks off the metaphor. God does not enter Israel with a penis, but enters into a covenant with Israel by an oath. God's voice steps in to displace the image of a divine phallus.[21] Given this linkage between the phallus and the divine mouth, it is interesting that Ezekiel tastes honey in his mouth when he eats the scroll God has given him (2:9–3:3)—an image that seemingly evokes associations to the vagina, as suggested by those passages mentioned earlier in which a woman's mouth is described as dripping with honey. Indeed, we have already seen how Ezekiel seems to play on the parallel between the mouth and vagina of Israel that is open to all passersby. It is as if Ezekiel has become the woman Israel who is receptive to the dissemination of God's word.

Another instance of feminization may be at work in the earlier narratives concerning the relationship of Moses and God.[22] The story of Moses veiling his face (Exodus 34:29–35) certainly is reminiscent of stories in which women, such as Rebecca and Tamar, don a veil (Genesis 24:65, 38:14). The purpose of veiling differs in the cases of the two women. Tamar veils so that Judah will not recognize her and so that she will be able to dupe him into intercourse with her. Rebecca, for her part, veils out of apparent modesty when she meets Isaac for the first time. It is true that Moses veils his face because it is transformed and initially frightens the people of Israel. And yet the image of Moses' veil does seem to carry other possible meanings as well. Moses is veiled after his most intimate moment with God. After forty days and nights on the mountain, during which time he neither eats nor drinks, Moses returns to the people with his face transfigured in some way, perhaps abeam with light. Indeed, the transformation of Moses' face points to the intimate and direct contact of his face with the glory of God, and thus is intended as a graphic sign of Moses speaking to God face to face. It also demonstrates his receptivity to God's word. It is almost as if Moses has become a bride to God in this most personal of contacts. Later Rabbinic traditions suggest that from this point onward Moses had no further sexual contact with his wife.

If fidelity in a man involves taking God's words in his mouth, then faithlessness is opening the mouth to other gods. "You sons of a sorceress, you offspring of an adulterer and harlot, with whom do you act so familiarly, at whom do you open your mouth and stick out your tongue [French kiss]? Are you not children of iniquity, offspring of treachery, you who inflame yourselves among the terebinths, under every verdant tree?" (Isaiah 57:3–5). As this passage unfolds, the sexual imagery becomes still more explicit: "You have made a covenant with them [i.e., the terebinths], you have loved bedding with them; you have chosen lust" (57:8).[23] In this image of whoring, it is not the vagina of Israel that is inappropriately open, but the mouths of the sorceress's sons. The male mouth is homologous to the vagina of Israel, collectively imagined.

The possible gender reversals of Ezekiel and Moses make sense given the frequent personification of Israel as a female in Israelite imagery. The idea that males are women with respect to God is simply a logical extension of the idea that collectively Israel is female. This phenomenon of gender reversal is well known from contexts of other sorts. In Freud's study of Schreber, for example, we meet a man who sometimes imagines becoming a woman so he can be penetrated by God. Similar reversals are discussed by Caroline Bynum in the imagery of Jesus as mother. It may be precisely this sort of slippage that the metaphor of Moses' uncircumcised lips (Exod. 6:12(P)) attempts to counteract. By linking the lips and the penis, this metaphor reasserts the masculinity of Moses' mouth, a masculinity which was in jeopardy in the early J-text narrative of his veiling (Exod. 34:29–35).

In the narratives recounting the relationship between Moses and God, there is no explicit equation of the divine mouth and phallus like that which occurs later in Ezekiel. And yet a careful reading of these sources suggests that such a displacement may actually be at work. As I have argued in other contexts,[24] the genitals of the deity are unimaginable in Israelite religion. In those passages that involve sightings of God there is an obvious hesitancy about identifying the divine sex. This is not to deny that God is generally conceptualized as of masculine gender. But there is evident a desire to hide the sex of God. Thus when Moses, Aaron, Nadab, and Abihu see God, the text only describes what is under God's feet (Exod. 24:10). And when Moses asks to see God's glory, God turns away, as if to keep all sexual characteristics hidden (Exod. 33:23). This veiling of the divine sex is the result of a number of basic dilemmas lying at the heart of monotheism.[25] Since God has no consort, the idea of divine genitals is incoherent; if God has a penis, what does he do with it? Moreover, there is a potential homoerotic relationship between God and the male Israelites with whom He is intimate. But this poses a problem for a tradition which links masculinity to heterosexual desire and procreation. To escape these conceptual dilemmas, therefore, the gaze is averted from those parts of the deity's form that normally signal a body's sex. The ambivalence about thinking about God's genitals is thus shifted to the face of God. Here we have something analogous to a Freudian displacement: because the genitals cannot be thought, the ambivalence is transferred to the face. The face is a perfect screen. Hiding the face is itself an act that veils the divine sex, since the face is an indicator of a body's sex. At the same time, the veiling of God's face also averts attention from God's lower body, which poses a problem within monotheism. The reasons for this displacement, however, are not psychological, as in the Freudian model. They are cultural. The transference to the face veils a problem that arises within monotheism as a cultural system. That the face replaces the phallus is also suggested by the importance in later narratives (P) of God's speech in creating the world. It is the word of God that replaces the generativity of the phallus.

This substitution of the face and mouth for the phallus returns us to the image of God speaking mouth to mouth with Moses. It is difficult to know how far to push this line of analysis. We are dealing here with innuendos, cultural connections, and displacements. And yet to ignore these connections and linkages is to miss the ways in which culture operates. Conceptual domains are always being constructed through reference to other domains. To the extent that the image of God speaking to Moses does have erotic overtones, as well it might, a number of possibilities come to mind that seem scandalous for a system that otherwise embraces heterosexuality. One is reminded of Irigaray's (1985) image of "when our lips speak to each other." As Jane Gallop comments on Irigaray's image: "Whose lips (plural even in one [female] body), not to mention which lips, speak to whose (which)?"[26] Is it really surprising that Moses is feminized after this encounter with God?

This analysis, I would also suggest, exposes another reason for the feminine personification of Wisdom in Israelite religion. Some interpreters see the image of a female Wisdom as deriving in part from the positive role of women as advisers in households, or simply as satisfying a need for a mother figure.[27] But given the dilemmas of homoeroticism, the image of Wisdom as a female intervenes in and thereby mediates between a male God and a male Israelite whose mutual encounter may threaten to become too intimate. It is thus significant that a female Wisdom tends to appear in Proverbs when individual men are being addressed. They should open their mouths to wisdom and not to other, foreign women. The gender and body imagery is here completely reversed. Whereas in Ezekiel a feminized and collective Israel lusted after the large phalluses of the Egyptians (Ezek. 16:26), in Proverbs (10:31) it is the mouths of Israelite men that should be open to a feminized Wisdom. The thought of a male with his mouth open to a male god has been veiled once more.

CONCLUSION

The transference from the vagina to the mouth is not simply a result of psychic repression. Such matters are complex cultural issues that involve ideas about gender, reproduction, and revelation and that dialectically play in and out of one another at various cultural levels. In this case, the eroticization of the female voice is deeply entangled in notions of masculinity—and masculinity, as is now evident, is not just about the phallus. It is also very much about the mouth and the role that the mouth plays in the dissemination of God's word. To be sure, the male mouth is phallic in an important sense. It is, after all, symbolically constructed from meanings that are related to the penis. But it also signals a repression of the penis: because God's penis cannot be imagined, the continuity between God and men must be oral. It is not at all clear, therefore, that an eroticization of the female lips could disrupt this form of phallogocentrism, as Irigaray suggests. Rather, the link between the vagina and the female mouth is part of the very structure that seems to make such phallogocentrism possible. Yet this construction of masculinity is also inherently unstable, for the male must be feminized in the very constructions that attempt to exclude women from the intimate and exclusive relationship between God and men. And when the male is feminized, and his mouth now full of honey takes in the word of God, the human male has nearly disappeared and is, at the level of symbolism, rendered invisible.

NOTES

I would like to thank David Biale, Daniel Boyarin, Tikvah Frymer-Kensky, Martin Jaffee, and Riv-Ellen Prell, all of whom made important suggestions on a previous draft of this essay.

1. See Freud 1905:30, 83. On some of the ideas that led Freud to this insight, see Geller 1992.

2. See, for example, Gearhart 1979, Hertz 1983, Lewin 1973, Marcus 1976, Moi 1981, Muslin and Gill 1978, Ramas 1980, Rose 1978, and Sprengnether 1985.

3. Some of the ideas in this essay are anticipated in Mary O'Brien's *Politics of Reproduction* (1981). O'Brien explores how images of reproduction and continuity are appropriated for certain activities of male creativity in general, such as philosophizing. My disagreement with O'Brien concerns her ideas about why and how this occurred. She links this development with a shift to a newfound discovery of paternity. The notion that paternity is discovered rather than constructed is problematic, as has been suggested by Carol Delaney 1986. As my own analysis suggests, such symbolism becomes important precisely when paternity in the physical sense ceases to be so important (see Eilberg-Schwartz 1990:195–234).

4. Quotations from the Hebrew Bible generally follow the Jewish Publication Society translation (1985). In a few cases I have translated more literally to illustrate a point.

5. There is an ambiguity running throughout this passage as to whether a woman's voice is defined as indecent exposure exclusively with regard to reciting the Shema or as a general pronouncement. Samuel's statement about a woman's voice is repeated (B. Qidushin 70a) in a completely different context that has nothing to do with prayer.

6. That is, even though the menstrual impurity should itself serve as a deterrent, gazing at one's wife's heel is problematic even if she is in a state of menstrual impurity.

7. "The place of decay" seems to be a reference to the vagina. But it is not clear what it means to say that the vagina is opposite the heel. Alternatively, the place of decay could mean the rectum.

8. Rashi interprets this expression to mean that the woman is on top.

9. See Eilberg-Schwartz 1990:229–34.

10. The Mishnah and later Rabbinic sources, for example, discuss the maximum

amount of time that a sage may be away from his wife for the purposes of Torah study. See Biale 1992:33–59 and Boyarin 1993:134–66.

11. On this image, see Setel 1985.

12. See, for example, Andersen and Freedman 1980:224 and Wolff 1974:33.

13. Eichrodt 1970:216–17 argues that this passage was not originally part of Ezekiel.

14. See Camp 1985:81–84.

15. At the outset, the narrative suggests that an angel of the Lord appears to Moses in the bush (Exod. 3:2). But subsequently the text says that God Himself speaks to Moses from the bush (3:4).

16. I have translated this passage more literally than the JPS rendition to convey the importance of the mouth in this discussion.

17. Eilberg-Schwartz 1990:141–76. See also Delaney 1977.

18. See, for example, Eichrodt 1970:205 and Greenberg 1983:277. Both of these interpreters note numerous difficulties in assuming that this is simply a marriage vow or oath.

19. Greenberg 1983:278 notes that nowhere except in this passage is this declaration called an oath and nowhere is marriage expressly called a covenant.

20. I have discussed this practice elsewhere (Eilberg-Schwartz 1990:169–70).

21. See my fuller argument in Eilberg-Schwartz 1994:113–14.

22. On the feminization of Moses more generally, see Eilberg-Schwartz 1994:142–48.

23. The last two words of the Hebrew text read *yād ḥāzît*. Some commentators take *yād* (normally "hand") in the sense "phallus"; others, relying on Ugaritic, translate it as "lust."

24. Eilberg-Schwartz 1991, 1994. I would like to acknowledge the important discussions I had with Tikvah Frymer-Kensky when first formulating this idea.

25. I have developed this point in more detail in Eilberg-Schwartz 1994.

26. See Gallop 1982:81.

27. See Camp 1985 and Patai 1967:23.

REFERENCES

Andersen, Francis I., and David Noel Freedman
1980   *Hosea.* The Anchor Bible Series. Garden City, N.Y.: Doubleday.
Biale, David
1992   *Eros and the Jews.* New York: Basic Books.
Boyarin, Daniel
1993   *Carnal Israel: Reading Sex in Talmudic Culture.* Berkeley and Los Angeles: University of California Press.
Camp, Claudia
1985   *Wisdom and the Feminine in the Book of Proverbs.* Sheffield: Almond.
Delaney, Carol
1977   "The Legacy of Abraham." In *Beyond Androcentrism,* ed. by Rita Gross, 217–36. Missoula, Mont.: Scholars Press.
1986   "The Meaning of Paternity and the Virgin Birth Debate." *Man* 21(3):494–513.

Eichrodt, Walther
    1970   *Ezekiel.* London: SCM Press.
Eilberg-Schwartz, Howard
    1990   *The Savage in Judaism: An Anthropology of Israelite Religion and Ancient Judaism.* Bloomington: Indiana University Press.
    1991   "People of the Body: The Problem of the Body for the People of the Book." *Journal of the History of Sexuality* 2(1): 1–24.
    1994   *God's Phallus and Other Problems for Men and Monotheism.* Boston: Beacon Press.
Freud, Sigmund
    1905   "Fragment of an Analysis of a Case of Hysteria." *Standard Edition,* ed. by James Strachey, 1–122. London: Hogarth Press.
Gallop, Jane
    1982   *The Daughter's Seduction: Feminism and Psychoanalysis.* Ithaca: Cornell University Press.
Gearhart, Suzanne
    1979   "The Scene of Psychoanalysis: The Unanswered Questions of Dora." In *The Tropology of Freud. Diacritics* 9(1):114–26.
Geller, Jay
    1992   "(G)nos(e)ology: The Cultural Construction of the Other." In *People of the Body: Jews and Judaism from an Embodied Perspective,* ed. by Howard Eilberg-Schwartz, 243–82. Albany: State University of New York Press.
Greenberg, Moshe
    1983   *Ezekiel, 1–20.* Anchor Bible Series. Garden City, N.Y.: Doubleday.
Hertz, Neil
    1983   "Dora's Secrets, Freud's Techniques." In *A Fine Romance: Freud and Dora,* ed. by Neil Hertz. *Diacritics* 13(1):65–76.
Irigaray, Luce
    1985   "When Our Lips Speak Together." In *This Sex Which Is Not One.* Trans. Catherine Porter with Carolyn Burke, 205–18. Ithaca: Cornell University Press.
Jewish Publication Society
    1985   *Tanakh: The Holy Scriptures.* Philadelphia: Jewish Publication Society.
Lewin, Karl Kay
    1973   "Dora Revisited." *Psychoanalytic Review* 60:519–32.
Marcus, Steven
    1976   "Freud and Dora: Story, History, Case History." In *Representations: Essays on Literature and Society,* 247–310. New York: Random House.
Moi, Toril
    1981   "Representation of Patriarchy: Sexuality and Epistemology in Freud's Dora." *Feminist Review* 9:60–73.
Muslin, Hyman, and Merton Gill
    1978   "Transference in the Dora Case." *Journal of the American Psychiatric Association* 26:311–28.
O'Brien, Mary
    1981   *The Politics of Reproduction.* Boston: Routledge and Kegan Paul.

Patai, Raphael
　1967　*The Hebrew Goddess.* New York: Ktav.
Ramas, Maria
　1980　"Freud's Dora, Dora's Hysteria: The Negation of a Woman's Rebellion."
　　　Feminist Studies 6:472–510.
Rose, Jacqueline
　1978　"Dora—Fragment of an Analysis." *m/f* 2:5–21.
Setel, T. Drorah
　1985　"Prophets and Pornography: Female Sexual Imagery in Hosea." In *Feminist Interpretation of the Bible,* ed. by Letty M. Russell, 86–95. Philadelphia: Westminster.
Sprengnether, Madelon
　1985　"Enforcing Oedipus: Freud and Dora." In *The Mother Tongue,* ed. by Shirley Nelson Garner et al., 51–71. Ithaca: Cornell University Press.
Wolff, Hans Walter
　1974　*Hosea.* Philadelphia: Fortress.

~~~oᴓᴓo~~~

Making Up a Woman

The Face of Roman Gender

Amy Richlin

> *I talk on the telephone for hours*
> *With a pound and a half of cream upon my face.*
> *I'm strictly a female female . . .*
> RICHARD RODGERS AND OSCAR HAMMERSTEIN II,
> "I ENJOY BEING A GIRL" (*Flower Drum Song*)

It is noticeable in many societies, of which ancient Rome is certainly one, that women wear makeup and men do not.[1] Sometimes, where this is so, it seems as if wearing makeup is almost constitutive of femaleness, or of femme-ness. Why should this be so?

One explanatory model would posit a social reason: women wear makeup to look beautiful and so to attract lovers. But this reasoning is circular—it amounts to saying that women wear makeup to show that they are female. This is an instance of what Judith Butler describes as the performative aspect of gender; it is as if, in the Rodgers and Hammerstein tune "I Enjoy Being a Girl," the verb "being" were transitive. As the character Linda Low says shortly before launching into the song, "I want to be a success as a girl. . . . The main thing is for a woman to be successful in her gender."[2] Thus the terms "look beautiful," "wear makeup," and "attract lovers" become interchangeable, synonymous; and beauty seems to lie, not only in the eye of the beholder, but in the labor of the beheld: the pure act of applying makeup becomes a token of the lengths to which the beheld is willing to go for the beholder. And thus in the current transsexual beauty contest known as "voguing," the assumption of women's clothing and makeup pushes biological males over the line into femaleness. Makeup then becomes the mark of gender—or *a* mark of gender.[3]

Of course, the usual mark of gender is elsewhere, lower down; perhaps this suggests a better model to explain why women wear makeup and men do not. Perhaps the reason women paint their *faces* is to hide something: by painting the outside, they contain what is inside; by painting the top, they conceal (but mark) the bottom. Nancy Vickers writes, apropos of the face of Medusa as a sign of her rape, "The obsessively spoken part—the face—[becomes] the other side of the obsessively unspoken . . . part—the genitalia . . . and fear of the female body is mastered through polarized figurations that can only denigrate or idealize."[4] And the reason *women* paint their faces is to hide something men do not have. After all, the faces of women are like the faces of (clean-shaven) men, with eyes, nose, mouth; you would not know to look at them that there was something completely different down there. Or perhaps women use makeup to mark something they are missing that men do have; hence the erotic allure of the bearded lady.[5] A man wearing makeup and long hair, or a woman wearing no makeup and short hair, can in this culture provoke the fascinated question "Is that a boy or is it a girl?" Once the signs on top are blurred, the real question comes out: what is the bottom line?

Likewise the application of makeup—cosm-etics—has implications for the universe—the cosm-os. The Greek root *kosm-* means "order," and the same double use of the root had symbolic meaning in Greek culture. In Rome, the word for makeup, *medicamina*, had a different set of associations: with medicine, poison, and witchcraft. Both sets of meanings resonate with the concealment and marking of gender; the female body becomes the site of gender's dirty work: "The female body is revealed as a task, an object in need of transformation."[6] Medicine, poison, witchcraft, and makeup are all crafts or skills aiming at a certain kind of control over the body and its surroundings; keeping the female body in order is an important aspect of keeping the universe in order.[7] Both Greeks and Romans saw the universe itself as gendered, so that the marks their culture imposed on people as determinants of gender formed part of a larger system. The ordering of people into males and females tallied with categorizations of classes into free and slave, of nations into civilized and barbarous, and of the world into heaven, earth, and underworld, center and edge.

In this system, as Howard Eilberg-Schwartz notes in the Introduction to this volume, women's own subjectivity is hard to find. Indeed, as has been remarked by feminists studying women's relation to their own bodies, women's choice to beautify themselves is particularly problematic, peculiarly self-deconstructing, since this focus on the surface calls into question the existence of any underlying self. As Eilberg-Schwartz argues, in cultures where woman is aligned with the body anyway, painting over the face and mouth obscures the one part of the body from which a female self might speak. Roman sources consistently link women's use of makeup with deception, covering a body often described by men as inherently repugnant; moreover, free women who use makeup are said to align their bodies with the open bodies of slaves and prostitutes. As will be seen, the exceptional cases where men use cosmetics point to areas of danger, disorderly zones in the order of Roman culture.

VANISHING CREAM: (UN)MAKING WOMEN

Consider Ovid's fragmentary poem *Medicamina Faciei Femineae*—"Medicines/Cosmetics for the Female Face." Like some of his other works—the three books of the *Ars Amatoria* ("The Art of Love," 1 B.C.), and the briefer *Remedia Amoris* ("Remedy for Love")—the *Medicamina* is a mock-didactic poem. The Romans were fond of didactic, and Ovid often takes this impulse and runs with it; the *Ars Amatoria* is an instruction manual on how to pick up a lover (two books addressed to men, one to women), the *Remedia* tells the reader how to get rid of a lover no longer wanted. As has been amply demonstrated by Molly Myerowitz, the instructor/narrator of the *Ars Amatoria* treats the woman and her body as the *materia* of his *ars*, and esteems women more highly than men precisely because women's relationship to their own bodies is more (literally) artificial.[8]

Thus the opening of the *Medicamina* (written by Ovid at a time between the writing of books two and three of the *Ars*) sets the reader on familiar ground (1–10):

> Learn what care [*cura*] will recommend your face, girls,
>> and by what means your beauty should be watched/guarded.
> Cultivation [*cultus*] has ordered sterile soil to pay out the bounty
>> of Ceres, and the toothed brambles have died;
> *Cultus* also remedies the bitter juices in fruits,
>> and the split tree takes in adopted aid.
> *Culta* things are pleasing: lofty roofs are smeared [*linuntur*] with gold,
>> the black earth hides under its superimposed marble.
> Fleeces are dyed [*medicantur*] over and over in the purpling cauldron;
>> India offers ivory to be carved for our delectation.

Throughout his writing, Ovid plays with the conventional elegiac preference for urban over rural, toilette over dishabille; in the lines that follow these, he contrasts the women of today favorably with the rustic matrons of the mythical Italian countryside. On one level, this is a send-up of the traditional Roman privileging of country over city, agriculture over all other ways of life. But on another level, the poet is setting up a symbolic opposition between control and cultivation—*cultus*, culture—and the physical nature that is its *materia*, its raw material. City then is to country as *cultus* is to chaos.

Thus when the analogy is extended to the female body, as in the just-cited proem, that body is likened to nature in the raw, and in some unpleasant forms. The woman's *forma* ("beauty," 2) is here compared with "sterile soil" (3) and its "toothed brambles" (4); to "bitter juices" in fruit (5), which can be amended by grafting onto the tree—here described as "split" in the process (6). High things are made pleasing by being "smeared" with gold (7; the same word is used elsewhere of putting on makeup); the "black earth" below is hidden by means of a marble covering (8). Wool, like hair, is dyed; ivory, like flesh, is to be shaped. These half-similes summon up a half-vague map of a woman's body, aided by the commonness of the ancient use of plowing (*cultus*) as a metaphor for sexual intercourse.[9] The sterile soil, with its brambles and bitter juices, is to be cured or amended by *cultus;* this is the black earth that needs to be dressed, covered over, in marble (hard, bright, not dark), as the higher parts are smeared with the golden mark of value.

These themes announce programs which Ovid develops at much greater length in Book 3 of the *Ars Amatoria.* Ovid himself cues his reader back to the *Medicamina* at *AA* 3.205–8:

> I have, in which I told the *medicamina* for your *forma*,
> > a little booklet, but a great work in its *cura:*
> In it, too, you should seek aid for your damaged form;
> > my art is not artless/impotent [*iners*] on your behalf.

This third book of the *Ars* was, so the poem claims, added on at women's popular request (2.745–46); women, too, says the narrator in his new proem, deserve and need instruction. After a gloomy reminder of the imminence of old age and wrinkles (3.59–82), concluding with the remark that having babies shortens youth and "the field grows old with continual harvest" (82), and after further reflection to the effect that, though iron and flint wear out with use, a woman's "part" need fear no such loss (91–92), the poet launches into his new book with the words *ordior a cultu* "I commence from *cultus*" (101). This gives him the occasion for his most famous rejection of Roman ancestral simplicity and embrace of the sophistication of present-day Rome (113–28); here again, the polish of the well-kempt body is aligned with the gilded architecture of the modern city, as opposed to wattle huts and cow pastures.[10]

After remarks on the best style of dress and coiffure for different kinds of figures (135–92, including a tip on where to buy a wig), the narrator goes on to give detailed instructions on makeup and personal hygiene. The armpits should not smell (literally, "no fierce goat should go into your armpits") (193); no rough hair on your legs (194); brush your teeth (197), wash your face (198); make yourself fair with powder (199), make yourself blush by *ars* (200), and by *ars* fill out your eyebrows (201), and mask your cheek with a little patch (202). And "there's no shame" in marking your eyes with a thin line of ash (203) or saffron (204). (Here follows the author's "plug" for the *Medicamina,* quoted above [205–8].) Then the narrator explains how vital it is to conceal the whole cosmetic process from the lover (209–34):

> But don't let your lover catch, exposed on the table,
> > your *pyxides* [makeup jars]; a feigned art helps the face.

Who would not be offended by scum smeared all over your face,
    when it runs into warm folds, slipping with its weight?
Oesypa—what do they smell like, though sent from Athens,
    the juice taken from the unkempt fleece of a sheep?
Nor would I approve if you put on your deer-marrow mixture
    in his presence, or brushed your teeth, either.
These things give you beauty [*forma*], but they are ugly [*deformia*] to look at,
    and many things foul to do please once they are done.

. . . .

[examples from the work of smith and sculptor]

. . . .

You also, while you are being cultivated, let us think you are sleeping;

. . . .

Why should I know the cause of the fairness of your complexion?
    Close the door of your bedroom; why do you give away the unfinished
        work?
There are many things it's proper for men not to know; most things
    would give offense, if you did not conceal the things inside [*interiora*].

In its developed form, then, Ovid's instructions include a strong recommendation to hide the process itself from its intended audience—for
two reasons. First, the lover should believe no effort has been involved; this
idea is a familiar one in Ovid, for whom *ars est celare artem* (art is the hiding
of art) is a motto, though a somewhat paradoxical one for such a consciously artificial poet. More important for us, and more taken for granted
by the poet: the actual ingredients used in the effort are repellent. The
"inside," the bedroom, conceals *pyxides* full of scum (*faex*), in fact runny
scum; *oesypa* (grease from wool); deer-marrow paste; as well as ash, saffron,
and chalk powder.

Ovid repeats the same themes, more strongly, in the *Remedia Amoris,*
which gives advice to lovers on how to fall out of love. Recommending that
the lover go to his girlfriend's house early in the day, before she has performed her toilette, he explains (351–56):

Then also, when she is smearing her face with her poison [*venenis*]
    concoctions,
    go to your mistress's face, and don't let shame stand in your way;
You will find *pyxides* and a thousand colors of things
    and slopped *oesypa* running into tepid folds.
Phineus, *medicamina* like that stink of your tables;
    nausea has come to my stomach from this more than once.

The identification of makeup as *venena*, literally "poisons," aligns this description with the placement of makeup in the Roman *materia medica*
(below); *venena* and *veneficia* are, with *medicamenta,* among the words en-

compassing the range of meanings poison/potion/medicine. The makeup box, the *pyxis*, reappears here in close association with its repulsive contents. And the whole picture is linked to the monstrous via an image from Greek mythology: the tables of Phineus, the blind king plagued by the Harpies, who steal food from his tables and befoul them with their excrement. Vergil describes these creatures as birds with women's faces (*Aeneid* 3.216–18): "Maiden-like the faces of these birds, but most foul / the offpouring of their bellies, and their hooked hands, and their countenance / always pallid with hunger." The contrast between the maiden-like face and the foul belly structures Ovid's picture of the mistress's dressing table, which causes his nausea.

Such themes are hardly unique to Ovid in Roman culture. A serious didactic poet, Lucretius, had fifty years earlier produced a picture of a woman's boudoir that was to proceed down the ages, via Ovid to Swift and beyond (*De Rerum Natura* 4.1174–91).[11] *Inside* the house, the woman "fumigates her wretched self with foul smells" (*miseram taetris se suffit odoribus,* 1175), as her maids run to get away from her, giggling; *outside,* the proverbial *exclusus amator* ("shut-out lover") hangs flowers and garlands on the doorway, anointing the doorposts with perfume, kissing the doors. Lucretius sums up: women know that if men realized what it was like inside, they would run away; "so all the more / they conceal from [their lovers] all the backstage [*poscaenia*] of life" (1185–86). Here the woman's body, as often, is mapped onto the parts of the house; this jibes especially well with Robert Brown's comments on *suffit,* which he argues must mean here, not "reeks" (the usual interpretation), but literally "fumigates" in the medical sense. Fumigation as a medical process "involved the application of strongsmelling fumes to the nostrils or, commonly in the case of gynecological complaints, to the womb by means of a tube introduced into the vagina."[12] Thus the lover kisses, perfumes, and garlands the door, the face of the house, while in an inner room the mistress pipes smells up her vagina (Brown notes that favorite fumigations included sulphur, burnt hair, urine, and dung).

Latin invective insists that makeup is itself horrible and must be covering something horrible, cataloguing the flaws of the female body.[13] The august Augustan poet Horace, in one of two *Epodes* describing a repellently ugly woman who is in bed with the narrator, lists among her unpleasant physical features (goat in armpits, sweat, bad smell) her "wet powder" slipping off and her complexion "colored with crocodile dung" (12.10–11). The firstcentury A.D. epigrammatist Martial lists what he suspects lies beneath the clothing of a woman who refuses to bathe with him (3.72): wrinkled breasts, wrinkled belly, deformed genitalia. Old age makes women both sexually repellent and greedy for sex. An old woman wears a coating of chalk on her face (8.33.17). A woman rejected by the poet's penis (9.37) "lies stored away in a hundred *pyxides*": her hair, her teeth, her dresses, her face, her eyebrows, all are removed at night, and her "white-haired cunt" can be numbered among her ancestors. An old woman is recommended (10.90) not to bother using depilatories on her crotch anymore, since it has ceased to be of interest. The anonymous poet of the *Priapea* (46) describes a girl "not whiter than a Moor, / shorter than a pygmy . . . / rougher and hairier than bears, / looser than Median or than Indian trousers"; he says he would need a powerful aphrodisiac to enter her groin, which he depicts as "swarming [with] worms." That such perceptions were shared by elite and popular culture alike is attested by a misspelled Pompeian graffito (*CIL* 4.1516; misspellings in the translation reflect those in the Latin):

> hic ego nu[nc f]utuii formosa fo[r]ma puella
>   laudata a multis set lutus intus eerat.

> Here I have now fuckid a gril beatiful too see,
>   prased by many, but there was muck inside.

Makeup itself could be directly connected with the vagina. Depilation of the female genitalia is said to make for attractiveness (Mart. 3.74); Martial says such *munditiae* are for *puellae*, not for an old woman (10.90), though one Pompeian graffitist prefers hair (*CIL* 4.1830). Depilation was carried out by plucking (Mart. 10.90), ointments (Mart. 3.74), or resin (Mart. 12.32.21–22, where the resin is "foul" and the property of the "wives" of the red-light district, i.e., whores). In this context it is helpful to remember that the depiction of the female genitalia in Roman texts is overwhelmingly negative; like the leaky Greek women described by Anne Carson, the vagina in Latin is smelly, dirty, wet, loose.[14]

Thus, by extension, the box that contained the makeup becomes sexualized. A famous and obscure dirty joke in the court case between Clodia and Caelius depended on what was contained in a *pyxis* sent by the young aristocrat to his equally aristocratic ex-mistress—possibly a depilatory, as Marilyn Skinner suggests.[15] Or possibly *unguentum*, "ointment" or "perfume"; Catullus (poem 13) praises Clodia's *unguentum* and says it would make the addressee wish to become "all nose"—a facial/genital transformation much remarked by modern commentators.[16] Certainly, as seen in Ovid's prohibitions above, *pyxides* were strongly associated with women and with makeup. Moreover, makeup boxes often were decorated with scenes of women applying makeup (Wyke 1994:143–44), so that, pretty on the outside, they would often have contained substances arousing the uneasy horror evoked by pollutants. They might contain spare body parts, as in the *Satyricon*, where Tryphaena's slave restores Giton and Encolpius to their former good looks by producing her mistress's wigs, and "eyebrows from a *pyxis*" (110.1–5; cf. Mart. 9.37). One of the Augustan declaimers remembered by the Elder Seneca, and cited by him as particularly gauche, used *pyxides* and *medicamina* as emblems of the female (*Suasoriae* 2.21):

> This is the Corvus who, while he was running a *schola* at Rome, . . . declaimed the *controversia* about the woman who was preaching to the *matronae* that children should be abandoned at birth, and so was on trial. . . . In this *controversia* this line of his raised a laugh: "Among the *pyxides* and *medicamina* for fragrant breath there stood the turbaned assembly [*mitrata contio*]."

These *controversiae* were something like moot-court cases in a modern law school, improbable situations used to train young men to argue in court. What is notable here is the representation of a convocation of women of the respectable class as a "turbaned assembly," i.e., with headgear also Asiatic and foreign, and surrounded even in public with their pots of makeup.[17]

Pyxides, as part of the personal possessions legally allowed to women (Paulus *Sententiae* 3.6.83), belonged to the *mundus muliebris,* the "woman's equipment." *Mundus* as a legal term could be used without the qualifying adjective *muliebris* with this meaning; it is notable here that the word *mundus* = "sky, universe, world" may have developed from the legal *mundus* in the same way the Greek *kosmos* developed. Another *mundus,* possibly the same word, was a ritual pit, the "gateway to Hell" (*ostium Orci*), associated with the goddess Ceres; when it was opened, it let out the spirits of the dead, and public activities were curtailed.[18] Indeed, the Roman grammarian Varro himself derives the legal *mundus* from *munditia* (*De Lingua Latina* 5.129)—the noun form of an adjective *mundus* "free from dirt or impurities, clean; cleared of superfluous growth; elegant" (*Oxford Latin Dictionary* s.v.).

Although my focus here is primarily on Rome, a few important Greek precursors should be noted. Paramount among these is the scene of the dressing of Pandora in Hesiod's *Theogony* and *Works and Days* (eighth century B.C.). Hesiod leaves his audience in no doubt that the first woman was a bad thing. In fact what he really stresses is that she was paradoxical in this regard, a *kalon kakon,* a "beautiful bad thing" (*Th.* 585). She is beautiful on the outside, especially when Athena has dressed her (*kosmēse, WD* 72, *Th.* 573), but bad on the inside (*WD* 60–82): a "trick" (*dolon, WD* 83, *Th.* 589), delighting in her *kosmōi* (*Th.* 587). The form of Pandora—beautiful and beautified on the outside, bad on the inside—serves as a paradigm for the general shape of things in Hesiod. Not only does she carry a jar with evils inside it; she is herself a miniature of tricky Gaia, the deified Earth who contains a hollow space from which Kronos reaches out to castrate his father (*Th.* 158, 174, 178). Her crown, moreover, carries monsters on it (*Th.* 582, *knōdal'*), so that she also recapitulates the horizontal shape of Hesiod's universe: the map with monsters at its margins, for example

Medusa (*Th.* 276), or Echidna, pretty nymph on top and slithering snake on the bottom, who lives in a cave and eats raw meat (*Th.* 295–305). Women, at least in Hesiod's version of the Greek origin myth, are a snare and a delusion, and their nature is writ large in their bodies; their *cultus* both constitutes them as pitfalls and is necessitated by their bad insides. Anne Carson suggests that this idea of the duplicitous nature of women may be connected with the Greek perception of women as wet, prone to rotting via sexuality, and hence unbounded, polluted. This would certainly tally with the Roman perception of makeup as something icky put over something icky.[19]

Working from the same premises on women's nature, the model husband Ischomachus in Xenophon's *Oeconomicus* (Athens, ca. 362/1 B.C.) instructs his wife that she should avoid wearing makeup, which will not make her as attractive to him as a rosy complexion derived from vigorous housework (10.2–13). His wife, in the dialogue, brings on his lecture by wearing white lead on her face, alkanet juice on her cheeks, and boots with platform soles; these he condemns as deceitful, like falsified material goods, and liable to be found out. According to the dialogue, she obeys his recommendations with alacrity; indeed, his final remarks indicate the presence of certain class/gender motivations:

> But [a wife's] looks, when she tries to outdo her servant, being more pure/ clean and clothed in a more seemly fashion—it's exciting, especially when the fact that the one willingly gratifies [you] is compared with the fact that the [other] one has to serve [you]. But women who are always sitting grandly around offer themselves to be judged next to adorned [*kekosmēmenas*] and seductive/cheating women. And now, Socrates, he said, you may well believe that my wife lives her life decked out just as I taught her and just as I now tell you.

Here the writer portrays the husband as the focus of efforts on the part of three classes of women to arouse his sexual interest: wives, slaves, prostitutes. The text shows a marginal consciousness of the bitterness that may well have existed between women in the same household sharing—on very different terms—the same man. Roman texts suggest that such ill feeling may have been acted out precisely in the arena of the toilette. In the uppermost reaches of Roman society, the very application of makeup was a servile occupation. Ovid, in the *Ars Amatoria*, suggests that it isn't nice for a woman to scratch the face of her *ornatrix* (hairdresser) with her fingernails or stick hairpins in her arms, causing the servant to curse the head she works on (3.239–42). The late first-century A.D. satirist Juvenal picks up the same motif (6.487–507), in the context of the flogging of slaves by bored mistresses. A group of *ornatrices* represented with their mistress on a Gallic funerary monument shows baldly how class, gender, and ornament were interwoven in this society: four (slave) women stand, one holding a mirror, around a woman lounging in an elaborate wicker chair.[20] One of the sole surviving women's voices from Rome, that of the (upper-class) poet Sulpicia, expresses in one of her few extant poems jealousy of a slave woman (Tibullus 3.16).

The wife's misguided use of cosmetics in Xenophon at the same time shifts her over into the category of prostitutes—women who are both deceitful and sexual professionals. The distinction between the undisguised looks of respectable women and the deceptively dressed-up appearance of prostitutes became a topos in moral literature and satire.[21] The declaimer Latro, in another of the Elder Seneca's *Controversiae*, delivers a catalogue of the proper outdoor behavior of a *matrona* in contrast with that of a recognizable *adultera;* the latter's "look" includes makeup or, as Latro puts it, "a face arranged for all kinds of pimping" (*Controv.* 2.7.3–4). In the second century A.D., Plutarch is still saying that an extremely virtuous wife might shun even a hint of pomade and makeup, avoiding what is "whorish," *hetairikon* (*Coniugalia Praecepta* 142a).[22] And the use of makeup did occasionally form part of the list of attributes of a prostitute in a Roman brothel. This can be seen, for example, in yet another *Controversia* (1.2), the point of which is to differentiate what makes a priestess from what makes a prostitute: "You stood ornamented [*ornata*] so as to please the people, in clothing a pimp gave you" (1.2.7); compare Juvenal 6.131, Messallina going home from work at the brothel "foul with her darkened cheeks."

Thus the subsequent appearance of the same theme in Christian tirades constitutes, not a new attitude (despite the Christians' claims against the wicked pagan Other), but a reworking of an old one. Tertullian's short two-book work *De Cultu Feminarum* ("On Women's Dress," late 2nd century A.D.) is the locus classicus here (cf. also Cyprian *De Habitu Virginum* ["On Maidens' Dress"], and see D'Angelo's essay, this volume). Blaming the female sex, in a famous exordium, for all the ills of humankind starting from Eve (1.1.1–2), Tertullian asserts that the inventors of women's adornment were the fallen angels who mated with the daughters of men (Genesis 6:1–2, *Book of Enoch* 8.1, 3). They are the ones who invented the worldly arts, including metallurgy, herbs, charms, science, and astrology; likewise they are the ones who gave women jewelry, dyed wool, and eye makeup (also at 2.10.3). To dress, Tertullian attributes the vice of ambition; to makeup, that of prostitution. Covering dress in Book 1, he proceeds to makeup in Book 2. His point is that the purpose of makeup is to entice men to desire women; women should be responsible for avoiding both the lust and the temptation (2.2.1), and not lead others astray. He lists "anointing the face with cream, staining the cheeks with rouge, and lengthening the eyebrows with antimony" as sins against God (2.5.2), and equates "having a painted face," "lying in your appearance," and "committing adultery in your appearance" (2.5.5). He concludes with a section on the association between makeup and whores (2.12): "The alluring display of beauty is invariably joined with and appropriate to bodily prostitution" (2.12.2). Likewise, the outer appearance should betoken what is inside (2.13): "Let whiteness come from simplicity, modesty produce your rosy complexion, paint your eyes with demureness, your mouth with silence, hang on your ears the words of God, bind on your neck the yoke of Christ, bow your heads to your husband—that's ornament enough. . . . Dress in . . . the purple of chastity . . . and you'll have God Himself for a lover" (2.13.7).[23] As in other cultures, and as previously and contemporaneously in Greco-Roman culture, the painted face here serves as an index to the woman's freedom with her genitalia.

Similarly, the Christian poet Prudentius, writing in the late fourth century A.D., includes the wearing of makeup by women in his catalogue of sins, the *Hamartigenia* (258–76). The poem moves from the *mundana machina* ("earthly machine") wobbling under the burden of sins, to women's deceitful devotion to bodily artifice, to the effeminacy of men who reject their position as *caput muliebris corporis et rex* ("head and king of the woman's body," 279). Here again the emphasis is on deceit and falsity: the woman "falsifies her outer [or: another] form" (*externam mentitur . . . formam*, 265); women "dye [*inficiunt*] / their forms with stain, so that their skin, smeared with pigment, / loses what it had been, not to be recognized under its false color" (274–76).

COSMETOLOGY AND BEAUTY CULTURE

So far, we have seen ample evidence that the female body in Roman culture was considered intrinsically disgusting; that makeup itself and the use of it were considered disgusting; and that women were often enjoined not to use makeup, or at least not to let themselves be caught putting it on. As the female genitals are at the bottom of all this disgust, so (male-authored) moralizing texts repeatedly claim that makeup is used by women to increase their opportunities for sexual activity—a bad thing, of course. Ovid's advice to women on how to use makeup and maximize their sex life is in keeping with his general (tongue-in-cheek?) flouting of cultural norms, his mocking of Augustan moral edicts. Meanwhile, the displacement of the disgust from the genitals, concealed both by clothing and by physiology, to the face, which in Rome was normally not even veiled, parallels the repeated claims that makeup is deceitful, is hiding what is really there. Makeup is part of a female trickiness that is fundamentally determined by the structure of the female genitals: hence the jokes about what's in the *pyxis*, the makeup box.

Lo and behold, despite all the disgust, a second and large group of texts consists of recipes and recommendations for making makeup, locating makeup within the body of scientific and didactic works that merged what we would consider chemistry, botany, pharmacology, medicine, and magic. And of these works, all those extant have male authors. We see here how the moralizing texts coexisted in tension with a contemporary technology, a science in cahoots with industry—literally, to use Teresa de Lauretis's term, a technology of gender (de Lauretis 1987). Yet these texts, along with the material remains of the Roman cosmetics industry—sometimes decorated, as noted above, with depictions of painted women—provide us with a fossilized indication of the real women who were the real market for Roman cosmetics, with scattered traces of women's own beauty practices. There are even fragments of texts by female experts in *medicamina* for women, though, as with most ancient women writers, most of their writing is lost.[24] Thus, in Roman culture as today, real women can be said both to implicate themselves in a system by which they beautify themselves, and to be implicated in a system that conceals, disguises, derides, and silences them. Such processes of co-optation seem indispensable to patriarchal societies, of which Rome was certainly one. The term "beauty culture" incorporates the paradox whereby a cultural practice simultaneously constructs and erases its practitioners.

Ovid again provides a starting point. After his cosmogonical introduction, the instructor of the *Medicamina Faciei Femineae* goes on to give some specific tips for how to achieve the desired *forma* (35–100, where the fragmentary poem breaks off). Significantly, he begins with a warning that women should not rely on magic arts to achieve the desired end (35–42):

> Thus rather should love [   ] than by powerful herbs,
>   which the magical hand cuts with awesome art;
> Don't you believe in plants nor in mixed juices
>   and don't you try the hazardous poison of the loving mare.
> (Nor are the middles of snakes split with Marsic chants
>   nor does the wave run backward to its sources;
> And even if someone has moved the Temesean bronze,
>   the moon will never be shaken off her horses.)

This standard list of magical acts—the cutting of special plants, the making of potions, the use of the *hippomanes* (a membrane from the forehead of a newborn foal), the Marsic snake-charm, forcing streams to flow backward, drawing down the moon—calls to the reader's mind a whole field of methods for attracting a lover.[25] The instructor continues with a pious recommendation that "girls" (*puellae*) should please instead by their good morals, which will last even after age has devastated their *forma* and they are ashamed to look in the mirror because of their wrinkles (43–50). But the initial rejection of magic (in the literal sense: *maga . . . manus*, "magical hand," 36) anticipates the whole next section of the poem, in which the instructor, after his nod to good conduct, proceeds to concoct potions of his own. He clearly wishes his recipes to suggest a field other than magic: medicine. That the border between these two fields was a contested one can clearly be seen in the texts, and is underscored by the range of meanings of the term *medicamina* itself: what cures, what amends, something concocted.

In its present incomplete form, the *Medicamina* gives only four recipes and the beginning of a fifth (and even these are not sharply divided one from the other, so that the effect is of a long grocery list). The first (51–68) recipe is for a night cream for the complexion, and calls for African grain, vetch, ten raw eggs, stag's horn, pounded narcissus bulbs, gum with spelt, and honey; "whatever woman will apply this *medicamen* to her face, / will shine more smoothly than her mirror" (67–68). The second (69–76), another skin cream, calls for lupines, beans, white lead, fine red soda, and Illyrian iris. A *medicamen* derived from birds' nests, called *alcyonea*, will "rout spots from the face" (78); this should be mixed with honey for better smearability. A fourth recipe (83–98) finds a new use for old incense, along with soda, gum, myrrh, honey, fennel, dried roses (a handful), Libyan salts, frankincense drops, and barley-water; "just let this be smeared on your soft face for a little while, / there will be no color on your whole face" (97–98). The poem breaks off with a recommendation of poppy paste for the cheeks. The ingredients, largely vegetable and pleasant-smelling, contrast with the invective picture of makeup as disgusting. They range from the common to the expensive and exotic, and the labor entailed ranges from the girl's own pounding of poppies (99–100) to the hired labor of mills (58) and men (75). The effect is highly technical, combining the didactic with the catalogue, and represents a poetic version of the encyclopedias for which the Hellenistic world had such an affinity. Its application to makeup here might seem like an Ovidian send-up, except for the equally serious and much lengthier treatment in the work of the Elder Pliny.[26]

The effort to distinguish between magic and medicine is one of the primary concerns of Pliny's *Historia Naturalis* (Natural History).[27] This amazing encyclopedia (A.D. 77) describes the physical world from iron ore to human beings. Along the way Pliny includes illustrative anecdotes, tantalizing throwaway lines (for example, on women chewing gum [22.45], or the efficacy of wearing a woman's brassiere on your head to cure a headache [28.76]), but most of all he lists various elements and their medicinal use, lecturing on the difference between such use and the practices of the Magi (26.19–20, 27.57, 28.4–9, 30.1–16, 30.95, 37.54), whom he sees as unscrupulous eastern charlatans, "barbarians and outsiders" (*barbari externique,* 28.6).

In the course of his exegesis, he tells us some things about women's beauty aids which tally with the list of ingredients in the *Medicamina Faciei Femineae*. Some of his information is unique, and purports to tell about real women's real practices—beauty culture. He notes that some women have their eyelashes dyed every day (11.154), a practice he feels is excessive (*tanta est decoris adfectatio,* "so great is their yen for beauty"); he concludes by remarking that it is said that too much sex makes the eyelashes fall out, and deservedly so (*haut inmerito*). Antimony is used by women to make their eyes look larger (33.102). Pliny lists some hair dyes (red: 28.191 [used in Germany; cf. Martial 8.33, Ovid *AA* 3.163 *Germanis . . . herbis*], 15.87; blonde: 26.164; black: 32.67–68 [by means of leeches, but you have to keep oil in your mouth or your teeth will turn black, too], 26.164; unspecified: 16.180, 35.194 [also used as mascara]), but does not associate this practice strongly with either gender. On the other hand, he says that he considers depilatories to be "women's *medicamenta,*" but that they are now used by men (26.164, also 36.154), a situation he deplores (14.123). As will be seen below, depilation was on the list of bad behaviors attributed to passive homosexuals (men who allowed themselves to be penetrated by other men).

By far the majority of Pliny's recipes have to do with women's skin. Most familiar might be the use of asses' milk, made notorious by Nero's wife Poppaea, who, Pliny says, used to travel with five hundred she-asses so that she could keep up her regimen of bathing in a tub of their milk (*Historia Naturalis* 11.238); the idea was that it "smoothed her skin." Elsewhere Pliny notes that some women bathe their faces in asses' milk seven times daily, emulating Poppaea (*HN* 28.183). Wrinkles, we recall, were the flaw in beauty singled out by Ovid to represent what ends beauty; as we have seen, male writers portray women as concerned not only about the wrinkles on their faces but about stretchmarks from childbirth, and Pliny has a remedy for stretchmarks: a lotion made from salt and melanthium (31.84). White earth of Chios is good for women's skin, and can also be used to touch up whitewash (35.194). Women use fat from a sow that has not littered for their skin (28.139); Pliny apologizes for giving a recipe for face cream made from the jelly of a bull calf's bone: *frivolum videatur, non tamen omittendum propter desideria mulierum,* "it might seem frivolous, but it should not be left out, because of the desires of women" (28.184). He appends to this a recipe employing bull's dung to make the cheeks red, though *crocodilea* (crocodile-intestine salve) is better (recall Horace's invective description of women's cosmetics, which includes crocodile dung; cf. von Staden 1992). Women also "nourish their skin" with the foam of the various kinds of beer made out of cereals from across the Empire: *zythum* from Egypt, *caelia* and *cerea* from Spain, *cervesia* and others from Gaul (22.164); they also use the red seed of osyris (27.111). Repeatedly here, Pliny appeals to women's own practices, even attributing "desires" to women.

Curiously, most of Pliny's skin-cream recipes have to do with the concealment or removal of freckles.[28] The ash of murex shell with a mixture of honey for seven days, followed by an eggwhite fomentation on the eighth day, clears spots off women's faces, takes away wrinkles, and fills out the skin (32.84); also recommended for spot removal (as well as a shampoo) is lead sulphide (33.110), while another lead derivative (34.176) gives women a bright complexion, the only drawback being that it is "deadly" (*letalis;* similar trade-offs faced nineteenth-century women).[29] Specifically for the removal of freckles, Pliny lists the following plant products: elaterium (cucumber juice) smeared on the face in sunshine (20.9); red bulbs in the sun with wine or vinegar (20.103); rocket and vinegar (20.125); wild cumin and vinegar (20.162); gith and vinegar (also good against leprosy, 20.183); corchorus (21.183); alkanet and vinegar (22.49) and bugloss-root ointment (22.52), both also good against leprosy; *sium* (22.84), also used as a night-cream for "flaws on women's faces"; barleymeal, vinegar, and honey (22.124); a decoction of wild lupines (22.156), also good for the skin generally; white grape juice (23.23, also good for "faults of the skin on the face" in general, and for bruises, scars, and warts); oil of ben nut (23.89); wild fig juice (23.126); decoction of white myrtle leaves (23.163); plane tree seed-balls in vinegar and honey (24.44, also good for cancerous sores and pustules); agnus castus seed, saltpeter, and vinegar (24.63, also good for lichens); rosemary seed (24.100); paste of arum and honey (24.145); fenugreek meal and sulphur (24.186, also good for leprous sores); *telephion* ointment (27.137). Non-vegetable cures include soda (31.122, also good for leprosy) and the marshy *adarca*, which "removes freckles from women's faces" (32.140). At 32.85 Pliny lists ways to remove freckles and "other flaws" with cuttlefish bones (other fishy remedies at 32.87, 97, 98). Orache is said to *cause* freckles and pimples (20.219). Lest there be any puzzlement as to why anyone would want to go out and get some orache, another suggestion of Pliny's hints at an answer: he notes that a *stelio* (spotted lizard) drowned in urine makes a *malum medicamentum* that causes freckles on the face of one who drinks this potion; hence "those plotting against the *forma* of a lover's mistress" kill such a lizard in her face cream (29.73). The remedy is egg yolk, honey, and soda. Real women, real rivals, real heartbreak, real home remedies?

That women themselves were indeed particularly concerned about freckles and other marks on their faces is claimed by Celsus, the paramount medical authority of the first century A.D.: *Paene ineptiae sunt curare varos et lenticulas et ephelidas, sed eripi tamen feminis cura cultus sui non potest,* "It is almost silly to treat [*curare*] pimples and freckles and moles, but the concern [*cura*] for their *cultus* cannot be torn away from women" (6.5.1). Again, this gives us a rare insight (if we believe it) into women as consumers with desires of their own. Two surprising asides from Pliny suggest that more than vanity was at stake: he says that divinities (*numina*) do not obey those with freckles and cannot be seen by them (30.16); and after a list of freckle cures, he comments: *Invenio apud auctores his qui lentigines habeant negari magice sacrificiorum usum,* "I find in my sources that to those who have freckles is denied, in Magic custom, the practice of ritual offerings" (28.188). The latter comment brings us around from the *materia* of Pliny's *ars*—the women whose faces need to be cured—to his rival and rejected *ars,* that of the Magi. Not only are freckles an outward bad sign, a *vitium,* to be worked on by Pliny's science; they suffice in themselves to vitiate extra-scientific practice.

It is as if freckles were like the bad spots on a piece of fruit: repellent in themselves, also perhaps indicative of inner decay. Compare Kathy Peiss on a similar idea in the early twentieth century:

> For beauty culturists, as for many nineteenth-century Americans, the face was a window into the soul, and complexion problems were indicative of a life that was disordered, out of balance. Thus Susanna Cocroft asked women: "Is your complexion *clear*? Does it express the clearness of your life? Are there discolorations or blemishes in the skin—which symbolize imperfections within?"[30]

A parallel to this may be suggested by Pliny's recommendation for getting back at your rival. What must Roman face cream have been like, we wonder, if your rival would not notice that a lizard had been killed in it? As seen above, Latin invective portrays the very makeup on a woman's face as repellent, crumbling, decaying. Makeup itself is to be concealed, hidden, kept inside, made up as it is of repellent ingredients: crocodile dung, scum, smelly wool grease, lizards.

Martial's contemporary, Juvenal, touches on this aspect of makeup in his immense sixth satire on women (457–73). A woman in a facial mask made of bread is described as *foeda aspectu,* "foul to see," and *ridenda,* "laughable" (461); her face cream smears the lips of her "wretched husband" (463; elsewhere he is befouled by her urine [313] and nauseated by her vomit [432–33]), while her lover sees the clean end result (464–66), the product of exotic cosmetics. Like Poppaea, she bathes in asses' milk (468–70). Juvenal poses the rhetorical question (471–73), "But something that is covered and bathed in so many varied *medicamina,* and receives the lumps of cooked and soaked cream of wheat—should it be called a face or a wound?" The unifying idea linking the two senses of *medicamina,* "medicine" and "cosmetic," is here shown to be the notion that the woman's face, like a wound, is something that is being cured—or that needs to be cured. Yet implied in these cosmetological texts are real women, briefly visible to us—women who literally bought into a system that labeled a woman's face a wound.

MAKING UP GENDER, MAKING UP EMPIRE

If makeup is a sign of the female—of the difference between outside and inside, top and bottom—and the makeup itself is a paradoxical substance—repellent in content but producing beauty—it makes sense that the (imputed) wearing of makeup should have been used in Roman culture by extension to mark other kinds of difference as well: among males, to mark off those who wanted to be penetrated sexually by other males ("pathics," or *cinaedi*); and among nations, to mark off barbarians from their conquerors.

Roman ethnographic travelogues of the tribes on their borders who painted themselves in various ways confirm the Greco-Roman definition of barbarians as Other, as women are Other in relation to men.[31] Those at the center (Rome) are normal and do not paint themselves; those at the margins are abnormal and do. This is only one example of the more general Roman use of accounts of barbarians to talk about what it meant to be Roman, most notably in Tacitus's *Germania* (early second century A.D.). The tone of these accounts is well represented by the locus classicus on the Britanni painting themselves with woad. Caesar writes, in his *Gallic Wars* (5.14.3):

> Indeed, all the Britanni dye themselves [*se . . . inficiunt*] with woad, which produces a blue [*caeruleus*] color, and by this means they are a more horrible sight when they go into battle; their hair is long and flowing, and every part of the body is shaven, except the head and the upper lip.

This blue color, the color of the ocean at the margin of the world (see *Oxford Latin Dictionary* s.v. *caeruleus*), recurs in other accounts of distant peoples: Pliny describes the Agathyrsi as having "blue hair" (*HN* 4.88); the first-century A.D. poet Silius Italicus writes of the "blue inhabitant of Thule" (17.416). Painting the face or body is attributed indifferently to both male and female barbarians; thus Pliny (22.2):

> Likewise I notice that, for the sake of beauty [*forma*] and of traditional rituals, some of the foreign [*exterarum*] races use certain herbs on their bodies. Indeed, the women among the barbarian peoples smear their faces, some with one [herb], some with another, and among the Dacians and Sarmatians even the males inscribe their bodies. There is in Gaul [a plant] like the plantain, called *glastum* [woad], and the wives and daughters-in-law of the Britanni, smeared over their whole bodies, walk naked in certain rites, reproducing the color of the Ethiopians.

The Ethiopians here connote the extreme of exoticism. Vergil cites the *picti Agathyrsi* in one list of exotic peoples (*Aeneid* 4.146) and the *picti Geloni* in another (*Georgics* 2.115). The word *picti* can mean "painted"; it can also, however, mean "embroidered," and there is a chance that these exotic skin decorations, as with Pliny's "inscribed" Dacians and Sarmatians, were achieved by tattooing rather than by paint. The fourth-century A.D. poet Claudian, in his *Getic Wars* (416–18), speaks of Roman soldiers who have read the "figures marked with iron" on the body of a dying Pict; and the third-century A.D. historian Herodian thinks the Britanni tattoo themselves with designs and pictures of animals (3.14.7). In classical Greek culture, decorative tattooing is reported and depicted as a practice of the paradigmatically barbaric Thracians. Like the long, unkempt locks and checkered trousers of barbarians and Amazons, marking of the skin provides an easy means of differentiating marked from unmarked groups of people.[32]

The content of Caesar's description of the painted Britanni presents them as antithetical to the female, extremely warlike. Similarly, Tacitus says that the savage and half-known Harii paint themselves (black?) and carry black shields when they make their sneak attacks in the dead of night (*Germania* 43.5). Yet it is the paradox of these outsiders that they combine an ultravirile proficiency in war with qualities and external attributes considered female by the Romans. The long, loose locks of barbarian men are described with phrases usually used in Latin to describe the hair of a distraught or grieving woman (e.g. *crinibus effusis,* Lucan 1.443). Such warriors associate themselves with women in battle; the tribesmen defending the island of Anglesey against the Romans are, according to Tacitus, accompanied by Druids and by women looking like Furies, with their hair hanging down (*crinibus deiectis, Annals* 14.30.1).[33] At the extremes of the known world, some even sink so low as to be ruled by women (Tacitus *Germania* 45.9—"to such a degree do they degenerate not only from freedom but even from slavery"). Thus Tacitus, describing the elaborate chignons of the Suebi, feels called upon to defend them from suspicions that they may be more interested in romance than is consistent with virility (*Germania* 38.4):

> [T]his is their beauty regimen [*cura formae*], but it is not harmful; for they are adorned not in order to make love or to be loved, but to create terror as they go into war, their hair arranged for the eyes of the enemy.[34]

Conversely, barbaric *cultus* is contrasted in Roman texts with the proper beauty of Roman women. Martial writes of the good wife and mother Claudia Rufina (11.53):

> Though Claudia Rufina is descended from the blue [*caeruleis*] Britanni,
>   how she displays the breast of the Latin race!
> What beauty of form [*decus formae*] she has!

He goes on to praise her for her conformity to Roman ideals of behavior for married women. On the other hand, the elegist Propertius (first century B.C.) scolds his mistress (2.18.23–32):

Now, crazy woman, you even imitate the dyed [*infectos*] Britanni,
    and you fool around, staining your head with foreign colors?
As nature made it, that's the right shape for everyone:
    a Belgic color is foul on a Roman face.
May many bad things happen under the earth to that girl
    who foolishly changes and falsifies her hair!
Take it away; to me you will certainly seem pretty,
    to me you are pretty enough, if only you visit me often.
But if some girl has stained her temples with blue dye
    then is a blue form/beauty [*forma*] good?

It is hard to be sure even what the poet is accusing his mistress of: painting her face with woad? Dyeing her hair? Using blue shadow to contour her face? What is clear here is that her makeup aligns her with the barbarian Other, and that the practice of using makeup itself is aligned with barbarian "staining." In the poet's eyes, what the *puella* has intended to make herself beautiful is wrong; he can tell her what is right, what will give her the correct *forma*.[35]

Whereas barbarians paint themselves because they are barbarians, men who like to play the part of women sexually—*cinaedi* (passive homosexuals), who let themselves be penetrated by other men—are said to mark this by wearing makeup like women, along with women's clothing.[36] Petronius vividly describes the decaying makeup of a *cinaedus* who is sexually molesting the narrator: "Streams of perfume ran down his forehead as he was sweating, and there was so much chalk in the wrinkles of his cheeks that you'd have thought a wall uncovered by rain was falling down" (*Satyricon* 23.5). Elsewhere, a slave woman takes the narrator, Encolpius, for a prostitute because of his styled hair, makeup (*facies medicamine attrita*), use of his eyes, and walk (126.2). Juvenal, in an extended vignette of passive homosexuals at home (2.83–114), imagines them wearing women's clothing; one applies eye makeup (93–95), his eyebrow "painted with wet soot" (*madida fuligine tinctum*), another wears a hairnet. Similarly, in a description of passives who insinuate themselves into your (i.e., a man's) home and corrupt your wife, the poet claims that "this adulterer in a hairnet feeds his eyes with soot" (*oculos fuligine pascit . . . reticulatus adulter,* 6.O.21–22). The effeminate emperor Otho bequeaths to the group in *Satire* 2 a mirror (typically a woman's accoutrement) in place of armor, and the poet pictures him using it to apply a facial mask (2.99–109).

Over two hundred years earlier, the statesman Scipio Aemilianus (quoted by Aulus Gellius, 6.12) had defined a passive homosexual by his appearance:

For a man who daily is adorned before his mirror [*adversum speculum ornetur*], covered with perfumes, whose eyebrows are shaven, who walks around with

his beard plucked out and his thighs depilated . . . does anyone doubt about
him, that he has done the same thing that *cinaedi* do?

Gender here is again performative. Compare another of the Elder Seneca's
moot-court cases (5.6), which debates whether a young man who has
dressed up as a woman on a bet and then been gang-raped should suffer
the restrictions on civil rights of an *inpudicus,* literally an "unchaste man."
One orator, arguing against the young man, declaims: "He put on wom-
anish clothing, he arranged his hair in a woman's style, he circled his eyes
in girlish pimping, he colored his cheeks." Another: "Give him girl's clothing, give him night: he'll be raped." The speakers assume both the inevi-
tability of the rape of women and the permeability of a man who could
pass as a woman. In this stereotype, the feminization of the passive and the
foreigner become conflated in the image of the effeminate (Greek) eas-
terner, as for example in a poem of Martial which contrasts the addressee,
a Greek with oiled hair and depilated skin, with the poet, a shaggy Spaniard
(10.65).[37] We might compare here the description in Seneca, discussed
earlier, of a gathering of women as a "turbaned assembly" (*Suasoriae* 2.21).

Thus, in Book 1 of the *Ars Amatoria,* when still addressing men, Ovid
makes it clear what they are *not* to do: curl their hair (1.505), depilate their
legs with pumice (506) — this is for the eunuch priests of Cybele (507–8).
Forma viros neglecta decet, "neglected beauty is becoming to men" (509);
munditie placeant, fuscentur corpora Campo, "let them be pleasing by their
neatness, let their bodies be painted/tanned from the playing fields"
(513). Men's togas should fit well and be clean (514), their teeth should
be clean (515), their shoes should fit well (516), their hair should not be
cut too short so that it is bristly (517), but hair and beard should be nicely
cut (518). Fingernails should be cut short and clean (519), no hairs should
stick out of the nose (520); no bad breath (521), no goat in the armpits
(522). The poet concludes: "Let wanton girls do the rest, / and whatever
not-really-a-man [*male vir*] seeks to have a man" (523–24). Makeup makes
the woman, and unmakes the man.

SLIPPAGE IN THE COURTROOM

It is, then, quite startling to read among the letters of the Younger Pliny, a
cheerful, kindly millionaire and civil servant under the emperor Trajan,
the following reminiscence of the accomplished orator and informer, Marcus Regulus (*Letters* 6.2):

> The very fact that he used to outline either his right eye or his left (the right
> if he was about to act for the claimant, the other if he was about to act for
> the defendant); that he used to move a white plaster to one or the other
> eyebrow; the fact that he always used to consult soothsayers on the outcome
> of the case; [all this] used to come from an excess of superstition, to be sure,
> but also from the great seriousness with which he took these endeavors.

This extraordinary (and, to my knowledge, unparalleled) example of an orator in makeup points to an interesting area of slippage in Roman gender construction.[38] For there is something of an overlap in Roman culture between the behavior of an orator in the courtroom—that quintessential proving ground of Roman manhood—and the sexually suspect movements of a dancer. The orator's movements, known as *actio*, were influenced by the practice of actors, though the great first-century A.D. professor of rhetoric Quintilian repeatedly distances the proper behavior of the orator from that of the stage performer (11.3.89, 103, 123, 184). *Mollis* (effeminate) *actio* is "to be put as far away from you as possible" (11.3.128); the orator is to exhibit "firmness of the body, lest our voice be attenuated to the weakness of eunuchs, women, and sick people" (11.3.19). Again, such behavioral marking connects the sexual and the ethnic; the flamboyant style in Roman oratory was known as "Asian" (connoting the effeminate East), the minimalist as "Attic" (here connoting severe style rather than Greekness). Thus one of the great practitioners of the forensic art, Quintus Hortensius, was attacked for his effeminacy (Aulus Gellius 1.5); his rival in a court case called him "Dionysia," after a famous danseuse.[39] Ironically, the definitively manly Roman art of oratory, enacted in the Forum at the center of the city of Rome, itself incorporated certain marginal elements.

CONCLUSIONS

In Roman thought, the use of makeup seems primarily to be connected with the idea that the female body is something that needs to be fixed. This idea appears to underlie both the real use of makeup by real women, as far as we can know about it, and the references to makeup in the works of male authors. Cosmetics are assimilated to the medical-magical substances catalogued by the Elder Pliny and others, which were assembled and marketed by both male and female practitioners. Disgust with the lower parts of the female body—what Bakhtin calls the "material bodily lower stratum"—is generalized to the whole body, dealt with palpably on the face, and generalized further to the cosmetics applied to the face and body, even to the pot they come in.[40] Makeup is not to be used by men; painted men become Other, categorizing themselves with women and/or as barbarians. The adjective *externus/a/um* appears sometimes applied to the surface of the body and sometimes applied to the marginal areas of the world; the *interiora* are paradoxically troublesome in the same way.

What are we to make of the variety of personal categories associated by Roman male writers with the use of cosmetics—women, but also barbarians, *cinaedi*, and the odd orator? Here it may help to move from the symbolic to law, and to recall this volume's theme of decapitation. Appropriately for our purposes, citizenship at Rome was sometimes called, in law, *caput*—"head." Change in a person's social status was termed *capitis deminutio,* literally "lessening of head." This could happen, for instance, with the loss of freedom through sale into slavery, or the loss of citizenship through exile; *caput,* as "civil honor," was stained by the censors' black mark which denoted official *infamia*—incurred, for example, by passive homosexuals. A slave's *caput* had no rights.[41] Free Roman women, who were citizens of a sort—owning property, moving about in public, acting as parties to contracts, literate—nonetheless could not vote or hold office, and their right to public speech was highly problematical; when women did make forensic speeches, they were often written about as if they had opened their bodies to penetration.[42] (Indeed, within the Roman sexual system, the face and mouth are seen as peculiarly vulnerable to sexual violation and staining; Latin has a word for oral rape, *irrumare,* and there are many Roman jokes about the mouth tainted by oral intercourse.)[43] The extremes of invective against Roman women astonish us, considering their degree of social power; as I have argued in detail elsewhere, Roman invective against women must have constituted a form of extra-legal social control.[44] Roman cosmetic culture, then, forms an elaborate part of that control. Like barbarians, who have no *caput,* and passive homosexuals, whose *caput* is dishonored, Roman women indeed lived in a state of partial decapitation. Even the hinted presence of orators in this group thus seems odd, unless we realize the extent to which Roman oratory played with the boundaries of manhood. Yet for male orators it was always a game; they, by definition, spoke—women did not.[45]

A recent commentator on the cross-cultural construction of masculinity writes:[46]

> Although women, too, in any society are judged by sometimes stringent sexual standards, it is rare that their very status as woman forms part of the evaluation. [R]arely is [women's] right to a gender identity questioned in the same public, dramatic way that it is for men. . . . It usually involves questions of body ornament or sexual allure, or other essentially cosmetic behaviors that enhance, rather than create, an inherent quality.

But this misses the point. To return to Butler's notion of the performative aspect of gender: it is clear that in Roman culture, and arguably in others, femaleness is not only problematic but precarious. The invective poems against old women make it clear that it is possible to cease being a woman, to be even more repulsive; I think of Martial's poem in which he tells an old woman to stop believing that what she has is a *cunnus,* since a phallus no longer will have anything to do with it. In this sense, the *medicamina* for the female face are cures that can never succeed, able neither to make nor to mend.

NOTES

Many thanks to Howard Eilberg-Schwartz for stimulating me to think about this topic; to my colleagues Martha Malamud and Donald McGuire for their helpful reading; to T. Corey Brennan, Cindy Weinstein, Marshall Cohen, and audiences at Bryn Mawr College, Caltech, and the University of Southern California for kind reception; and to Molly Myerowitz Levine for ongoing discussion. Translations throughout are my own, unless otherwise noted.

1. Maria Wyke has recently discussed the "Roman rhetoric of adornment" as a way of using the "surface of the female body to define the social and sexual identity of woman as non-male, non-citizen, and seductive trap" (1994:148); see especially her concluding section, on "the adorned body's dangers" (146–48).

2. In *Flower Drum Song*, music by Richard Rodgers, lyrics by Oscar Hammerstein II, book by Oscar Hammerstein II and Joseph Fields (New York: Farrar, Straus and Cudahy, 1959). The full song and setting appear on pp. 33–37.

3. Butler 1990:25, 128–41. On gender as makeup, see Bartky 1988:68–86, esp. 68–71; Heath 1986; Rivière 1986. On voguing, see Livingston 1990. For an extended argument on cross-dressers as a third category that calls into question sexual categories themselves, see Garber 1992.

4. Vickers 1985:220.

5. See Gubar 1987 on Magritte's *Le Viol* (The Rape), and comments by Eilberg-Schwartz in the Introduction to this volume.

6. Bartky 1991:40. For feminist theory on the politics of the female body, see also Bartky 1988, Chapkis 1986.

7. For this model in Greek culture, see Winkler 1990. For an application of this model to women's ritual masks in Sierra Leone, see Lamp 1985.

8. Myerowitz 1985:104–28.

9. DuBois 1988:65–85, Carson 1990.

10. On *Ars Amatoria* 3, see Myerowitz 1985:41–149, and esp. p. 58 on *AA* 3.113–28.

11. See Nussbaum 1989:41–47; she argues that Lucretius is not misogynistic but an advocate of equality in love between men and women: "Male illusion forces the female too to live a dishonest life, staging herself as in a theatre, and concealing the stage machinery" (43). For a late third-century A.D. version of this theme, see pseudo-Lucian *Amores* 38–42.

12. Brown 1987:296. For discussion of fumigation and the control of the female body, see King 1994:109. On ancient dung therapy for women, see the excellent discussion in von Staden 1992.

13. Richlin 1983:109–16; 1984.

14. Carson 1990; Richlin 1983:67–69, cf. 46–47.

15. Skinner 1982. Though *not* because Cicero depicts Clodia as a whore and Martial associates the use of resin with whores at 12.32.21–22, as Skinner argues; there is no other evidence to restrict resin to whores (Pliny, in fact, says it is used primarily by men, 14.123), and other sorts of women depilated themselves, as in the Martial poems discussed above. On the connection between women's use of cosmetics and the social meaning of the implements themselves, see further Wyke 1994:143–44, with illustrations.

16. See, e.g., Dettmer 1989.

17. On the *scholae*, see Bonner 1949.

18. See Scullard 1981:180–81.

19. Carson 1990. On *cultus*, deceit, and women in Hesiod, see discussion in Boyarin 1993. For a consideration of the semiotics of Pandora in film, see Mulvey 1992.

20. For the image, with discussion, see Kampen 1985, plate 15 (also Wyke 1994, plate 1). For epigraphic evidence on *ornatrices*, see Treggiari 1976. Both are discussed in Wyke 1994:142.

21. See Henry 1992, Richlin 1983:176–77. On the historical shift on this point in the late nineteenth century, see Banner 1983:42, 133, Peiss 1990.

22. Discussed by Carson 1990:150.

23. Trans. Edwin A. Quain; text and translation from *Tertullian: Disciplinary, Moral, and Ascetical Works*, trans. Rudolph Arbesmann, Emily Joseph Daly, and Edwin A. Quain, in *The Fathers of the Church*, 40:117–49 (Washington, D.C.: Catholic University of America Press). On this work of Tertullian, see Clark 1989.

24. For female practitioners and their recipes in Pliny, see for example 28.38, 66, 262, 32.135 (all from the female practitioner Salpe); 28.67 ("midwives"); 28.70 ("midwives and prostitutes"). Holt Parker, in his work in progress on ancient women medical authorities, cites also Cleopatra (not *the* Cleopatra), who wrote a *Cosmetics* (Galen 12.403–5K); also Elephantis (Galen 12.416K); and the sixth-century woman medical writer Metrodora (her sections 1.55–63, 4.19 bis A).

25. On Hellenistic love charms, see Winkler 1990.

26. For a detailed assessment of the ingredients Ovid lists in the *Medicamina* and their effectiveness in the light of "modern chemical and dermatological knowledge," see Green 1979 (with bibliography). Green's attitude is that Ovid gives serious scientific advice, while Pliny is "one of the worst offenders" among ancient sources "riddled with old wives' tales and outré, if not downright disgusting materials"; Pliny "seems quite incapable of distinguishing between the functional and the spurious, between scientifically based prescriptions and those dictated by the analogies of sympathetic magic"; Ovid is no "rehash of stale superstitions," measures up to "modern scientific criteria," and "will have no truck with this kind of hocus-pocus" (381–83, 391). Green's expert advisers were a chemist and a "cosmetologist." It is my premise that the division between science and magic which Green uses as a criterion is anachronistic for the culture in which Ovid and Pliny lived.

27. So Lloyd 1979:13; cf. 37–49, on the overlap of medicine and magic; further on Pliny, in Lloyd 1983:135–49.

28. The preoccupation with the removal of freckles shows up in modern fiction for young women in the Anne of Green Gables books (in *Anne of Avonlea*, first published in 1909, Anne dyes her nose red with carpet dye, mistaking it for a freckle lotion she had "compounded" herself from a recipe in a magazine). In the 1950s, Beany Malone, in the books by Lenore Mattingly Weber, is always trying a new freckle cream.

29. Banner 1983:40–42.

30. Peiss 1990:147.

31. For Roman attitudes toward northern tribes, see Sherwin-White 1967, Balsdon 1979. For the barbarian Other in Athenian ideology, see duBois 1982a, 1982b.

32. On Thracian tattooing, see Jones 1987:145–46. On barbarians and Amazons, see duBois 1982a:35.

33. Barbarian women in battle: Caesar *Gallic Wars* 1.51.3; Tacitus *Annals* 4.51.2, 12.30.3, 34.4, *Germania* 7–8, *Histories* 4.18; Plutarch *Marius* 19.

34. For representations of the hairstyles of the Germans in contemporary Roman art, see Anderson 1938, plates 21–23. The alignment between conquered status and exotic appearance shows up in many Roman depictions of northern Europeans—for example, in Anderson's plate 8 (Roman cavalryman riding over man naked except for a light cloak), plate 17 (dejected woman wearing checked tunic and trousers), plate 24 (man wearing checked trousers, no shirt, and a chignon, with his hands bound behind his back).

35. For more on Propertius 2.18, and on the interrelationship between gender construction, the exotic, and ornament in Latin love poetry generally, see Fredrick 1992, chap. 3, pp. 52–61.

36. On these men, see Edwards 1993:63–97; Richlin 1993, esp. 541–54.

37. See Richlin 1983:44, 136–37.

38. Sherwin-White, in his commentary (1966:357), concentrates on what Pliny says about Regulus's "superstition."

39. Modern critics sometimes replicate the perceptions they study; one of the foremost commentators on Roman oratory, A. D. Leeman, calls *actio* "certainly the most amusing department, especially to the northern reader who is not accustomed to the opera-like performances of the mediterranean orator" (1963:27). On the sexual ambiguity of dancers, see Richlin 1983:92, 98, 101; on actors generally, see Edwards 1993:98–136, Dupont 1985:95–110. On *actio* and Asianism, see Bonner 1949:20–22, 63.

40. Bakhtin 1984:303–436.

41. Paulus at *Digest* 4.5.3.1, 4.5.11; Gaius *Institutes* 1.160–62; see Edwards 1993:63–136, Richlin 1993:556.

42. See Richlin 1992a on Roman women and public speech.

43. Richlin 1983:26–29, 53, 69, 82–83, 93–94, 99, 108–9, 123, 128, 132, 148–51, 169, 170; Edwards 1993:71.

44. Richlin 1984.

45. Richlin 1992b; contrast Corbeill n.d., chap. 3, who discusses the reality of orators' claims against each other.

46. Gilmore 1990:11.

REFERENCES

Anderson, J. G. C.
   1938   *Cornelii Taciti de Origine et Situ Germanorum.* Oxford: Clarendon Press.
Bakhtin, Mikhail
   1984   *Rabelais and His World.* Trans. Hélène Iswolsky. Bloomington: Indiana University Press.

Balsdon, J. P. V. D.

1979 *Romans and Aliens.* Chapel Hill: University of North Carolina Press.

Banner, Lois W.

1983 *American Beauty.* Chicago and London: University of Chicago Press.

Bartky, Sandra Lee

1988 "Foucault, Femininity, and the Modernization of Patriarchal Power." In *Feminism and Foucault,* ed. by Irene Diamond and Lee Quinby, 61–86. Boston: Northeastern University Press.

1991 *Femininity and Domination.* New York: Routledge.

Bonner, S. F.

1949 *Roman Declamation in the Late Republic and Early Empire.* Berkeley: University of California Press.

Boyarin, Daniel

1993 *Carnal Israel: Reading Sex in Talmudic Culture.* Berkeley and Los Angeles: University of California Press.

Brown, Robert D.

1987 *Lucretius on Love and Sex.* Leiden: E. J. Brill.

Butler, Judith

1990 *Gender Trouble: Feminism and the Subversion of Identity.* New York and London: Routledge.

Carson, Anne

1990 "Putting Her in Her Place: Woman, Dirt, and Desire." In *Before Sexuality,* ed. by David M. Halperin, John J. Winkler, and Froma I. Zeitlin, 135–69. Princeton: Princeton University Press.

Chapkis, Wendy

1986 *Beauty Secrets: Women and the Politics of Appearance.* Boston: South End Press.

Clark, Elizabeth A.

1989 "Devil's Gateway and Bride of Christ: Women in the Early Christian World." In *Women and a New Academy,* ed. by Jean F. O'Barr, 81–102. Madison: University of Wisconsin Press.

Corbeill, Anthony

n.d. *Controlling Laughter.* Forthcoming.

de Lauretis, Teresa

1987 *Technologies of Gender.* Bloomington: Indiana University Press.

Dettmer, Helena

1989 "Catullus 13: A Nose Is a Nose Is a Nose." *Syllecta Classica* 1:75–85.

duBois, Page

1982a *Centaurs and Amazons: Women and the Prehistory of the Great Chain of Being.* Ann Arbor: University of Michigan Press.

1982b "On the Invention of Hierarchy." *Arethusa* 15:203–20.

1988 *Sowing the Body: Psychoanalysis and Ancient Representations of Women.* Chicago and London: University of Chicago Press.

Dupont, Florence

1985 *L'acteur-roi, ou, Le théâtre dans la Rome antique.* Paris: Société d'Edition "Les belles lettres."

Edwards, Catharine
    1993   *The Politics of Immorality in Ancient Rome.* Cambridge: Cambridge University Press.
Fredrick, David
    1992   "Self-consuming Artifacts: The Representation of Women in Catullus, Propertius, and Ovid." Ph.D. diss., University of Southern California.
Garber, Marjorie
    1992   *Vested Interests: Cross-dressing & Cultural Anxiety.* New York: Harper-Collins.
Gilmore, David D.
    1990   *Manhood in the Making.* New Haven: Yale University Press.
Green, Peter
    1979   "Ars Gratia Cultus: Ovid as Beautician." *American Journal of Philology* 100:381–92.
Gubar, Susan
    1987   "Representing Pornography: Feminism, Criticism, and Depictions of Female Violation." *Critical Inquiry* 13:712–41.
Heath, Stephen
    1986   "Joan Rivière and the Masquerade." In *Formations of Fantasy,* ed. by Victor Burgin, James Donald, and Cora Kaplan, 45–62. London: Methuen.
Henry, Madeleine M.
    1992   "The Edible Woman: Athenaeus's Concept of the Pornographic." In *Pornography and Representation in Greece and Rome,* ed. by Amy Richlin, 250–68. New York: Oxford University Press.
Jones, C. P.
    1987   "*Stigma:* Tattooing and Branding in Graeco-Roman Antiquity." *Journal of Roman Studies* 77:139–55.
Kampen, Natalie
    1985   "Social Status and Gender in Roman Art: The Case of the Saleswoman." In *Feminism and Art History,* ed. by Norma Broude and Mary D. Garrard, 63–78. New York: Harper and Row.
King, Helen
    1994   "Producing Woman: Hippocratic Gynaecology." In *Women in Ancient Societies,* ed. by Léonie J. Archer, Susan Fischler, and Maria Wyke, 102–14. New York: Routledge.
Lamp, Frederick
    1985   "Cosmos, Cosmetics, and the Spirit of Bondo." *African Arts* 28(3): 28–43, 98–99.
Leeman, A. D.
    1963   *Orationis Ratio.* Amsterdam: Hakkert.
Livingston, Jennie (director)
    1990   *Paris Is Burning* [motion picture]. Off-White Productions.
Lloyd, G. E. R.
    1979   *Magic, Reason and Experience: Studies in the Origins and Development of Greek Science.* Cambridge: Cambridge University Press.

Lloyd, G. E. R.
  1983   *Science, Folklore and Ideology: Studies in the Life Sciences in Ancient Greece.*
          Cambridge: Cambridge University Press.
Mulvey, Laura
  1992   "Pandora: Topographies of the Mask and Curiosity." In *Sexuality &*
          Space, ed. by Beatriz Colomina, 53–71. Princeton: Princeton Architec-
          tural Press.
Myerowitz, Molly
  1985   *Ovid's Games of Love.* Detroit: Wayne State University Press.
Nussbaum, Martha
  1989   "Beyond Obsession and Disgust: Lucretius' Genealogy of Love." *Apeiron*
          22(1): 1–59.
Peiss, Kathy
  1990   "Making Faces: The Cosmetics Industry and the Cultural Construction
          of Gender, 1890–1930." *Genders* 7:143–69.
Richlin, Amy
  1983   *The Garden of Priapus: Sexuality and Aggression in Roman Humor.* New Ha-
          ven: Yale University Press. (Rev. ed. New York: Oxford University Press,
          1992.)
  1984   "Invective against Women in Roman Satire." *Arethusa* 17:67–79.
  1992a   "Roman Oratory, Pornography, and the Silencing of Anita Hill." *South-*
          ern California Law Review 65:501–12.
  1992b   "Making Gender in the Roman Forum." Paper delivered to the Amer-
          ican Philological Association, New Orleans.
  1993   "Not before Homosexuality: The Materiality of the *Cinaedus* and the
          Roman Law against Love between Men." *Journal of the History of Sexuality*
          3(4): 523–73.
Rivière, Joan
  1986   "Womanliness as a Masquerade." In *Formations of Fantasy,* ed. by Victor
          Burgin, James Donald, and Cora Kaplan, 35–44. London: Methuen.
Scullard, H. H.
  1981   *Festivals and Ceremonies of the Roman Republic.* Ithaca: Cornell University
          Press.
Sherwin-White, A. N.
  1966   *The Letters of Pliny.* Oxford: Clarendon Press.
  1967   *Racial Prejudice in Imperial Rome.* Cambridge: Cambridge University
          Press.
Skinner, Marilyn B.
  1982   "The Contents of Caelius' *Pyxis.*" *Classical World* 75:243–45.
Treggiari, Susan
  1976   "Jobs for Women." *American Journal of Ancient History* 1:76–104.
Vickers, Nancy J.
  1985   " 'This Heraldry in Lucrece' Face.' " In *The Female Body in Western Cul-*
          ture, ed. by Susan Rubin Suleiman, 209–22. Cambridge: Harvard Uni-
          versity Press.

von Staden, Heinrich
    1992   "Women and Dirt." *Helios* 19(1–2):7–30.
Winkler, John J.
    1990   "The Constraints of Desire: Erotic Magical Spells." In his *The Constraints of Desire,* 71–98. New York and London: Routledge.
Wyke, Maria
    1994   "Woman in the Mirror: The Rhetoric of Adornment in the Roman World." In *Women in Ancient Societies,* ed. by Léonie J. Archer, Susan Fischler, and Maria Wyke, 134–51. New York: Routledge.

CONTRIBUTORS

Mary Rose D'Angelo is Associate Professor of Theology at the University of Notre Dame, and serves on the editorial boards of the *Journal of Biblical Literature* and the *Toronto Journal of Theology*. She is the author of *Moses in the Letter to the Hebrews* and of a number of articles on women and on issues of gender and theological language in the origins of Christianity. She is currently editing *Women and Christian Origins: A Reader* (Oxford University Press, forthcoming) with Ross Shepard Kraemer.

Carol Delaney is Associate Professor of Anthropology at Stanford University. She received her Ph.D. from the University of Chicago in 1984. Her dissertation research concerned the symbolic interrelations between gender and religion in Turkey and resulted in a book, *The Seed and the Soil: Gender and Cosmology in Turkish Village Society,* published by the University of California Press, 1991. Co-editor with Sylvia Yanagisako of *Naturalizing Power: Essays in Feminist Cultural Analysis* (Routledge, 1994), she has also completed a manuscript to be published by Princeton University Press, tentatively titled *Abraham's Trial: Essays on Paternity, Power and Patriarchy,* which reflects a long-standing interest in the story of Abraham and the "sacrifice" of Isaac. Another important publication is "The Meaning of Paternity and the Virgin Birth Debate" (*Man,* September 1986).

Wendy Doniger (formerly Wendy Doniger O'Flaherty) is the Mircea Eliade Professor of the History of Religions at the University of Chicago. Her writings range from translations of Sanskrit poems and Hindu myths to books about hallucinogenic mushrooms, phallic worship, evil, karma, women, dreams, folklore, horses, and myths. Among her many books are *Women, Androgynes, and Other Mythical Beasts,* 1980; *Dreams, Illusion, and Other Realities,* 1984; *Tales of Sex and Violence: Folklore, Sacrifice, and Danger in the Jaim-*

iniya Brahmana, 1985; and *Other Peoples' Myths: The Cave of Echoes,* 1988. In progress are *The Mythology of Horses in India; The Bed Trick: Sex, Myth, and Masquerade;* and a novel entitled *Horses for Lovers, Dogs for Husbands.*

Howard Eilberg-Schwartz is Associate Professor and Director of Jewish Studies at San Francisco State University and a Guggenheim Fellow. His interdisciplinary work on ancient Judaism draws on anthropology, gender criticism, and the study of the body. He is author of *God's Phallus and Other Problems for Men and Monotheism* and *The Savage in Judaism: An Anthropology of Israelite Religion and Ancient Judaism,* winner of an Award for Academic Excellence from the American Academy of Religion. He is editor of *People of the Body: Jews and Judaism from an Embodied Perspective* as well as of a series entitled The Body in Culture, History and Religion, and serves on the editorial boards of the *Journal of the American Academy of Religion* and *Religion.*

Karen Lang is Associate Professor of Religious Studies at the University of Virginia. Her research focuses on textual and thematic studies of early Indian Buddhism. She is the author of *Āryadeva's Catuhśataka: On the Bodhisattva's Cultivation of Merit and Knowledge.* She is currently completing a book that will include a translation of Candrakīrti's *Bodhisattva's Practice of Spiritual Discipline.* Her articles have appeared in *Feminist Studies in Religion, Buddhist-Christian Studies,* and other journals and collaborative volumes.

Molly Myerowitz Levine is Associate Professor of Classics at Howard University. Known in some circles as "the hair lady," her research includes a focus on the cultural grammar of Greek, Roman, and Jewish hair codes as part of her broader interest in classical culture of the ancient Mediterranean. Her publications include *Ovid's Games of Love,* 1985; *The Challenge of Black Athena,* 1989; "The Use and Abuse of Black Athena," *American Historical Review* 97; "Multiculturalism and the Classics," *Arethusa* 25; "The Domestication of Desire: Ovid's *Parva Tabella* and the Theater of Love," in Amy Richlin, ed., *Pornography and Representation in Greece and Rome,* 1992.

Amy Richlin is Professor of Classics and Women's Studies at the University of Southern California. She is the author of *The Garden of Priapus: Sexuality and Aggression in Roman Humor,* 1983, editor of *Pornography and Representation in Greece and Rome,* 1992, and co-editor of *Feminist Theory and the Classics,* 1993. Her current projects include a book on gender construction in the Roman rhetorical schools. But it is a long-standing work in progress, *Roman Witches,* that has led her into the world of religion and so, indirectly, to the article that appears herein.

INDEX

Compositor: Impressions
Text: 10/12 Baskerville
Display: Baskerville
Printer and Binder: Edwards Brothers, Inc.